THE FAC-1 FRAMEWORK ALLIANCE CONTRACT: A HANDBOOK

THE FAC-1 FRAMEWORK ALLIANCE CONTRACT: A HANDBOOK

David Mosey

LONDON PUBLISHING PARTNERSHIP

Published by London Publishing Partnership
www.londonpublishingpartnership.co.uk

ISBN: 978-1-913019-83-9 (hbk)
ISBN: 978-1-913019-84-6 (iPDF)
ISBN: 978-1-913019-85-3 (epub)

A catalogue record for this book is
available from the British Library

This book has been composed in
Adobe Garamond Pro

Copy-edited and typeset by
T&T Productions Ltd, London
www.tandtproductions.com

Printed and bound by TJ Books Ltd,
Padstow

Contents

Introduction

F AC-1 provides the foundations for a new approach to contracting that fills important gaps and creates new opportunities for improving economic, environmental and social value. Its multiparty structure and collaborative systems connect multiple parties in ways that create an integrated team and improve the planning and delivery of a complex project or a programme of works, services or supplies. This standard form has been adopted on projects and strategic programmes worth more than £100 billion in the UK and other jurisdictions.

FAC-1 offers a major step forward in modern procurement practices. It describes agreed processes for planning, joint working, contract award, performance review, problem-solving and shared learning that align the different commercial objectives of multiple organisations. Its systems of joint evaluation and decision-making enable clients to take full advantage of added value in the proposals submitted by consultants, contractors and other specialists. FAC-1 integrates any number of different contracts governing individual appointments without overriding what is separately agreed with each party, and it supports a collaborative approach to strategic management.

Without FAC-1 as a contractual integrator, the members of a team are divided from each other by their separate contracts in ways that increase the risk of misunderstandings and disputes. The absence of integrated contractual commitments leaves the parties no choice but to rely on defensive positions that do not facilitate progress or success. Meanwhile, to seek collaboration only through general declarations of good faith leads to confusion and mismatched expectations that often need to be unravelled by the courts.

FAC-1 provides a route map for collaboration that shows how contracts can do more than just allocate risks. Its shared systems enable team members to manage and reduce those risks, and to build up the information they need to agree intelligent solutions when new risks arise rather than just look for someone else to blame. Over the lifecycle of a complex project or a series of multiple projects, FAC-1 provides for the performance measurement and shared learning that generate improved practices, and it describes new supply chain relationships that show how the contributions from all participants can be maximised. These contractual processes are essential for industries such as construction, engineering and facilities management to meet the challenges of successfully combining fair profits with efficiency savings, improved safety, net zero carbon, community benefits and dispute avoidance.

The purpose of this handbook is to help all parties involved in delivering projects or programmes of works, services or supplies in any jurisdiction to understand how FAC-1 works and to get the best out of using it in practice. The handbook is designed for use by framework providers, clients, designers, managers, contractors, specialists, operators and legal advisers. The expression 'framework provider' may not be familiar in some jurisdictions – it denotes organisations that procure, create and manage frameworks for use by multiple clients.

The handbook and its case studies and practice notes provide an introduction for those who are new to FAC-1, a refresher for current users, and practical tips that can be used by teams engaged on any project or programme of works, services or supplies in any sector.

An FAC-1 *Alliance* draws together a range of *Alliance Members*, who also enter into separate *Project Contracts* using forms such as FIDIC, JCT, NEC and PPC, and it provides the foundations for integrated working practices that are essential to the modernisation of the construction, engineering and facilities management industries. This handbook is designed to help clients, advisers and other industry team members to answer the following questions.

- **How** is an FAC-1 *Alliance* created, between which *Alliance Members*, and how can new *Alliance Members* be added?
- **What** is the scope of the *Alliance* and how are the different interests of *Alliance Members* protected?
- **Why** is the FAC-1 *Alliance* created; what are the measures, targets and rewards for its success; and how is it brought to an end if it does not succeed?
- **How** is each stage of the agreed scope of FAC-1 works, services and supplies authorised, in what stages, and among which *Alliance Members*?
- **What** will FAC-1 *Alliance Members* do together or individually in order to improve economic, environmental and social value, by means of what contributions, and by what deadlines?
- **How** do FAC-1 *Alliance Members* reach decisions, manage risks and avoid disputes?

This handbook contains

- an overview of FAC-1 and what it can achieve in Chapters 1–10;
- examples of how FAC-1 is being used in practice in Chapters 11–15;

- a clause-by-clause explanation of how FAC-1 works in Chapters 16–40;
- the defined words and expressions used in FAC-1 in Annex A;
- the features of FAC-1 as a 'Gold Standard' framework contract in Annex B;
- a template for completing an FAC-1 *Framework Alliance Agreement* in Annex C;
- a list of FAC-1 time limits in Annex D;
- a schedule of amendments for using FAC-1 in Italy in Annex E; and, finally,
- the sources of case studies and other relevant guidance in Annex F.

Many aspects of collaborative procurement through FAC-1 can be explored in more detail by referring to *Collaborative Construction Procurement and Improved Value* (2019), and I am grateful to the publishers Wiley for allowing me to use quotes and case studies taken from that book. The features of FAC-1 that provide the basis for Gold Standard framework contracts and actions plans are also explored in 'Constructing the Gold Standard' (2021), my independent review for the UK government, and I am grateful for the work undertaken by the 120 contributors to that review.

I owe a great deal to all the users of FAC-1 who have demonstrated its value, and to the members of the Alliance Steering Group who offer guidance and training on successful FAC-1 practices. Please read this handbook alongside a copy of FAC-1, which can be purchased in paper or digital form at allianceforms.co.uk.

Table of case studies

The case studies in this handbook illustrate the use of FAC-1 and of earlier FAC-1 prototypes on a wide range of procurements, and they summarise the benefits that have been achieved. Sources of further information in relation to each case study appear in Annex F.

The majority of case studies were led by public sector clients, and a significant number were led by private sector clients. All the case studies describe crucial private sector commitments.

Table of practice notes

The practice notes in this handbook show how clients and industry can use specific FAC-1 relationships and processes to deliver improved results on their projects and programmes of works, services and supplies. Many of the practice notes cross-refer to case studies from which they are drawn.

Table of figures and checklists

FIGURES

The figures in this handbook illustrate how specific FAC-1 relationships and processes operate in practice and how these support Gold Standard frameworks.

CHECKLISTS

The checklists in this handbook summarise specific FAC-1 processes, provisions and benefits.

PART I

WHAT IS DIFFERENT ABOUT FAC-1?

CHAPTER 1

What is FAC-1?

The FAC-1 *Framework Alliance Contract* (FAC-1) integrates the activities of consultants, contractors, suppliers and other industry organisations engaged on a project or a programme of works, services or supplies of any size or type, and it aligns their interests with the interests of clients. It creates important connections between other contracts and sets out agreed processes for planning, value improvement, contract award, performance review, problem-solving and shared learning. FAC-1 is an established and successful contract form that describes a range of systems designed to achieve value improvement, risk management and net zero carbon targets in any sector and any jurisdiction.

FAC-1 is a toolkit: a working document through which to understand and integrate the needs and expectations of clients and industry. It provides the foundations for trust based on the agreed activities that are necessary for successful strategic collaboration, which in turn create and sustain a collaborative contractual environment for projects and programmes of works, services or supplies.

FAC-1 has been adopted on procurements worth more than £100 billion and has attracted widespread recognition in the UK and internationally because it creates clear commercial systems that reach beyond the traditional role of contracts and that enhance the work of individual team members. FAC-1 was developed by King's College London Centre of Construction Law & Dispute Resolution and the Association of Consultant Architects through consultation with 120 organisations in 14 jurisdictions; it was published in 2016. It has been used by private and public sector organisations on projects and programmes of works, services and supplies ranging in value from £5 million to £30 billion, and it is recognised by the UK government as exemplifying a new 'Gold Standard'.

FAC-1 is a multiparty umbrella contract that is designed to be used in conjunction with any number of consultancy agreements, construction contracts and specialist appointments, such as the published FIDIC, ICC, JCT, NEC, PPC, RIBA, RICS and TAC-1 forms, and it describes the relationships and processes that these contracts are not designed to cover. The structure of FAC-1 is illustrated in Figure 1, and it comprises a range of proven contractual systems for

- **integrating** the roles of *Alliance Members* through shared *Objectives, Success Measures* and *Targets* linked to agreed *Incentives*;
- **awarding** any number or range of *Project Contracts* for works, services or supplies comprising the *Framework Programme*;
- **planning** the early engagement of *Alliance Members* and of wider *Supply Chain* members in advance of each *Project* commencing on site;
- **programming** a *Timetable* of *Supply Chain Collaboration* and other *Alliance Activities* designed to achieve *Improved Value*;
- **capturing** learning and improvement from one *Project* to another; and
- **managing** risks through a shared *Risk Register*, and avoiding disputes through shared preparatory measures, through an *Early Warning* system and through reference to a *Core Group* of individuals who seek agreed solutions.

FAC-1 enables the agreement and sharing of improvements in quality, safety and net zero carbon while protecting the *Intellectual Property Rights* and other commercial interests of *Alliance Members*. It creates mutual confidence between *Alliance Members* and wider *Supply Chain* members, and it helps to accelerate essential progress through the learning gained from exchanges of experience.

FAC-1 is a versatile contract that can be used as a strategic integrator governing a programme of multiple projects or as a single project contractual integrator. It is an umbrella contract that establishes direct links between one or more clients and one or more consultants, contractors, suppliers and other industry organisations as *Alliance Members*, supporting shared systems for improving value and reducing risks and avoiding the fragmentation of relying only on separate two-party contracts.

FAC-1 is distinct from stand-alone alliance contracts, such as the 'PPC2000' project alliance contract and the 'TPC2005' or 'TAC-1' term alliance contracts, and the distinctions can be summarised as follows.

- A 'framework alliance contract' links multiple other contracts and integrates a multiparty team engaged on one or more projects, so that the team can use lessons learned on each project to improve the delivery of other projects.

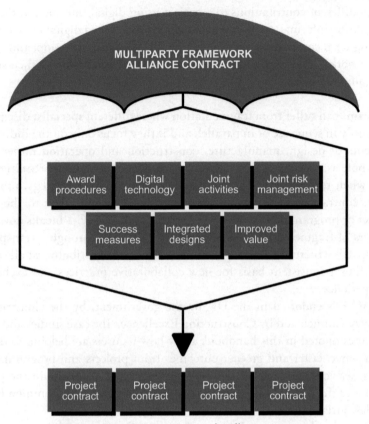

Figure 1. FAC-1 as an umbrella contract.

- A 'project alliance contract' such as PPC2000 is a stand-alone contract that integrates a multiparty team who are brought together to deliver a single project.
- A 'term alliance contract' such as TPC2005 or TAC-1 is a stand-alone contract that integrates a multiparty team through multiple orders placed for agreed tasks so that the team can use lessons learned on each order to improve the delivery of other orders.

FAC-1, as a framework alliance contract, describes the multiparty relationships, commitments and systems that improve the procurement, integration, management and delivery of

- the multiple projects comprising one or more programmes of works, services or supplies;
- the multiple parts of one or more complex projects;

- the different contributions to a project using digital information through building information management (BIM) and related digital technologies;
- long-term commitments through a public–private partnership; and
- the works, services or supplies awarded by tier 1 contractors to their supply chain members.

Teams can suffer from fragmentation where different specialist disciplines work only in sequence or in parallel, and if they focus only on the individual elements of design, manufacture, construction and operation rather than the whole asset and its life cycle. Gaps, errors and missed opportunities also arise when teams compartmentalise the skills applied to strategy, procurement, contracting and management, as if they do not relate to the same project or programme of works, services or supplies. FAC-1 breaks down the barriers of fragmentation and compartmentalisation through a transparent multiparty structure that integrates the skills of all contributors at all stages, providing a consistent basis for new collaborative practices and exchanges of experience.

FAC-1 is endorsed in the UK by the government, by the Construction Industry Council and by Constructing Excellence. The case studies and practice notes quoted in this handbook show how its users are helping to deliver better, safer, faster and greener outcomes from projects and programmes of works, services and supplies. FAC-1 is equally suitable for use in the public sector and the private sector, and it is designed for use in any common law or civil law jurisdiction.

FAC-1 has been adopted on a wide range of projects and programmes of works, services and supplies in sectors that include airfields, asset management, custodial, education, energy, environmental, health, highways, housing, infrastructure, maritime and public buildings. Examples include the following.

- Alliances governing construction works and services, modern methods of construction (MMC) and materials/equipment supplies such as those led by Crown Commercial Service (see Case Studies 1, 7 and 21).
- Sub-alliances integrating multiple complex projects (each a 'Sub-Alliance'), such as the Sub-Alliance led by the Ministry of Justice under a Crown Commercial Service overarching alliance (see Case Study 16).
- Energy alliances and other alliances for a complex project such as those led by Enel Green Power (see Case Studies 11 and 20).
- Health sector alliances such as those led by NHS Improvement and NHS Shared Business Services (see Case Studies 1 and 14).
- Housing alliances such as those led by Futures Housing Group and Haringey Council (see Case Studies 3 and 30).

- Highways alliances such as those led by Surrey County Council and Oxfordshire County Council (see Case Studies 5 and 9).
- Manufacturing and offsite construction alliances such as those led by the Football Foundation and Building Better (see Case Studies 25 and 26).
- Regional alliances and alliances for small and medium-sized enterprises (SMEs) such as those led by LHC (see Case Studies 2 and 13).
- Public–private partnership (PPP) alliances such as the one led by the University of Milan and Lendlease (see Case Study 17).
- *Supply Chain* alliances such as those led by Kier (see Case Study 22).

A total of 30 case studies and 46 practice notes in this handbook illustrate how FAC-1 *Alliances* operate in practice and what they are achieving.

CHAPTER 2

What is a Gold Standard framework alliance contract?

The UK 'Construction Playbook', published in 2020 and updated in 2022, sets out a range of government policies through which to deliver 'better, safer, faster and greener project outcomes'. It sets out principles and practices for efficient construction procurement that are equally applicable in the public and private sectors and that can be applied in any jurisdiction. The 'Construction Playbook' promotes frameworks as an efficient method for procuring public works, goods and services, and it states that a 'successful framework contract should be based around principles that align objectives, success measures, targets and incentives so as to enable joint work on improving value and reducing risk'. It recognises FAC-1 as 'a good example of a standard form framework contract that can achieve many of the ambitions set out in this Playbook'.

In January 2021 the UK government commissioned an independent review of construction frameworks and framework contracts, and the result was published in December 2021 as 'Constructing the Gold Standard'. The 24 Gold Standard recommendations are endorsed by the UK government, they are supported by the 49 industry signatories to the 'Construction Playbook', and they are quoted in this handbook. The contributors to the Gold Standard review recognised the power of a standard form multiparty framework alliance contract and supported the wider adoption of the relationships and systems that are described in FAC-1.

Practice Note 1. A Gold Standard framework contract.
'Constructing the Gold Standard' recommends that a Gold Standard framework contract

- expresses the client's strategy through objectives, success measures, targets and incentives;

- provides contractual systems through which to achieve objectives and success measures, with agreed rewards linked to improved outcomes by reference to clear targets;
- provides targets for each success measure that are transparent and objectively measurable, stating the method of recording relevant data, the parties responsible for measuring that data, and the systems for reporting to the other framework clients and suppliers;
- creates an environment in which clients and suppliers can work together and individually to improve outcomes, earn incentives and undertake agreed activities designed to improve value and reduce risk; and
- sets out the timing of agreed actions, the systems of joint risk management and the collaborative support provided by the framework manager and by a joint decision-making forum.

All of the 120 contributors to 'Constructing the Gold Standard' supported frameworks as the best procurement and contracting medium through which to improve results, but many expressed frustrations regarding

- the lack of objective standards to help clients and industry assess the merits of different frameworks;
- the cost and waste of creating and responding to onerous and inconsistent framework contracts;
- complex performance measurement systems that are not used for rewarding excellence, awarding work or sharing improved practices;
- limited understanding and adoption of digital technologies, modern methods of construction, early supply chain involvement and whole-life procurement; and
- limited strategic commitments to deliver improved social value, net zero carbon targets and other environmental value.

Gold Standard Recommendation 1. 'Use the Gold Standard features of frameworks, framework contracts and action plans to measure Construction Playbook implementation on a "comply or explain" basis.'

Gold Standard Recommendation 2. 'Ensure that all Gold Standard features are adopted by clients and suppliers when comparing the different construction frameworks on offer.'

Gold Standard Recommendation 17. 'Integrate the mutual commitments of framework providers, clients, managers and suppliers through the terms of a Gold Standard framework alliance contract.'

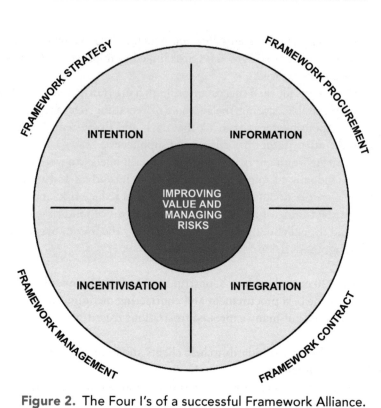

Figure 2. The Four I's of a successful Framework Alliance.

'Constructing the Gold Standard' examines the role of frameworks and framework contracts and the potential for binding action plans under existing framework contracts. It recommends ways to deliver improved value and risk management at each of the four key stages that comprise framework strategy, procurement, contracts and management. These stages comprise the 'Four I's' of intention, information, integration and incentivisation, which are illustrated in Figure 2, and FAC-1 governs improved performance across the 'Four I's' as specified below.

- **Intention**. A framework strategy that establishes the intention of a *Client* in terms of credible plans and commitments, clear requirements for *Project* outcomes, and clear expectations for *Improved Value* and successful *Risk Management*.
- **Information**. Procurement processes for the *Framework Programme* and for each *Project* that exchange information between a *Client* and prospective industry *Alliance Members*, forming the basis on which to implement agreed plans and commitments, to achieve required *Project* outcomes, and to meet expectations for *Improved Value* and successful *Risk Management*.

- **Integration**. A contract that creates and sustains integration of the mutual commitments of the *Client,* any *Additional Clients* and the selected industry *Alliance Members* to implement agreed plans and commitments, to achieve required *Project* outcomes, and to meet expectations for *Improved Value* and successful *Risk Management.*
- **Incentivisation**. Framework management that incentivises *Alliance Members* through instructions, support, guidance and motivation for the *Client,* any *Additional Clients* and the industry *Alliance Members* to integrate their mutual commitments, to implement agreed plans and commitments, to achieve required *Project* outcomes, and to meet expectations for *Improved Value* and successful *Risk Management.*

The 24 recommendations from 'Constructing the Gold Standard' are quoted in the relevant sections of this handbook, and the full text of these recommendations is set out in Annex B. The following features of a Gold Standard framework contract are also quoted in Annex B, with cross-references to relevant FAC-1 provisions.

- An outcome-based strategic brief that drives economic, social and environmental value with strategic supplier proposals for delivering that brief.
- Multiparty relationships that align objectives, success measures, targets and incentives with commitments to joint work on improving value and reducing risk.
- Enterprise contract systems and a timetable of strategic actions that improve information, integration, value and outcomes, e.g. using MMC, *BIM* and related digital technologies, early supply chain involvement (ESI) and *Supply Chain Collaboration.*
- Transparent costing, call-off, performance measurement and incentives that provide a fair return for consultants, contractors, suppliers and other industry organisations and drive value rather than a race to the bottom.
- Framework management systems that support collaboration and dispute avoidance.

This handbook illustrates how the recommendations set out in 'Constructing the Gold Standard' are equally relevant in the public and private sectors and can be applied in any jurisdiction.

CHAPTER 3

How does FAC-1 improve strategic contracting?

Framework alliances are recognised by the contributors to 'Constructing the Gold Standard' as the best medium through which procurement and contracting can deliver transformational improvements in construction efficiency and sustainability. Without the integrated relationships created by a framework alliance, the good practices that are developed and proven on one project are not easily transferable to other projects, and the contributions to a complex project remain isolated from the other contributions. A 'groundhog day' of lost learning can hold back the modernisation and efficiency of the construction sector because

- short-term commitments to a single project, and failure to connect the contributors to a complex project, place limits on the potential for industry investment and modernisation;
- people engaged on unconnected projects and unconnected project components have limited shared experience and limited opportunities to develop mutual confidence and shared practices; and
- organisations engaged on unconnected projects and unconnected project components cannot agree the licences through which innovations and improvements can be reused on other projects.

FAC-1 connects learning between multiple projects and between the components of a complex project. It is a multiparty contract that draws together multiple contracts governing the delivery of works, services and supplies and that describes the commitment of all parties 'to work in an *Alliance*, to fulfil their agreed roles and responsibilities and to apply their agreed expertise in relation to the *Framework Programme*, in accordance with and subject to the *Framework Documents*' (see page i of the *Framework Alliance Agreement*).

Practice Note 2. *Clients, Additional Clients* **and Framework Providers.** This handbook uses the defined FAC-1 terms *'Client'* and *'Additional Client'*, which are explained in Chapter 16.

FAC-1 can deliver *Framework Programmes* and *Projects* procured by or on behalf of one or more client organisations, including where

- the named FAC-1 *Client* is a 'framework provider' who establishes and operates the FAC-1 *Alliance* expressly for the benefit of other client organisations; and
- these other client organisations join the FAC-1 *Alliance* at any time and are identified as FAC-1 *Additional Clients*.

The expression 'framework provider' is used extensively in 'Constructing the Gold Standard', whereas the expressions *'Client'* and *'Additional Clients'* are used in this handbook to include reference to a framework provider.

FAC-1 governs activities that improve value, manage risks, improve performance and embed learning. It answers the following questions.

- **How** is an FAC-1 *Alliance* created, between which *Alliance Members* and how can *Additional Alliance Members* be added?
  - ○ An FAC-1 *Alliance* is created following selection of *Alliance Members*, either in advance of awarding *Project Contracts* or, in certain cases, at the same time as awarding *Project Contracts* or even after their award.
  - ○ The *Alliance Members* include the *Client,* an in-house or external A*lliance Manager* and any combination of contractor, consultant, supplier and other industry *Alliance Members*, with the facility to add *Additional Clients* and other *Additional Alliance Members*.

- **What** is the scope of the *Alliance* and how are the different interests of the *Alliance Members* protected?
  - ○ The FAC-1 *Framework Brief* states the scope of the *Framework Programme* and is issued by the *Client* (and any *Additional Clients*) at the time of selecting other *Alliance Members*.
  - ○ *Framework Proposals* and *Framework Prices* are submitted by each industry *Alliance Member* and are confidential between the *Client*, the *Alliance Manager* and the *Alliance Member* who submits them.
  - ○ *Intellectual Property Rights* are protected and licensed by agreement between *Alliance Members* according to the information agreed to be shared as part of the *Alliance Activities*.

- **Why** is the FAC-1 *Alliance* created, what are the measures, targets and rewards for its success, and how is it brought to an end if it does not succeed?
  - o FAC-1 states the agreed *Objectives, Success Measures, Targets* and *Incentives.*
  - o FAC-1 provides for joint review, possible adjustment of work awarded or other agreed actions and ultimately termination of an *Alliance Member's* appointment if agreed *Targets* are not achieved.

- **How** is each stage of the agreed scope of works, services and supplies authorised, in what stages and among which *Alliance Members*?
  - o Works, services and supplies are awarded to *Alliance Members* following a *Direct Award Procedure* and/or a *Competitive Award Procedure* and under agreed forms of *Project Contract* and/or early standard form *Orders* for *Pre-Contract Activities.*
  - o FAC-1 *Framework Prices* can identify *Profit and Overheads* separately from other costs so that *Improved Value* gained from *Supply Chain Collaboration* and other joint *Alliance Activities* does not erode margins.

- **What** will the *Alliance Members* do together or individually to improve economic, environmental and social value, by means of what contributions and by what deadlines?
  - o The *Alliance Members* seek *Improved Value*, working together through *Supply Chain Collaboration* and other *Alliance Activities* in accordance with an agreed *Timetable.*

- **How** do the *Alliance Members* reach decisions, manage risks and avoid disputes?
  - o The *Alliance Members* make decisions, manage strategic risks and avoid disputes through a *Core Group*, an *Early Warning* system and a shared *Risk Register.*

Practice Note 3. Collaborative, Outcome-Focused and Flexible.
Gold Standard contributors commented that 'the advisers who draft framework contracts seem remote from strategic commercial objectives', and that 'their work seems to focus primarily on the fear of regulatory challenge and the illusory attraction of risk transfer'. Instead, clients and industry support 'a Gold Standard framework contract that is collaborative, outcome-focused and flexible, with standard form provisions that drive improved value by integrating the work of the framework provider, clients, manager, suppliers and supply chain members, for example through shared approaches to MMC, digital technologies, ESI and joint risk management'.

An FAC-1 *Framework Alliance Contract* embodies the UK 'Construction Playbook' requirements for 'transparent performance measurement and work allocation procedures' and for 'principles that align objectives, success measures, targets and incentives so as to enable joint work on improving value and reducing risk'. Key strengths of a framework alliance contract are illustrated in Figure 3.

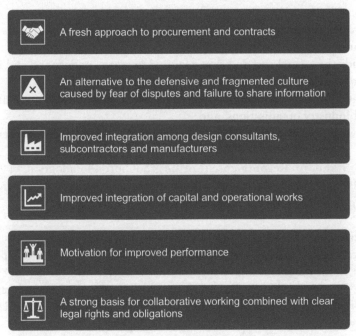

A fresh approach to procurement and contracts

An alternative to the defensive and fragmented culture caused by fear of disputes and failure to share information

Improved integration among design consultants, subcontractors and manufacturers

Improved integration of capital and operational works

Motivation for improved performance

A strong basis for collaborative working combined with clear legal rights and obligations

Figure 3. Strengths of a *Framework Alliance Contract*.

Gold Standard review participants expressed concerns over the cost, duplication and confusion created by the wide range of bespoke framework contracts because

- each bespoke contract requires clients, managers and industry organisa-tions, and their advisers, to familiarise themselves with a new set of terms and conditions, which increases the cost and time required for framework procurement;
- it is distracting for clients, managers and industry organisations to invest significant resources in understanding how to implement each new bespoke form; and
- industry organisations, and their advisers, remain suspicious of hidden risk transfer in a bespoke framework contract created on behalf of a client, and this can inhibit their commitment to collaborative framework activities.

Gold Standard Recommendation 4. 'Reduce procurement costs, improve value and reduce risks by wider adoption of a standard form Gold Standard framework alliance contract.'

'Constructing the Gold Standard' found that the use of a published standard form framework alliance contract

- provides consistent foundations on which to construct the specific client requirements and industry proposals;
- avoids the wasted cost and time required to create, understand and implement multiple bespoke forms;
- creates mutual confidence between framework providers, clients, managers and industry organisations; and
- provides a consistent basis for training, guidance and exchanges of experience.

Gold Standard Recommendation 24. 'Support the adoption of Gold Standard frameworks, framework contracts and action plans through government-led training and guidance.'

Practice Note 4. A New Standard Form.
The contractor GRAHAM reports: 'Most frameworks that we operate under adopt the use of a bespoke Framework Agreement for appointment to the Framework. Exceptions to this are the Crown Commercial Service and NHS Shared Business Services Frameworks that adopt the FAC-1 Alliancing agreement. This is an approach we support.'

Case Study 1. Crown Commercial Service framework alliances integrating works, services and supplies.
Crown Commercial Service uses FAC-1 for a wide range of framework alliances, including:

- **Construction Professional Services** with a total potential value of £1.3 billion in 6 lots (built environment & general infrastructure; urban regeneration; international; high rise; defence; environmental and sustainability technical services). Services in all lots include project management, cost consultancy, architectural, *BIM*, building services, civil and mechanical engineering.
- **Construction Works and Associated Services** with a total potential value of £30 billion in 11 lots comprising five generalist value-banded lots and six specialist lots (residential works; high-rise; maritime; airfield; demolition; construction management).

- **Modular Building Solutions** with a total potential value of £1.2 billion, covering design consultants, project managers, principal contractor and building manufacturers in 5 lots (education purchase; health purchase; education hire; health hire; general buy or hire).
- **Building Materials and Equipment** with a total potential value of £900 million, comprising manufacturers, merchants and subcontractors in 9 lots (heavy building materials; plumbing, heating & bathrooms; electrical products; paints and solvents; flooring; kitchens; PPE and workwear; tools and equipment purchase; tools and equipment hire).

The range of more than 300 clients who have joined Crown Commercial Service FAC-1 framework alliances include the BBC, the Defence Infrastructure Organisation, the Department for Education, the Department for Transport, the Environment Agency, Forestry England, the London Fire Brigade, Manchester Airport, the Metropolitan Police Service, the Museum of London, the National Gallery, National Highways, Natural Resources Wales, Network Rail, the Nuclear Decommissioning Authority, the Scottish government, Transport for London, the UK Atomic Energy Authority, the UK Parliament and numerous housing associations, local authorities, NHS Trusts and universities.

Crown Commercial Service is also using FAC-1 for additional Construction Works and Associated Services with a total potential value of £30 billion, which includes framework alliances procured in partnership with NHS England through ProCure23 (P23), providing a range of design, construction and building services for

- NHS capital projects, which refer to the money spent on investing in buildings and infrastructure, including the maintenance and repairs of buildings and facilities;
- major and minor building works;
- general construction; and
- civil engineering projects.

The Crown Commercial Service framework alliances use FAC-1 in conjunction with *Project Contracts* based on a range of JCT, NEC and PPC standard forms.

The options under all the Crown Commercial Service FAC-1 framework alliances enable clients to procure works, services and supplies as self-managed FAC-1 'Sub-Alliances'. For guidance in relation to Crown Commercial Service Sub-Alliances, see Practice Note 5, Chapter 12, Case Study 16 and references to Case Study 16 in other practice notes.

See also Case Study 16 regarding the implementation of a Crown Commercial Service FAC-1 'Sub-Alliance' by Ministry of Justice with Kier, ISG, Laing O'Rourke and Wates.

See also Case Study 7 regarding the Department for Work & Pensions CCS framework alliance and Case Study 21 regarding the 'action plan' under a Crown Commercial Service transitional FAC-1 consultant alliance.

Case Study 2. LHC framework alliances integrating works, services and supplies.

Local government framework provider LHC uses FAC-1 to provide frameworks that include:

- **Off-site Construction** of New Homes with a total potential value of £1.1 billion.
- **Housing Construction** and **Consultancy** in
  - Scotland with a total potential value of £150 million (Consultancy) and £1.5 billion (Services);
  - Southwest and Wales with a total potential value of £70 million (Consultancy) and £1.2 billion (Construction); and
  - North and Mid-Wales with a total potential value of £1 billion.
- **Schools & Community Buildings** with a total potential value of £6.92 billion.
- **Modular Buildings** with a total potential value of £1 billion.
- **Whole House Refurbishment and Improvement** with a total potential value of £1.3 billion.
- A range of related frameworks including supply of kitchen units and worktops, heating services, energy efficiency, general refurbishment works and offsite project integrators.

The LHC framework alliances use FAC-1 in conjunction with *Project Contracts* based on a range of JCT, NEC and PPC standard forms.

See also Case Study 13 regarding the FAC-1 alliance created by LHC and London Borough of Southwark with micro-SMEs.

CHAPTER 4

How do you navigate FAC-1?

FAC-1 is a flexible contract form that is designed to be compatible with any *Project* procurement and award processes and with any *Project Contract Conditions* and *Template Project Documents* that govern the delivery of each *Project* comprising a *Framework Programme*.

The FAC-1 *Framework Alliance Contract* comprises a set of *Framework Documents*, as summarised in Checklist 1, that are listed in the *Framework Alliance Agreement* (page i) and that are 'subject to addition and amendment in accordance with any *Joining Agreements* and the *Contract Terms*'.

The *Contract Terms* can be grouped around the themes of:

- *Alliance* integration: clauses 1, 10, 11 and 13; Schedules 1 and 6; Annex 2.
- *Project* procurement: clauses 4, 5 and 7; Schedules 4 and 5; Annex 3.
- *Improved Value*: clauses 2, 6 and 8; Schedules 1 and 2.
- *Alliance* management: clauses 3, 9, 12, 14 and 15; Schedule 3; Annex 4.

The *Framework Alliance Agreement* is designed for the insertion of details that cross-refer to the numbered clauses of the *Contract Terms* (pages i–v) and is signed by all *Alliance Members* (pages vi and vii). The FAC-1 *Contract Terms* and their relationship to the other *Framework Documents* are explained in Chapters 16–40.

The FAC-1 *Framework Brief* is issued to prospective industry *Alliance Members*, in response to which each prospective industry *Alliance Member* submits its *Framework Proposals* and *Framework Prices*. The contents of the *Framework Brief* and the *Framework Proposals* are described in Chapter 18, and the contents of the *Framework Prices* are described in Chapter 26.

FAC-1 provides for controls over the *Framework Documents*, including:

- under clauses 1.3.3 and 13.3.2, the *Framework Prices* and *Framework Proposals* are binding only between the *Client*, the *Alliance Manager* and the

The *Framework Alliance Agreement* (pages i–xiv)

The *Contract Terms* (pages 1–24)

The *Objectives, Success Measures, Targets* and *Incentives* (Schedule 1)

The *Timetable* (Schedule 2)

The *Risk Register* (Schedule 3)

The *Direct Award Procedure* and *Competitive Award Procedure* (Schedule 4)

The *Template Project Documents* (Schedule 5)

Any *Legal Requirements* and *Special Terms* (Schedule 6)

The *Framework Brief* of the *Client* and any *Additional Clients*

The *Framework Prices* and *Framework Proposals* of each industry *Alliance Member*

Any *Alliance Manager Services Schedule* and *Alliance Manager Payment Terms*

Additonal/amended *Framework Documents* in a *Joining Agreement* (clause 1.11.4)

Additional *Framework Documents* listed in the *Framework Alliance Agreement* (page i)

Checklist 1. FAC-1 *Framework Documents.*

other individual *Alliance Member* who submits them, and they are confidential between that limited group of *Alliance Members*;

- under clause 1.4, the responsibility of each *Alliance Member* is limited to those *Framework Documents* that it prepares or contributes to, except to the extent of its stated reliance on information provided by other *Alliance Members*; and
- under clause 1.5.3, in the event of any discrepancy, a *Project Contract* takes precedence over the *Framework Documents*.

Each *Project* comprising the *Framework Programme* is governed by its own *Project Contract*, which comprises

- a *Project Brief* issued by the *Client* or an *Additional Client* as described in the Schedule 5 *Template Project Documents*;
- the *Project Proposals* and proposed *Agreed Prices* submitted by the relevant *Alliance Member* or *Alliance Members* and finalised in accordance with the Schedule 4 *Direct Award Procedure* or *Competitive Award Procedure*; and
- the *Project Contract Conditions* described in the Schedule 5 *Template Project Documents*.

The contents of the *Project Brief* and *Project Proposals* are described in Chapter 28 together with the processes for the award of *Project Contracts*, and the contents of the *Agreed Prices* are described in Chapter 27.

The *Framework Documents* are intended to be consistent but there may be a need to resolve discrepancies between different *Framework Documents* and also a need to align the provisions under the *Framework Documents* with those under the documents that govern the award of a *Project Contract*. Under clause 1.5, the *Framework Documents* are complementary, and FAC-1 clauses 1.5.1 and 1.5.2 set out an *Early Warning* procedure and a default order of priority in the event of any error, omission or discrepancy.

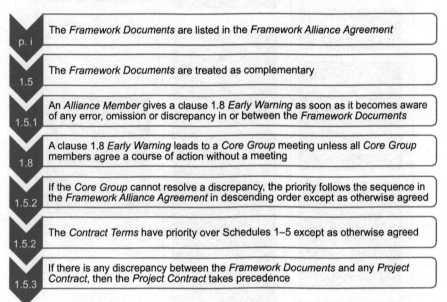

p. i — The *Framework Documents* are listed in the *Framework Alliance Agreement*

1.5 — The *Framework Documents* are treated as complementary

1.5.1 — An *Alliance Member* gives a clause 1.8 *Early Warning* as soon as it becomes aware of any error, omission or discrepancy in or between the *Framework Documents*

1.8 — A clause 1.8 *Early Warning* leads to a *Core Group* meeting unless all *Core Group* members agree a course of action without a meeting

1.5.2 — If the *Core Group* cannot resolve a discrepancy, the priority follows the sequence in the *Framework Alliance Agreement* in descending order except as otherwise agreed

1.5.2 — The *Contract Terms* have priority over Schedules 1–5 except as otherwise agreed

1.5.3 — If there is any discrepancy between the *Framework Documents* and any *Project Contract*, then the *Project Contract* takes precedence

Checklist 2. Priority of *Framework Documents*.

The systems for resolving errors, omissions and discrepancies in or between different *Framework Documents* are summarised in Checklist 2, and the relationship between the *Framework Documents* and the *Project Contracts* is illustrated in Figure 4.

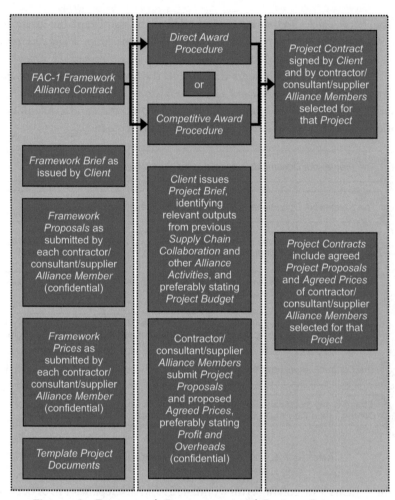

Figure 4. *Framework Documents* and *Project Contracts.*

CHAPTER 5

How and when do you procure FAC-1?

The following three stages of FAC-1 procurement are designed to ensure that the right parties are selected as *Alliance Members* and *Supply Chain* members, and to ensure that the selection processes demonstrate how *Alliance Members* and *Supply Chain* members will deliver best value in accordance with the agreed *Objectives, Success Measures* and *Targets*:

- the process leading to the selection of the *Alliance Members* when creating the *Alliance,* as described in this chapter;
- the process leading to the selection of the *Alliance Members* when awarding *Project Contracts*, as described in Chapter 28; and
- the process leading to the selection of *Supply Chain* members for strategic appointments by industry *Alliance Members* in accordance with *Supply Chain Collaboration,* as described in Chapter 30.

FAC-1 can support a complex project or a programme of related or unrelated projects in any sector and in any jurisdiction. It can be used

- for an *Alliance* led by one or more clients (the FAC-1 *Client* and *Additional Clients*) working with industry *Alliance Members* from one or more professional disciplines and industry specialisations (see Chapters 11 and 12);
- for a 'Sub-Alliance' within the scope of an FAC-1 *Alliance* led by one or more clients working with industry *Alliance Members* from one or more professional disciplines and industry specialisations to deliver part of the *Alliance* programme of works, services or supplies (see Chapter 12); or
- for an *Alliance* led by one or more industry *Alliance Members* working with one or more tier 2 and tier 3 *Supply Chain* members from one or more professional disciplines and industry specialisations (see Chapter 30).

FAC-1 can create a contractual 'ecosystem' of related *Alliances* through which a *Client/Additional Clients* and industry *Alliance Members* agree and implement

- interconnected and consistent *Alliances* governing strategic relationships and creating interfaces between the *Project Contracts* awarded under each *Alliance* (see Chapter 11);
- Sub-Alliances for the delivery of part of an *Alliance* programme of works, services or supplies (see Chapter 12);
- 'integrated information management contracts' (see Chapter 14) integrating the contributions of *Alliance Members* through *BIM* and related technologies; and
- *Supply Chain Alliances* between tier 1 industry *Alliance Members* and tier 2 and tier 3 *Supply Chain* members (see Chapter 30).

Practice Note 5. FAC-1 *Alliances* and Sub-Alliances.
Crown Commercial Service has created systems in its FAC-1 *Framework Alliance Contracts* for its users to create a range of 'Sub-Alliances' under separate FAC-1 *Framework Alliance Contracts* that can be procured through a *Direct Award Procedure* or *Competitive Award Procedure* within the scope of the overarching FAC-1 *Alliance*.

These Sub-Alliances enable collaboration between teams created at call-off stage in accordance with terms set out in, and consistent with, the overarching FAC-1 *Framework Alliance Contract* by which a *Client* or *Additional Client* can

- use the *Direct Award Procedure* or *Competitive Award Procedure* under the overarching FAC-1 to agree *Objectives, Targets, Success Measures* and *Incentives* with the other *Alliance Members* that it selects for one or more specific *Projects*;
- use the *Direct Award Procedure* or *Competitive Award Procedure* under the overarching FAC-1 to establish with those other *Alliance Members* the *Alliance Activities, Supply Chain Collaboration,* joint *Risk Management* and other FAC-1 systems that meet the particular needs of one or more specific *Projects*;
- describe the agreed *Objectives, Targets, Success Measures* and *Incentives*, and the agreed *Alliance Activities, Supply Chain Collaboration,* joint *Risk Management* and other FAC-1 systems, in a separate FAC-1 *Framework Alliance Contract* governing the Sub-Alliance; and
- collaborate with those other *Alliance Members* through the agreed FAC-1 systems using a *Timetable* and a *Risk Register* applicable to the particular

needs of one or more specific *Projects*, supported by a separate *Alliance Manager* and *Core Group*.

The Crown Commercial Service FAC-1 *Framework Alliance Contract* defines industry *Alliance Members* as '*Supplier Alliance Members*' and states in the Schedule 5 *Template Project Documents* that

'An additional FAC-1 *Framework Alliance Contract* may be used in con-junction with any of the [JCT, NEC, PPC, SBCC, TAC-1 *Project Contract*] forms if and where any one or more *Additional Clients* propose to increase the potential for consistency, efficiency, *Improved Value* and lessons learned by integrating or connecting:

- A programme of work comprising more than one *Project*, to be awarded to one or more *Supplier Alliance Members*; or
- The capital and operational phases of any one or more *Projects*, to be awarded to one or more *Supplier Alliance Members*, for example as a whole life approach to procurement; or
- The *BIM* contributions of one or more *Supplier Alliance Members* and other team members in relation to any one or more *Projects*, to be awarded to one or more *Supplier Alliance Members*; or
- The contributions of the *Supply Chain* members used by different Sup-plier *Alliance Members* on any *Projects* or programmes of *Projects*, to be awarded to one or more *Supplier Alliance Members*.'

An example of an FAC-1 Sub-Alliance is described in Case Study 16.

Each FAC-1 *Alliance* enables

- increased transparency and improved efficiency through consistent data shared among *Alliance Members*,
- stronger joint commitment to shared *Objectives* and closer working rela-tionships on agreed *Alliance Activities*,
- improved joint engagement with the *Supply Chain* and with *Stakeholders*,
- collective self-regulation through the *Core Group*, and
- more open measurement against agreed *Targets* and more effective motiva-tion to earn agreed *Incentives*.

An FAC-1 *Alliance* is usually created in advance of the award of any *Pro-ject Contracts* so that it can enhance those *Project Contracts* through shared preparatory processes and lessons learned. However, if it is agreed that the selection of industry *Alliance Members* for each *Project Contract* is undertaken using a separate process not governed by the FAC-1 Schedule 4 *Direct Award Procedure* or *Competitive Award Procedure*, then an FAC-1 *Alliance* can also be created

- at the same time as the *Project Contracts*, in order to integrate the relationships and processes established by those *Project Contracts* (as illustrated in Chapter 12); or
- after the *Project Contracts*, in order to govern an 'action plan' for improvement of the relationships and processes established by those *Project Contracts* (as illustrated in Chapter 13).

Practice Note 6. Award of *Project Contracts* comprising a complex project.
As described in Chapter 12, an FAC-1 Alliance can be created by a *Client* with the participants in a complex project, such as the designers, the managers, the site remediation and preparation team, one or more contractors and their *Supply Chain* specialists and manufacturers, and the operator of the completed facility. It may be that the *Project Contracts* governing the appointments of some of these *Alliance Members* are awarded in advance of or at the same time as signing FAC-1.

'Constructing the Gold Standard' recommends that the *Client/Additional Clients* use pre-procurement consultation to inform the framework strategy that leads to the FAC-1 *Framework Brief.* This consultation can explore emerging technologies and innovations, can obtain insights as to the potential for industry to deliver the best outcomes for the *Client/Additional Clients*, and can identify limitations and gaps in the relevant market. The prospect of a place on a framework alliance can attract new investment by prospective industry *Alliance Members* and can support investment in *Supply Chain* relationships that are necessary to access specialist expertise. FAC-1 framework strategies, procurements and contracts can then capture and embed this pre-procurement learning.

Gold Standard Recommendation 9. 'Use pre-procurement framework consultation to explore emerging technologies and innovations and to identify opportunities in the market.'

The selection process for FAC-1 *Alliance Members* should not tempt bidders to undercut each other on costs or to prioritise cost savings above other measures of value. Instead, the evaluation criteria used for selecting industry *Alliance Members* should invite them to demonstrate how their proposed costs will be deployed in ways that generate *Improved Value*, that achieve net zero carbon targets, and that implement successful *Risk Management*.

Contributors to 'Constructing the Gold Standard' proposed that more consistent and proportionate procedures for assessing the economic and financial standing of prospective industry *Alliance Members* should be adopted in order to reduce waste and duplication, creating efficiency savings for clients and the industry. For this purpose, duplications and inconsistencies can be avoided by the *Client/Additional Clients* and the *Alliance Manager* using the standard requirements set out in 'PAS91' or the 'Common Assessment Standard'.

Gold Standard Recommendation 20. 'Reduce procurement costs by consistent and proportionate assessment of economic and financial standing using "PAS91" or the "Common Assessment Standard".'

Contributors to 'Constructing the Gold Standard' proposed that more proportionate and consistent evaluation systems for framework procurement and call-off will reduce waste and duplication and will create efficiency savings for clients and industry. For this purpose, the FAC-1 *Client/Additional Clients* and the *Alliance Manager* should establish and apply balanced evaluation criteria for selecting industry *Alliance Members* and for appointing them to each *Project*. These criteria should examine all relevant aspects of value that enable differentiation between qualitative bids, that reflect expected *Project* outcomes, and that incentivise *Improved Value Objectives*.

Gold Standard Recommendation 21. 'Evaluate proposals for frameworks and call-offs proportionately and consistently using balanced criteria that include quality, social value and net zero GHG emissions.'

The Construction Innovation Hub 'Value Toolkit' recognises that each *Project* and *Framework Programme* has its own unique value profile by reference to the relative importance of four value categories:

- natural (air, climate, water, land, resource use, biodiversity),
- social (influence and consultation, equality and diversity, networks and connections),
- human (employment, skills and knowledge, health, experience) and
- produced (lifecycle cost, return, production, resilience).

The evaluation criteria for procuring an FAC-1 *Alliance* and for calling off each *Project* need to deal with the impact of qualitative proposals on cost, time, risk and other factors. Reconciling potential conflicts between costs and other measures of value requires a procurement process that allows sufficient time for the examination and agreement of proposals submitted by prospective industry *Alliance Members*. If bidders are asked to submit costed proposals without the benefit of full information, they may hold back or compromise good ideas in order to reduce their bid prices (see also Chapter 26).

Practice Note 7. Balanced evaluation (1).
Gold Standard participants expressed concerns that balanced evaluation can become skewed, and resources can be wasted, where:

- 'Quality differentials are marginal and lowest cost becomes the key criterion
- Quality criteria are subjective and not easily understood
- Qualitative proposals are requested which are not relevant to the client's needs
- Qualitative proposals are not implemented or kept under review for later adoption.'

'Constructing the Gold Standard' recognised that: 'A balanced approach to evaluating prospective suppliers for frameworks and framework call-offs lies at the heart of successful framework strategies, procurement processes and contracts. It enables framework providers and other clients to test supplier proposals against required and expected outcomes at framework level and at project level.'

Practice Note 8. Balanced evaluation (2).
LHC report that: 'Within recent frameworks we have introduced the LHC Lifetime Values which comprise a set of social, community and environmental measures. In designing the specification and evaluation criteria for the procurement of our frameworks we consider these Lifetime Values, and we ensure that our assessment of bidders' responses support the achievement of these values.'
See also Case Study 2.

Case Study 3. Futures Housing Group framework alliance integrating specialist contractors.
Futures Housing Group embarked on its FAC-1 framework alliance with predicted outcomes that included

- better service delivery through a stronger partnering approach built upon closer ties to the successful bidders;

- efficiency gains from the innovative approach to selecting and managing individual works;
- greater emphasis on employment and training and a greater impact on local economies;
- new standard contract terms providing lower risk through closer engagement criteria; and
- continued success in spending over 75% of contractor budget within 25 miles of its two regional offices, contributing to its 'Lean and Local' ambitions.

The tender included measures attractive to SMEs (small and medium-sized enterprises) but open to all, with cashflow-easing features that included the provision of key materials in certain lots on a free issue basis, such as heating installations, bathroom installations and electrical works. It also included proposals to have embedded payment cards with the contactors, enabling them to claim payment immediately on agreement of a final account. Throughout the tender process, the emphasis was on a collaborative approach via FAC-1. Of the 23 contractors invited to join the framework alliance, only two were not SMEs. The average size of the other companies was fewer than 25 employees.

Various tools were used to introduce the framework alliance, including a speed-dating session, ensuring that each contractor met their client counterpart and all the other contractors in the framework alliance. Every contractor welcomed FAC-1, its plain language and its sequential approach to each stage making it easy to understand.

Futures Housing Group used FAC-1 in conjunction with *Project Contracts* based on the TPC2005 (now TAC-1) standard form term alliance contract.

The client reported: 'The sense of truly belonging to a collaborative group is already apparent. Since launching on 1 August 2016, the framework has seen the first call off contracts by direct award for pilot programmes of heating installation, kitchen installation and bathroom installation. Site surveys have taken place and costs returned showing an average cost saving of 9.3% against the previous framework.'

Supply Management reported that: 'Futures Housing Group adopted the Framework Alliance Contract (FAC-1), which not only makes it easier for small businesses to bid for deals, it sets shared objectives for those on the framework. Alliance members are expected to work together to improve value, share information on suppliers, review and compare prices and tender or renegotiate subcontracts.'

CHAPTER 6

How does FAC-1 enable successful collaboration?

F AC-1 connects the objectives of collaboration with clear mutual commitments and detailed procurement, contracting and management systems. The FAC-1 collaborative systems are designed to be easily understood and commercially attractive. These systems are flexible as regards agreed options for costing (see Chapters 26 and 27), incentivisation (see Chapters 22 and 23) and risk management (see Chapter 34).

Collaborative procurement and contracting underpin a collaborative working culture. However, the objectives of collaboration can be difficult to translate into commercial procurement, contracting and management systems, with the result that collaboration is often expressed in general terms, such as 'good faith' and 'no blame', rather than through a set of agreed commitments. Without these agreed commitments it is not clear what collaboration actually involves, with the effect that clients, industry and advisers can see it as an exotic and risky option.

Confusion is also created when clients, industry and advisers suggest that collaborative procurement and contracting must adopt particular models for costing, incentivisation and risk sharing or must include specific limits on lability, exclusions of liability or additional insurances. These preconditions can be commercially unattractive and can prevent the wider adoption of collaborative approaches.

FAC-1 avoids confusion and unnecessary preconditions by combining the *Alliance Members'* commitment to 'trust, fairness and collaboration' in clause 1.1 with detailed provisions that are practical, commercial and legally enforceable. It describes approaches to collaborative strategies, procurement processes, contractual relationships and management practices that avoid collaborative relationships being lost in the 'Bermuda Triangle' of idealistic debate, cynical criticism and unrealised good intentions.

The 'Construction Playbook' emphasises the value of investing in and maintaining collaborative relationships and states that

- 'acting together with suppliers drives mutual understanding and helps to solve problems more effectively, leading to better and faster delivery';
- 'strategic supplier relationship management can unlock additional value and innovation'; and
- 'contracting authorities should place significant importance on the relationships they create with their supply chains at an organisational and portfolio-level'.

Practice Note 9. Limits of informal collaboration.
'Constructing the Gold Standard' recognises the arguments of framework providers that 'personal leadership and consultation are the best ways to ensure the adoption of their guidance' and that 'informal collaborative techniques can nudge clients and suppliers towards improved framework practices'. It notes that 'these arguments are fair insofar as most of us react better to human engagement than to cold legal obligations, but the evidence from Trial Projects and other case studies shows how the right framework contract joins up the dots among good framework practices and accelerates the progress of transformational efforts by giving them clearer shape and direction'.

FAC-1 clarifies the collaborative interactions between the *Alliance Members* and requires that 'in all matters governed by the *Framework Alliance Contract* they shall act reasonably and without delay' (clause 1.1). For example:

- the requirement to act reasonably is extended to individuals employed by *Alliance Members*, and FAC-1 requires that an *Alliance Member* 'shall promptly replace any individual who disrupts or adversely affects the *Framework Programme* or any *Alliance Activities* or any *Project*' (clause 3.4); and
- the requirement to avoid delay is made clear in the time limits set out in the FAC-1 *Contract Terms* and in the Schedule 2 *Timetable*, which 'states agreed deadlines, gateways and milestones in respect of the *Framework Programme* and achievement of the *Objectives* and the timescales for *Alliance Activities*' (see Chapter 24 and Annex D).

'Constructing the Gold Standard' highlights the importance of driving improved framework outcomes through collaborative relationship management systems that establish and sustain clear mutual understanding, effective problem-solving and dispute avoidance at all levels of the *Supply Chain*.
The FAC-1 collaborative systems for managing framework relationships include

- the duties of the *Alliance Manager* (see Chapter 25), who is required to exercise 'any discretion fairly and constructively' (clause 3.1);
- the operation of the *Core Group* (see Chapter 21) as a collaborative decision-making body; and
- the *Early Warning* and joint *Risk Management* systems (see Chapter 34) governing the joint assessment and agreement of appropriate actions and timelines.

These values are extended to the wider *Supply Chain* through *Alliance Activities* such as *Supply Chain Collaboration* that establish and support strategic collaborative relationships with *Supply Chain* members outside the FAC-1 *Alliance*, including joint reviews that explore the scope for the wider *Supply Chain* to offer *Improved Value* in exchange for improved commitments by *Alliance Members* (see Chapters 29 and 30).

> Gold Standard Recommendation 23. 'Improve framework outcomes by creating collaborative systems for the management of framework relationships and strategic supply chain relationships.'

FAC-1 provides for collaborative relationship management of *Alliance Members* and *Supply Chain* members through processes that build up more reliable design, cost and risk information. It enables joint reviews and exchanges of data through agreed contributions and interactions between *Alliance Members* that establish the scope for greater consistency and greater efficiency and the potential for revised and shared working practices, including reviews after completion of each *Project* that consider how improvements can be made in later *Projects*.

> **Practice Note 10. Features of an *Alliance*.**
> 'Constructing the Gold Standard' noted that confusion is created if clients, suppliers and advisers make assumptions as to the characteristics of a framework alliance. For example, a framework alliance is not obliged to adopt a particular cost model or particular exclusions or limitations of liability. There is no reason to restrict the features of a framework alliance in this way, and a rigid definition can be unhelpful if it leads to a framework alliance being seen as uncommercial.

The 'Construction Playbook' states that the Crown Commercial Service framework alliances are 'integrating FAC-1 and Project 13 principles'. The 'Project 13 principles' that are reflected in FAC-1 treat a collaborative team as an 'Enterprise', through which the *Alliance Members* can apply the following five pillars.

Capable owner

- Owner develops the Enterprise built on long-term relationships.
- The Enterprise is set up to deliver (1) clearly articulated customer outcomes and (2) long-term asset performance.

Governance

- Value is defined at outcome level (through baselines, benchmarks or affordability).
- The Enterprise is rewarded for outcome performance.
- Risk allocation is aligned with capability.
- Commercial arrangements provide the potential for sustainable returns.

Organisation

- All parts of the Enterprise are aligned with the outcomes to be delivered.
- Suppliers are engaged early in developing solutions.
- The Enterprise integrates capability in high-performing, collaborative teams.

Integration

- An Integrator brings together capabilities that translates solutions into production systems.
- The Integrator enables a platform approach to delivery.
- Strategic suppliers within the ecosystem are organisationally and commercially aligned with the outcomes.
- The Enterprise has a common and committed approach to health, safety and wellbeing.

Digital transformation

- The Enterprise digital transformation strategy enables an integrated digital approach to asset management and delivery.
- The Enterprise effectively integrates engineering and digital technology to deliver intelligent solutions.

FAC-1 adopts the 2017 ISO 44001 international standard for collaborative business relationship management in relation to

- 'Operational awareness: vison, values, leadership and objectives';
- 'Knowledge: specify strategy, outcomes, business case and implementation plan';
- 'Internal assessment: policies, people skills and collaborative maturity';

- 'Partner selection: capability, roles and responsibilities';
- 'Working together: governance, management systems and processes';
- 'Value creation: continual improvement processes';
- 'Staying together: team management, monitoring, measurement and behaviour'; and
- 'Exit strategy activation: disengagement triggers and processes'.

The evaluation of prospective *Alliance Members* can assess the collaborative commitments of organisations. The evaluation criteria for FAC-1 *Alliance* procurement and for *Project* awards can include assessment of

- collaborative profile and experience,
- cultural compatibility,
- *Client* relationship management,
- *Supply Chain* relationship management, and
- *User* and *Stakeholder* management.

Personal leadership and professional management are essential to creating and maintaining a collaborative culture, and the evaluation of prospective *Alliance Members* can also assess the collaborative commitments of individuals. A collaborative culture depends on *Alliance Members* allocating the right individuals to fulfil their strategic commitments, and the evaluation of prospective *Alliance Members* can include behavioural analysis.

FAC-1 enables productive collaborative engagement with parties outside the *Alliance* such as

- *Stakeholders*, who are defined in Appendix 1 as 'any one or more organisations or groups of individuals, as stated in the *Framework Alliance Agreement* by reference to clause 1.10, who are not *Alliance Members* and who have an interest relating to the *Framework Programme*'; and
- *Users*, who are defined in Appendix 1 as 'any person or party using a *Project*'.

Alliance Activities can allow the time and opportunity to take the needs and wishes of *Stakeholders* and *Users* into account, both at a strategic level and in the procurement of individual *Projects*. Benefits to *Stakeholders* and *Users* are included in the FAC-1 definition of *Improved Value*.

CHAPTER 7

How does FAC-1 drive *Improved Value* and *Risk Management*?

FAC-1 *Alliances* can generate significant *Improved Value* and effective *Risk Management*, as illustrated in the case studies and practice notes that form part of this handbook. The search for *Improved Value* and the organisation of effective *Risk Management* need to run through all four stages of framework strategy, procurement, contracting and management (see Chapter 2), starting with a strategy that is sufficiently clear and persuasive to attract industry commitments. With the motivation of a credible commercial strategy, FAC-1 provides many opportunities for the *Client/Additional Clients* to attract proposals for *Improved Value*:

- When prospective industry *Alliance Members* are seeking a place on the framework alliance.
- When industry *Alliance Members* are seeking appointment to a specific *Project* or group of *Projects*.
- When industry *Alliance Members* are undertaking *Alliance Activities* with the *Client/Additional Clients* and with other industry *Alliance Members*.
- When industry *Alliance Members* are undertaking *Supply Chain Collaboration* with the *Client/Additional Clients* and with *Supply Chain* members.
- When industry *Alliance Members* are providing feedback on lessons learned from each *Project* to the *Client/Additional Clients* and to other industry *Alliance Members*.

FAC-1 expresses the strategy of the *Client/Additional Clients* through the Schedule 1 *Objectives, Success Measures, Targets* and *Incentives*. It provides contractual systems through which to achieve the *Objectives* and *Success Measures*, with *Incentives* that can be linked to improved outcomes by reference to the *Targets*.

On the basis of these foundations, FAC-1 motivates the *Client/Additional Clients* and other *Alliance Members* to work both together and individually to improve outcomes, to earn *Incentives* and to undertake agreed *Alliance Activities* designed to improve value and reduce risk. It sets out the timing of *Alliance Activities*, the systems of joint *Risk Management* and the collaborative support provided by the *Alliance Manager* and by the *Core Group* as a joint decision-making forum. This cycle of *Improved Value* is illustrated in Figure 5.

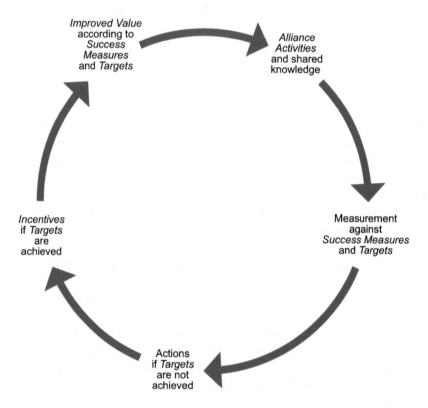

Figure 5. FAC-1 cycle of *Improved Value*.

Examples of how FAC-1 *Alliances* can achieve *Improved Value* and effective *Risk Management* were established by the FAC-1 prototypes used on UK government 'Trial Projects' such as the Ministry of Justice prisons programme (Case Study 4), the Surrey County Council highways programme (Case Study 5) and the SCMG housing programme (Case Study 12). In 'Constructing the Gold Standard', Crown Commercial Service identified a range of benefits from FAC-1, and these are listed in Checklist 3.

▶	Ability to influence design through earlier contractor engagement
▶	Connecting whole life considerations through an integrated supply chain
▶	Focus on newer and safer working practices in construction
▶	Options for innovative construction methods and technologies
▶	More opportunities for SMEs, specialists and local providers
▶	Sustainable solutions and environmental benefits
▶	Collaborative risk management and dispute avoidance
▶	Promoting standardisation in contracting through common 'boilerplate' clauses

Checklist 3. Crown Commercial Service FAC-1 benefits.

Practice Note 11. Benefits of a *Framework Alliance Contract*.
'Constructing the Gold Standard' found that: 'The transparency, clarity
and integration offered by multiparty framework alliance contracts has
a positive impact on outcomes, for example as recorded on the Ministry
of Justice, SCMG and Project Horizon Trial Projects. These framework
alliances achieved agreed efficiency savings averaging 18.5% combined
with design improvements, extended warranties, improved safety, new
opportunities for local and regional SMEs, environmental benefits,
improved employment and skills opportunities and improved whole
life value.'

FAC-1 *Alliances* have enabled a wide range of successful outcomes from
Projects and Framework Programme in terms of measurable *Improved Value*
and *Risk Management* solutions. Examples summarised in the case studies and
practice notes that form part of this handbook include

- improved cost certainty and agreed *Project* cost savings without eroding
  profits (see Case Studies 3, 4, 5, 6, 12, 15, 19, 22, 23, 24, 27 and 28);
- strategic time management and agreed *Project* time savings (see Case
  Studies 5, 6, 11, 12, 19, 20, 23, 24, 28 and 29);
- reduced carbon footprint and other improvements in *Sustainability* (see
  Case Studies 5, 7, 9, 10, 11, 14, 16, 19, 20, 23 and 30);
- shared innovations, design improvements and extended warranties (see
  Case Studies 4, 5, 8, 12, 16, 19, 23 and 24);
- improved use of manufacturing and offsite construction (see Case Studies 16, 19, 23, 25 and 26);

- improved digital information management through *BIM* (see Case Studies 16, 19, 23 and 24);
- improved *Risk Management* through agreed actions (see Case Studies 5, 8, 11, 14, 15, 16, 19, 23, 24, 27 and 29);
- reduced accidents and improved safety (see Case Studies 5 and 24);
- new local and regional business opportunities (see Case Studies 3, 5, 7, 12, 13, 19, 22, 23 and 30);
- new training and employment opportunities (see Case Studies 5, 6, 7, 11, 12, 15, 19 and 23); and
- problem-solving and dispute avoidance (see all of the case studies in this handbook).

Practice Note 12. Benefits of FAC-1.
The Ministry of Justice reports that, on its New Prisons alliance:

- 'FAC-1 encouraged use of innovative contract arrangements to procure projects or programmes of work as a strategic alliance';
- 'this approach increased consistency, efficiency, and improved value and performance';
- 'the alliance model was beneficial to the Ministry of Justice due to the scale and complexity of the project as well as the need for consistency in standard prison design'; and
- 'beyond the cost benefits of the singular tender exercise, the alliance approach aimed to drive benefits of collective buying power, sharing of good practice, and procurement efficiencies'.

See also Case Study 16.

Practice Note 13. Collaborative *Risk Management*.
NHS Shared Business Services report that

- 'at an overarching framework level, we chose to utilise the FAC-1 form of contract due to the prominence it gives to having a framework level *Risk Register* and also its core focus on collaboration'; and
- 'the collaborative nature of the FAC-1 helps us as it contains mechanisms within it that lean heavily towards a decision-making process that is embarked upon by all parties working together towards a common unified goal'.

See also Case Study 14.

The systems through which FAC-1 *Alliances* achieve *Improved Value* and *Risk Management* are explained in this handbook in

- Chapters 26 and 27 in relation to cost certainty and agreed cost savings;
- Chapter 24 in relation to strategic time management and agreed time savings;
- Chapter 8 in relation to reduced carbon footprint and other improvements in *Sustainability*;
- Chapters 29, 30 and 36 in relation to shared innovations, design improvements and extended warranties;
- Chapter 14 in relation to improved digital information management through *BIM*;
- Chapter 15 in relation to improved use of manufacture and offsite construction;
- Chapter 34 in relation to improved *Risk Management* through agreed actions;
- Chapter 7 (this chapter) in relation to reduced accidents and improved safety;
- Chapter 9 in relation to new local and regional business opportunities and new training and employment opportunities; and
- Chapter 40 in relation to problem-solving and dispute avoidance.

Powerful examples of the impact of FAC-1 *Risk Management* include the reduced accidents and improved safety illustrated in Case Studies 5 and 12. The need for a new procurement approach to improve building safety was highlighted by Dame Judith Hackitt's Independent Review of Building Regulations and Fire Safety following the Grenfell Tower disaster in 2017. Dame Judith concluded that

- 'the way in which procurement is often managed can reduce the likelihood that a building will be safe';
- 'the contracting process determines the relationships, competencies and processes that exist between all the parties in the build and management processes'; and
- 'issues at this stage, for example inadequate specification, focus on low cost or adversarial contracting, can make it difficult (and most likely, more expensive) to produce a safe building'.

Practice Note 14. Improved building safety.
Under their FAC-1 framework alliances, Crown Commercial Service 'facilitated alliance forums which included multiple stakeholders from MHCLG,

CCS alliance managers, CCS High Rise lot suppliers and CCS Construction Management suppliers, and which enabled better understanding of the practical implications of the Hackitt recommendations'. Dame Judith Hackitt stated in her 'Progress of Culture Change in the Construction Sector' report

- that she 'welcomed the Construction Works and Associated Services Framework established by the Crown Commercial Service';
- that 'the contract will enable CCS to mandate collaborative working, creating more integrated relationships and sharing of good practice'; and
- that this highlights how CCS is 'influencing and shaping a positive culture within the Construction Industry', as 'an exemplar to others who have yet to demonstrate the leadership we are looking for'.

See also Case Studies 5 and 24 and Practice Note 42.

FAC-1 provides for *Risk Management* in relation to improved health and safety as follows.

- It includes 'improved health and safety' in its definition of *Improved Value*, and this forms part of the shared *Objectives* and *Targets* against which performance is measured, and to which all signatories commit through agreed *Alliance Activities* in accordance with the shared *Timetable*.
- Its multiparty structure ensures that all *Alliance Members* are aware of each other's health and safety roles, expertise and responsibilities.
- Its strategic *Risk Management* actions capture responses to health and safety risks and improved health and safety practices through the knowledge and experience shared among *Alliance Members* on multiple *Projects*.
- Its *Intellectual Property Rights* and confidentiality provisions encourage the sharing of ideas for improved safety on agreed terms.

Case Study 4. Ministry of Justice framework alliances integrating consultants, contractors and supply chains.
The Ministry of Justice procured FAC-1 prototype framework alliances, which underpinned the HMP Berwyn and HMP Five Wells projects and which were credited in the 2012 'Effectiveness of Frameworks' report with achieving

- reduced operating costs of £10 million,
- reduced burden on industry of £30 million, and
- procurement risk mitigation of £2 million.

The HMP Berwyn Trial Project case study was procured through this FAC-1 prototype and showed how *Supply Chain Collaboration* combined with the integrated use of *BIM* and MMC helped project teams to achieve

- efficiency savings of up to 26%,
- reduced construction programmes,
- design innovations and more sustainable project solutions,
- appointment of local and regional supply chain members, and
- new local skills and employment opportunities.

Comparable achievements have been demonstrated on the HMP Five Wells project, which was a 'Construction Playbook' case study.

The Ministry of Justice used an FAC-1 prototype in conjunction with *Project Contracts* based on the PPC2000 standard form project alliance contract.

See also Case Studies 19 and 23.

Case Study 5. Surrey County Council and Kier Highways framework alliance and improved value.

Surrey County Council and Kier Highways created an FAC-1 prototype framework alliance contract with Aggregate Industries and Marshall Surfacing, using *Supply Chain Collaboration* led by Kier to generate agreed savings in excess of 12% over a period of five years in exchange for

- 'visibility and continuity of a larger-scale, longer-term pipeline of work',
- 'advance planning of work on each annual cycle',
- 'prompt payment at all levels of the supply chain',
- 'closer supply chain involvement in design and planning', and
- 'availability of storage facilities in client depots'.

The Surrey County Council FAC-1 prototype also achieved 'qualitative benefits' comprising

- 'improved whole life value, including 10 year warranties for 76% of schemes and 5–8 year warranties for 22% of schemes',
- 'improved quality control through joint risk management',
- 'improved apprentice commitments by tier 2 and 3 supply chain members',
- 'time savings through lean programming',
- 'innovations that increased recycling, reduced landfill and reduced cost for treating tarbound roads from £140 per tonne to £60 per tonne',

- 'no major remedial work required and no health and safety incidents', and
- 'over 100 complimentary letters received from residents and Council members'.

Surrey County Council used an FAC-1 prototype in conjunction with a *Project Contract* based on the TPC2005 (now TAC-1) standard form term alliance contract.

See also Case Study 22.

Case Study 6. Whitefriars Housing Group framework alliance and improved value.

Whitefriars Housing Group set up an FAC-1 prototype framework alliance with windows specialists Graham Holmes and Anglian Windows. This was expanded to comprise a total of £230 million of refurbishment work undertaken by Wates Construction and Lovell.

A three-way framework alliance contract between Whitefriars, Wates and Lovell awarded annual programmes of work according to available client funding, contractor performance on previous work and main contractor capacity for further work. When the framework alliance was set up, Whitefriars did not have sufficient funding to cover its entire programme, and efficiencies were essential in order to reduce anticipated costs. Lovell had obtained cheaper prices from its long-term kitchen supplier, and Wates agreed to utilise the same kitchen supplier, with all consequent savings reverting to the client. The resultant efficiencies reduced a five-year programme to four years and saved the client 10% of its £240 million expected cost.

In addition, the establishment of a steady volume of work enabled both constructors to operate using a stable workforce and to increase their efficiency on site, e.g. by reducing the turnaround time for the installation of new kitchens from three weeks to two weeks per flat. Reducing the time spent on site achieved savings in preliminaries costs of £2 million, all of which reverted to the client. The client – with both constructors and in partnership with Mowlem – established the Whitefriars Housing Plus Agency, which secured training opportunities for 38 people in the first year and a total of more than 200 over the duration of the whole programme.

Whitefriars Housing Group used an FAC-1 prototype in conjunction with *Project Contracts* based on the PPC2000 standard form project alliance contract.

Case Study 7. Department for Work & Pensions framework alliance and improved value.

The Department for Work & Pensions (DWP) worked through the CCS FAC-1 framework alliance to deliver engagement with the market that supported social value initiatives including increased employment opportunities for high-risk groups such as prison leavers, carbon reduction by more efficient heating systems, and other improved sustainability. The DWP Rapid Estates Expansion Programme used soft-market engagement to inform understanding of supplier scheduling capability and supply chain capacity among mid-tier contractors and contractors for smaller or medium-sized projects.

DWP focused on suppliers who recruited the unemployed as well as those who used apprenticeships. They used metrics for suppliers to report on the numbers of new start-ups, small and medium-sized enterprises, voluntary community and social enterprises, and mutuals. The alliance enabled support for military veterans entering the workforce, for apprenticeships, for SME supply chain members and for local supply chain members. It worked with local communities and monitored payment of the living wage via its contracts and supply chain.

DWP and CCS used FAC-1 in conjunction with *Project Contracts* based on the NEC4 Term Services Contract.

Case Study 8. Eden Project Core complex project alliance and improved value.

The Eden Project, in Cornwall, UK, created a framework alliance using an FAC-1 prototype as a multiparty integrator of a complex project. The *Alliance Members* comprised Nicholas Grimshaw & Partners, Buro Happold, Scott Wilson Kilpatrick, Anthony Hunt Associates, Haskoll Limited, Land Use Consultants, Davis Langdon and a McAlpine Joint Venture (Alfred McAlpine Construction and Sir Robert McAlpine), all of whom signed a multiparty alliance contract with provisions for preconstruction phase design development, pricing, risk management and programming prior to award of each construction phase contract. This ensured the team's early commitment to joint design of the innovative Education and Resource Centre (the 'Core') as well as a number of smaller projects while ensuring that construction operations did not interfere with the ongoing operation of the Eden Project as a visitor attraction.

The Core alliance project was to be constructed on an unstable site comprising the wall of a former clay pit, and the alliance contract governed shared systems for early supply chain involvement that included the instruction of surveys and other activities necessary to agree risk solutions ahead of work starting on site while finalising scope, price and programme. It also described the terms of reference for a *Core Group*, including an express duty to warn other team members of problems arising.

The Core alliance project won an 'Excellence in Collaborative Engineered Design' award, with a key contribution made by Swiss contractor Haring, who supplied unique glulam beams for the Fibonacci spiral design and implemented value engineering with the McAlpine Joint Venture and with architect Nicholas Grimshaw. The award citation observed that: 'Collaborative teamwork has been established over a long period of time at the Eden Project. Special mention should be made of how well Haring integrated into this environment.' The project also won an award for 'Best Structural Innovation', which noted that: 'The 100ft span of glulam timber roof was cut by computer in the form of the equiangular spiral found throughout nature, from sunflower seeds to galaxies. This was combined with the latest environmental technologies to make one of the most complex and sustainable structures ever built in Britain.' The Core was opened by HM Queen Elizabeth II in summer 2006.

The Eden Project used an FAC-1 prototype in conjunction with *Project Contracts* based on the NEC2 standard form building contract.

CHAPTER 8

How does FAC-1 drive net zero carbon and improved *Sustainability*?

Combatting climate change is the greatest challenge of our time, and there are key roles to be played by the construction industry, its clients and their advisers. The UK Department for Business, Energy & Industrial Strategy defines 'net zero carbon' outcomes as those where 'any emissions would be balanced by schemes to offset an equivalent amount of greenhouse gases from the atmosphere', and the 2016 Paris Agreement required that global carbon emissions must be at net zero by 2050.

The carbon reduction commitments and innovations of individual organisations need to be supported by a more integrated approach to procuring projects and programmes of work. A new approach is essential because important commitments and innovations are being lost or inhibited where

- net zero objectives are too vague to be converted into project deliverables,
- net zero proposals are not assessed in sufficient detail to establish their viability and are discounted as too costly or complex, and
- net zero achievements on individual projects are not shared in ways that create learning and develop new norms.

Clear carbon reduction measures need to be committed to by clients and industry at each stage in the strategy, procurement, contracting and management of a project or a programme of works, services or supplies. Carbon reduction can then be assessed transparently as part of an objective contractual performance measurement process, supported by agreed systems through which the team members can examine and seek to correct any shortfall in achieving agreed targets. The UK Green Building Council states that: 'Achieving net zero whole life carbon will require close collaboration within the supply chain to minimize embodied carbon and related liabilities for offsets. Similar to performance contracting for operational energy, this could involve a move towards carbon performance contracting with suppliers.'

'Constructing the Gold Standard' recommends that the *Client/Additional Clients* and industry use long-term strategic relationships to achieve improved net zero carbon targets and to align these with other agreed priorities. The means to align net zero carbon with other *Objectives* and *Success Measures* and to embed net zero carbon in each stage of framework strategy, procurement, contracting and management are set out in FAC-1.

> **Gold Standard Recommendation 3.** 'Require that all public sector construction frameworks prioritise safety, net zero carbon and the Compact with Industry.'

A cornerstone of achieving net zero carbon targets is to capture and apply incremental learning from project to project, and this learning depends on strategic procurement practices that create and support commercially robust systems of collaboration among multiple parties on multiple projects. Progress will be far too slow to meet net zero carbon targets if team members can only design, cost and offer net zero solutions for one project at a time.

In FAC-1's Appendix 1, improved *Sustainability* forms part of the definition of *Improved Value*, and the definition of *Sustainability* includes measures intended to

- reduce carbon emissions,
- reduce use of energy and or natural and manmade resources,
- improve waste management, and
- protect or improve the condition of the *Environment*.

Appendix 1 defines the *Environment* as 'all and any land, water and air within any natural or man-made structure above or below ground'.

FAC-1 supports implementation of the net zero recommendations set out in the King's College London research report that accompanies the 'Construction Playbook'. The research report was published by the Society of Construction Law in April 2022 and is referred to in UK government guidance on net zero procurement. These net zero recommendations are summarised in Checklist 4 and state the following:

- 'Clients, consultants, contractors and supply chain members should create multiparty "Gold Standard" framework alliances through which to integrate the net zero carbon commitments of multiple parties on multiple projects and through which to ensure shared learning while protecting intellectual property rights and other confidential information' (see Chapters 11 and 36).

- 'The construction procurement strategy should state clearly the client's commitments to tackling climate change and the ways in which the client expects these to be matched by commitments from the construction industry' (see Chapters 22 and 23).
- 'The system for the selection of construction team members should use balanced evaluation criteria that take into account net zero carbon proposals submitted by prospective consultants, contractors and supply chain members and should make clear the procedures by which the approved net zero carbon proposals from successful bidders will be developed, agreed and implemented' (see Chapters 4 and 28).
- 'Contractors and supply chain members should be appointed early during the pre-construction phase of a construction project on the basis of clear contractual systems through which they work with the client and consultants in developing and agreeing viable and affordable net zero carbon proposals in line with the client's stated brief and budget as preconditions to commencement of the construction phase of the project' (see Chapters 9 and 30).
- 'The construction procurement strategy, team selection processes and construction contracts should make clear how long-term pipelines of work will be awarded in order to attract industry investments in net zero carbon innovations such as offsite manufacture' (see Chapters 15, 17 and 28).
- 'Clients, consultants and contractors should commit to contractual systems by which they explore systematically the best ways for specialist supply chain members to contribute their net zero carbon expertise and the best ways for local and regional supply chain members to offer a lower carbon footprint' (see Chapters 9 and 30).
- 'Clients should ensure that their construction contracts include a definition of sustainability and describe systems of collaborative governance and joint risk management by which the client, consultants, contractors and supply chain members will work together and individually to achieve net zero carbon and other sustainable outcomes' (see Chapters 21 and 34).
- 'Clients, consultants, contractors and supply chain members should implement net zero carbon commitments to whole life procurement through digital information management governing exchanges of accurate data in relation to design, cost, time, risk and operation supported by a multiparty contractual integrator' (see Chapter 14).
- 'Clients and consultants should lead and manage the implementation of net zero objectives under new and existing construction contracts, including through the agreement and management of supplemental action plans with binding timetables' (see Chapter 13).

By the *Client/Additional Clients* inviting net zero proposals at a time when they can be assessed and developed on a framework alliance comprising multiple *Projects*, the *Alliance Members* can establish the full potential for significant reductions in environmental impact through

- proposals for design, supply, construction and *Operation* that reduce greenhouse gas emissions;
- proposals for the most buildable and least wasteful interpretation of designs;
- proposals for reduced waste and increased recycling;
- proposals for the efficient use of energy on site, including through offsite construction; and
- proposals for the efficient use of energy by reduced maintenance and repair in the *Operation* of the built facility.

Integrate the net zero carbon commitments of multiple parties on multiple *Projects*

Share learning while protecting *Intellectual Property Rights* and confidentiality

Create strategic *Objectives* and *Success Measures* for tackling climate change

Select *Alliance Members* on criteria that take into account net zero carbon proposals

Agree a process for *Client* review and approval of costed net zero carbon proposals

Create a *Framework Programme* pipeline that attracts investment in net zero carbon

Explore specialist, local and regional *Supply Chain* contributions to net zero carbon

Define *Sustainability* and agree systems for net zero carbon sustainable outcomes

Integrate contributions to whole life procurement through *BIM*

Agree contractual action plans with a binding *Timetable*

Checklist 4. FAC-1 and net zero carbon.

FAC-1 enables the net zero carbon proposals of individual organisations to be integrated into viable and affordable mutual commitments. It enables these net zero carbon proposals and other *Sustainability* initiatives to be evaluated by *Alliance Members*, to be costed accurately and objectively, and to be adopted on multiple *Projects*.

FAC-1 helps *Alliance Members* to develop net zero carbon *Objectives* under an existing contract into an 'action plan' describing *Alliance Activities* using a shared *Timetable*. A net zero action plan under FAC-1 can describe supplemental mutual commitments that do not change the overall scope of the existing contract, do not change its agreed terms, and comply with public procurement regulations (see Chapter 13).

Practice Note 15. FAC-1 options for net zero carbon.
Crown Commercial Service reports that its FAC-1 *Framework Briefs* 'emphasise delivery of sustainability through the design process, materials selection, construction techniques and construction methods implemented, supporting 2050 net zero commitments, and ultimately a whole life carbon approach'. These FAC-1 *Framework Briefs* explain how consultants/ccontractors/suppliers are mandated to identify opportunities to clients on achievement of sustainability objectives. Specifications also contain more detailed requirements, shoring-up these higher-level objectives, for example:

- 'Adopting the application of BRE's Environmental Assessment Methodology (BREEAM)
- Promoting, conserving and enhancing biodiversity, including use of Biodiversity Action Plans or equivalent, and the management of Sites of Special Scientific Interest (SSSIs)
- Following the principles of the Green Public Procurement (GPP) voluntary instrument
- Adherence to packaging regulations and the reduction of embedded carbon, particular important in Building Materials.'

Crown Commercial Service are using FAC-1 to procure their 2023 'Demand Management and Renewables' framework alliance, incorporating the following products and services:

- solar photovoltaic,
- battery (energy) storage,
- heat pumps,
- heat network technical support and
- net zero carbon consultancy.

See also Case Studies 1, 7, 16 and 21.

The net zero procurement strategy of the *Client/Additional Clients* should be made clear when procuring the *Alliance* by stating the following in the FAC-1 *Framework Brief*:

- How net zero proposals will form part of the quality criteria that shift the evaluation focus away from lowest price towards a deeper understanding of the capabilities of prospective industry *Alliance Members*.

- The purpose of seeking net zero proposals from prospective industry *Alliance Members*, including the processes by which these proposals are reviewed, developed and adopted when *Alliance Members* are appointed.
- How *Intellectual Property Rights* and confidentiality in net zero proposals will be respected.
- By what process *Alliance Members* will seek agreement to share approved net zero proposals with other *Alliance Members*.
- How the success of agreed proposals in delivering improved net zero outcomes will affect the award of future *Projects* and other *Incentives*.

Practice Note 16. Innovation and net zero carbon.
In relation to their FAC-1 New Prisons alliance, the Ministry of Justice report that innovation is driven through the design workstreams, joint review with representatives across all four tier 1 contractors alongside the Ministry of Justice and its consultant delivery partners. The design improvements include

- changes to increase offsite manufacture,
- improvements to health and safety onsite, and
- better efficiency in construction.

More than 60 opportunities were triaged for implementation through the *Alliance* change group.

Though there was a pre-existing standard design, the design for the four new prisons targets BREEAM 2018 Outstanding ratings, and routes to net zero carbon. The design of these new prisons, while based on that of Glen Parva, are expected to deliver better environmental outcomes because they

- achieve a significant reduction in operational energy consumption from the national grid compared to the Glen Parva baseline and
- achieve an 85% reduction in operational carbon emissions compared to the Glen Parva baseline and achieve BREEAM Outstanding.

See also Case Study 16.

FAC-1 *Supply Chain Collaboration* (see Chapter 30) is an effective system through which to evaluate and adopt proposals for net zero carbon targets and other *Sustainability* initiatives. By inviting proposals from tier 2 and tier 3 *Supply Chain* members at a time when they can be assessed at a strategic level, an FAC-1 *Alliance* can establish the full potential for significant reductions in environmental impact.

Case Study 9. Oxfordshire County Council and Skanska net zero carbon framework alliance action plan.
Oxfordshire County Council and Skanska supplemented their £40 million per annum contract for highways and infrastructure with a net zero carbon action plan using an FAC-1 transitional framework alliance contract through which to capture improved environmental value linked to extension of an underlying NEC term call-off contract. The team identified significant opportunities, including carbon consumption reductions and financial savings, and their strategic net zero carbon outputs using FAC-1 included:

- A suite of low carbon design solutions and associated action plans
- Development of a 'Partnership Carbon Reduction Strategy' and associated action plan
- Creation of a 'Whole Life Cost & Carbon' tool
- Focused training on lower carbon alternative materials
- Trials of new lower carbon materials.

Oxfordshire County Council and Skanska used FAC-1 in conjunction with a *Project Contract* broadly based on an NEC3 standard form.

Case Study 10. Stratford District Council/Wychavon District Council/Savills net zero framework alliance.
Stratford District Council, Wychavon District Council and Savills led 'a Social Housing Decarbonisation Demonstrator Programme' that complies with PAS2035 (retrofitting dwellings for improved energy efficiency), integrating their work with Rooftop Housing Group, Citizen Housing Group, Trent and Dove Housing, the Trident Group and the Orbit Housing Group. They used FAC-1 to maximise efficiencies through

- joint procurement and collaborative working to deliver shared best practice and innovation;
- early supply chain involvement to finalise surveys, designs, risks and costs; and
- consistent systems of project management, tenant engagement and education.

Stratford District Council, Wychavon District Council, Savills Rooftop Housing Group, Citizen Housing Group, Trent and Dove Housing, the Trident Group and the Orbit Housing Group used FAC-1 in conjunction with *Project Contracts* based on the PPC2000 standard form project alliance contract.

Case Study 11. Enel Green Power windfarm complex project alliance with EPC contractors in Spain.

Enel Green Power – an Italian multinational energy company – adopted FAC-1 in order to integrate the work of contractors and specialists engaged on their new-build windfarm projects. Enel Green Power used FAC-1 as a contractual integrator for the Campillo windfarms project in Spain, drawing together the separate EPC *Project Contracts* awarded to a range of specialist *Alliance Members*. Enel Green Power invested approximately €256 million in the construction of these three windfarms, employing around 350 people from the local area. The *Objectives* of the Campillo *Alliance* focused on time savings and health and safety issues, and the *Alliance Members* agreed financial *Incentives* linked to shared *Success Measures* that led to

- optimization of Campillo II and Campillo III being integrated in one site;
- cost savings from re-utilization of concrete pre-assembly slabs proposed by one of the EPC contractors;
- joint measures and proposals to advance the 'First Synchronization Date' resulting in connection to the Spanish grid two months ahead of schedule; and
- creation of a sustainable site by means of recycling, environmental protection and engagement with the local community.

Enel Green Power used FAC-1 in conjunction with *Project Contracts* that are bespoke EPC forms. Based on the results at Campillo, they have decided to use FAC-1 on all their European projects.

Enel Green Power is also using FAC-1 for a windfarm project in Brazil and is exploring its use for solar projects in the United States.

CHAPTER 9

How does FAC-1 support SMEs and social value?

F ramework alliances can play a crucial role in aggregating demand so that the specialist skills and experience of small and medium-sized enterprises (SMEs), including local and regional organisations, can be fully deployed. This aggregation can attract SMEs to roles as *Alliance Members* and *Supply Chain* members, can ensure that they are motivated to share their innovations and other ideas for *Improved Value* and *Risk Management*, and can provide a forum in which such ideas are voiced, tested, adopted and shared with others.

A framework alliance can obtain better *Client/Additional Client* outcomes by integrating the work of tier 1 industry *Alliance Members* alongside the work of tier 2 and tier 3 SME *Supply Chain* members, including local and regional *Supply Chain* members, in ways that can attract their maximum contributions, both strategically and in the pre-construction phase of framework *Projects*.

In order to capture *Improved Value* from the contributions of SMEs that include local and regional *Alliance Members* and *Supply Chain Members*, 'Constructing the Gold Standard' recommends that the *Client/Additional Clients* and *Alliance Manager*

- select prospective industry *Alliance Members* and award each *Project Contract* using evaluation criteria that identify SME strengths and
- use *Supply Chain Collaboration* (see Chapter 30) to create industry-led *Alliances* with *Supply Chain* members that include SMEs.

FAC-1 can provide for early SME *Supply Chain* involvement in several ways, both at *Framework Programme* level and at *Project* level, through

- FAC-1 *Alliance* selection and *Project* award processes that lead to direct *Client/Additional Client* appointments of SMEs as FAC-1 *Alliance Members*;

- FAC-1 *Alliance* selection and *Project* award processes that lead to the nomination of SME specialists as FAC-1 tier 2 and tier 3 *Supply Chain* members to be appointed by tier 1 industry *Alliance Members*;
- systems in the FAC-1 *Alliance* selection and *Project* award processes for tier 1 industry *Alliance Members* that describe how and when they will involve tier 2 and tier 3 SME *Supply Chain* members when implementing *Project Contracts*; and
- systems in the FAC-1 framework contracts of tier 1 industry *Alliance Members* that describe how and when they will work collaboratively with the *Client/Additional Clients* and other tier 1 industry *Alliance Members* to involve tier 2 and tier 3 SME *Supply Chain* members in advance of, and separate from, the award of *Project Contracts*.

An FAC-1 framework procurement can include evaluation criteria linked to proposals that draw out the particular strengths of SMEs, where these are relevant to required and desired *Client/Additional Client* outcomes from the *Framework Programme* and prospective *Projects*. For example, SMEs may offer relevant expertise based on local or regional knowledge, and may offer efficiency savings, improved social value and a reduced carbon footprint based on their local or regional location.

Aggregation of demand may create framework opportunities that exceed the capacity of SMEs. Pre-procurement market consultation can explore the capacity of prospective SMEs and can balance the benefits of aggregating framework *Projects* against the particular expertise and *Improved Value* offered by prospective SMEs. This will help the *Client/Additional Clients* to finalise the optimum framework strategy for engaging SMEs when calling off framework *Projects*.

> Gold Standard Recommendation 7. 'Capture improved value by identifying SME strengths and use Supply Chain Collaboration systems to maximise social value.'

An alternative way to access SME expertise, including contributions from local and regional businesses, is for the *Client/Additional Clients* to collaborate with tier 1 industry *Alliance Members* after they have been appointed to the FAC-1 *Alliance*. This collaboration involves the joint review of the tier 2 and tier 3 *Supply Chain* relationships recommended by each tier 1 industry *Alliance Member* and assessment of the value that can be delivered by aggregating these relationships and by optimising the scale and duration of *Supply Chain* appointments. These collaborative processes comprise *Supply Chain Collaboration*, which is described in Chapter 30.

FAC-1 *Supply Chain Collaboration* also provides systems during the pre-construction phase of *Projects* to ensure that the selection of tier 2/tier 3 *Supply Chain* members takes account of the particular benefits that local and regional SME businesses may offer in terms of cost, quality, *Sustainability* and other relevant factors. This is a major breakthrough for public sector clients who wish to support the local and regional economy in ways that comply with public procurement legislation.

Early strategic engagement with tier 2 and tier 3 SME *Supply Chain* members under FAC-1 helps establish and implement proposals for social value, for example in relation to

- employment and skills benefits, including the avoidance of Modern Slavery, given that the majority of the construction workforce is employed by tier 2 and tier 3 SMEs for whom a long-term framework alliance appointment provides important new opportunities to offer apprenticeships and jobs as well as predictability of workflow; and
- community benefits, given that local and regional tier 2 and tier 3 SME *Supply Chain* members are likely to know more about the communities they work in and to design and deliver meaningful contributions to those communities.

Employment and training opportunities and the improved well-being of people both fall within the FAC-1 definition of *Sustainability*, and FAC-1 includes machinery that can convert social value *Objectives* into shared action plans with timescales and expected outcomes.

The FAC-1 *Framework Brief* and *Framework Proposals* need to make clear how *Alliance Members* will seek to achieve social value, so as to avoid tier 1 industry *Alliance Members* simply passing extra obligations and costs down the *Supply Chain*. In order to manage these risks:

- an FAC-1 *Alliance* connects social value expectations and measures to the proposals put forward when tier 1 industry *Alliance Members* are appointed, it makes clear how these proposals will be implemented, and it explores the potential for greater social value benefits where the *Client/Additional Clients*, the *Alliance Manager*, the tier 1 industry *Alliance Members* and the *Supply Chain* members work together; and
- an FAC-1 *Framework Alliance Contract* supports social value through the collaborative contractual machinery described in this handbook, agreeing the actions by the *Client/Additional Clients*, the *Alliance Manager*, the tier 1 industry *Alliance Members* and the *Supply Chain* members that convert social value targets into agreed actions with clear timescales.

Case Study 12. Hackney Homes/Homes for Haringey framework alliance integrating contractors and SME supply chains.

Hackney Homes and Homes for Haringey created the Supply Chain Management Group (SCMG), which procured a multi-client, multi-contractor prototype FAC-1 framework alliance to deliver a £240 million housing improvement programme, working with Mulalley, Keepmoat, Mansell, Lakehouse, Lovell and Wates, and a wide range of tier 2 and tier 3 *Supply Chain* members spanning 30 disciplines. The SCMG alliance reported that 'early joint appointment of a comprehensive range of SME tier 2 and tier 3 supply chain members' has created 'new opportunities for SME subcontractors and suppliers' and has 'demonstrated a breakthrough in enabling public sector clients to deal directly with key subcontractors and suppliers so as to ensure they build up fully integrated working relationships'.

The SCMG alliance created systems under which 'The project teams have a clear process for exchanging information on a collaborative basis at an early stage, with participants in early supply chain involvement meetings working together to agree solutions that promote the best method of delivering the project. Often such discussions are led by the tier 1 contractor (with tier 2/3 support), so as to utilise experience from recent similar projects and to offer clear and well considered methods for the efficient delivery of the works.'

The SCMG alliance reported 'additional employment and skills opportunities for individuals, for example 46 new apprenticeships over the first 18 months of the Hackney programme, plus establishment of the Building Lives Training Academy where apprentices who have got NVQ Level 1 are engaged by constructors/specialists according to demand of ongoing work so as to achieve NVQ Level 2 after 15/18 months'.

SCMG agreed action plans with contractor *Alliance Members* and *Supply Chain* members under standardised *Supply Chain Collaboration* systems for joint planning, design, costing and risk management. Through these systems SCMG reported that the clients and tier 1 contractors worked with local SMEs and national manufacturers including Veka, Bauder, Sovereign and Birchcroft as integrated teams who, together, delivered agreed cost savings and social value combined with extended warranties and more sustainable solutions across the framework portfolio. Improved environmental value included

- future-proofing green roofs at no additional cost and upgrading windows from Grade C to Grade A at no additional cost;
- improved repairs and maintenance through, for example, self-cleaning glass on high rise blocks; and
- more sustainable solutions including external wall insulation.

SCMG demonstrated significant savings in tender costs for the clients and the industry *Alliance Members* when procuring a framework alliance. Their analysis revealed that procurement consultant costs incurred by the clients were substantially reduced as a result of pre-existing *Supply Chain Collaboration* data and documentation. Independent confirmation was also provided by a sample contractor, Keepmoat, who explained how their own tender costs on the prototype FAC-1 procurement were far lower than the bid costs they incurred under a comparable single-stage procurement, specifically £719 per £1 million of turnover under SCMG as against £4,808 per £1 million of turnover under the comparable traditional bid.

SCMG used an FAC-1 prototype in conjunction with *Project Contracts* based on the PPC2000 standard form project alliance contract.

See also Case Study 30.

Case Study 13. LHC and London Borough of Southwark framework alliance integrating micro-SMEs.
LHC and London Borough of Southwark created FAC-1 framework alliances of SME and micro-SME architects, engineers and other consultant disciplines, using evaluation criteria that identified relevant strengths such as innovations linked to community knowledge and experience.

The FAC-1 alliances

- create a community of framework clients and consultants with shared *Objectives*, *Success Measures*, *Alliance Activities* and *Timetables* to support and integrate their work;
- govern the sharing of innovations, community knowledge and other good practices through the FAC-1 *Core Group* and agreement of mutual *Intellectual Property Rights*;
- use *Supply Chain Collaboration* to combine the buying power of multiple SMEs and micro-SMEs; and
- use the FAC-1 *Early Warning* and *Core Group* systems to avoid a blame culture and collaborate in joint *Risk Management*.

LHC and London Borough of Southwark used FAC-1 in conjunction with *Project Contracts* based on a range of JCT, NEC and PPC standard forms.

See also Case Study 2.

CHAPTER 10

How does FAC-1 provide flexibility for different users and different countries?

D ifferent clients and advisers need flexibility in developing and adapting a standard form framework alliance contract so as to include the details and variations that reflect their specific requirements. Framework alliances should allow flexibility in the way that *Projects* are delivered, and FAC-1 is designed to accommodate a wide range of specific *Client/Additional Client* requirements.

In order to identify the best means of delivering each prospective *Project* forming part of a *Framework Programme*, 'Constructing the Gold Standard' recommends that the *Client/Additional Clients* include in their framework strategies an evidence-based 'delivery model' assessment for each type of *Project*; that they reflect the chosen delivery model or models in their framework procurement, call-off and management systems; and that the *Alliance Manager* should provide guidance to the *Client/Additional Clients* on how to choose the most appropriate delivery model when calling off each *Project*.

> Gold Standard Recommendation 15. 'Use delivery model assessments to inform and support framework strategies, procurement, contracting, management and call-off.'

FAC-1 provides scope for the bespoke drafting needed to reflect the details of the *Alliance* relationships and the underlying *Project Contracts*. These details are developed in

- the *Framework Alliance Agreement*;
- the *Framework Brief* and other *Framework Documents*;
- the agreed *Objectives, Success Measures, Targets* and *Incentives*;
- the *Timetable* of agreed *Alliance Activities*;

- the agreed award procedures for *Project Contracts* and the *Template Project Documents*; and
- specific amendments to the *Contract Terms* by way of *Legal Requirements* or *Special Terms*.

An FAC-1 framework alliance can be combined with any allocation of design, supply and construction responsibilities on each *Project* while enabling the *Project Contract* award processes and the *Pre-Contract Activities* to be supported by early integrated contributions from all *Alliance Members* and *Supply Chain* members. The FAC-1 *Direct Award Procedure* and *Competitive Award Procedure* are compatible with any combination of roles, responsibilities and warranties among the *Alliance Members* and *Supply Chain* members engaged on each *Project*. They can describe one or more *Project* procurement options, which

- integrate the contributors to a *Project* under one or more *Project Contracts* so as to govern a 'consultant-led design' or 'design and build' or 'construction management' procurement model, with any level or combination of design, construction and operation contributions from design consultants, contractors, subcontractors, suppliers, manufacturers and operators;
- integrate activities under related *Project Contracts* where these contribute to a single complex *Project* or combination of *Projects*; and
- integrate the capital and operational phases of each *Project* to create a whole-life procurement model.

FAC-1 provides for the issue of *Orders* in respect of *Pre-Contract Activities*, which can then be brought under the terms of a full *Project Contract* when it is awarded.

> **Practice Note 17. Flexibility and consistency.**
> VINCI report that: 'We see the benefit of frameworks that offer different models of "call off" contract (as can be facilitated by FAC-1) but also where there is consistency between the collaborative approach defined in the overarching framework agreement.'

FAC-1 is designed for use in any jurisdiction, and for this purpose it

- provides for the choice of the applicable law,
- does not include any *Contract Terms* that restate specific provisions of English law,

- provides for the *Contract Terms* to be supplemented or amended to state particular *Legal Requirements* in order to comply with the laws of the jurisdiction stated in the *Framework Alliance Agreement*, and
- has been adapted for use in a range of common law and civil law jurisdictions.

Collaborative work on adaptations of FAC-1 for use in Brazil, Bulgaria, Chile, Germany, Italy, Peru and Spain have shown that few amendments are required to reflect the *Legal Requirements* of these countries. For example, the FAC-1 Schedule 6 Part 1 *Legal Requirements* can clarify any required changes to

- the clause 10 duty of care,
- the Appendix 1 definitions of *Insolvency Events* or *Intellectual Property Rights*, or
- the clause 15 and Appendix 4 options in respect of dispute resolution.

The adjustments made for the use of FAC-1 in Italy are set out in Annex E of this handbook.

FAC-1 does not refer expressly to any aspect of English law. However, clause 8 dealing with payment and clause 15.3 and Appendix 4 Part 2 dealing with adjudication are drafted to conform to the requirements of the UK Housing Grants, Construction and Regeneration Act 1996 as amended without specifically referring to that legislation. When completing the FAC-1 *Framework Alliance Agreement*, the *Client* and its advisers need to decide whether it is necessary for specific legislative provisions to be restated in the Schedule 6 Part 1 *Legal Requirements*.

FAC-1 provides for the *Contract Terms* to be supplemented or amended by *Special Terms* that reflect the particular needs of the *Client* or other *Alliance Members* or are required by reason of the nature of the *Framework Programme*.

If required, FAC-1 *Special Terms* can be used to align certain *Contract Terms* with the wording of the selected *Project Contract Conditions*, provided that the *Client* has selected a single set of *Project Contract Conditions* to govern the award of all *Project Contracts* to all *Alliance Members*.

However, most FAC-1 users do not use *Special Terms* to align the defined terms used in FAC-1 and in *Project Contracts* because

- different *Project Contract Conditions* are often required for the appointment of different consultant/contractor/supplier *Alliance Members* to different *Project* roles and under different *Project* procurement models;

- FAC-1 is designed to draw together different *Project Contract Conditions* used for the appointment of different contractor/consultant/supplier *Alliance Members* and *Supply Chain* members;
- FAC-1 is designed to govern activities and relationships that are not governed by the *Project Contracts*; and
- FAC-1 makes clear that only the *Project Contracts* govern the *Projects*.

PART II

HOW IS FAC-1 USED IN PRACTICE?

CHAPTER 11

How does FAC-1 integrate a programme of multiple *Projects*?

The framework alliances reviewed in 'Constructing the Gold Standard' illustrate the different approaches that deliver successful *Projects* and successful *Framework Programmes* while exploring the potential for improved economic, social and environmental value. They include

- regional and national construction and engineering projects and pro-grammes of works, services and supplies procured through framework alliances led by Crown Commercial Service for multiple government departments and a wide range of other public sector clients;
- major infrastructure programmes procured through frameworks and alli-ances led by the Environment Agency, National Highways and Network Rail;
- national and regional programmes for the construction and improvement of schools, healthcare facilities and custodial facilities procured through frameworks and alliances led by the Department for Education, the National Health Service and the Ministry of Justice;
- large-scale programmes of improvement to government estates led by the Department for Work & Pensions and HM Revenue and Customs; and
- regional and national frameworks and framework alliances delivering construction and engineering projects and programmes of works, services and supplies procured by LHC and by the members of the National Asso-ciation of Construction Frameworks for local authorities and other public sector clients.

'Constructing the Gold Standard' reviewed frameworks designed for national and regional programmes of works, services and supplies in England, Wales, Scotland and Northern Ireland. Review contributors included clients, contractors, consultants, suppliers and advisers in each of the four nations. Frameworks vary according to whether they are procured by

- one client,
- a group of connected or unconnected clients or
- a framework provider on behalf of a range of identified and unidentified clients.

'Constructing the Gold Standard' reviewed how frameworks also vary according to whether they are designed to govern

- committed or speculative programmes of works, services or supplies;
- generic types of works, services or supplies;
- works, services or supplies in a single sector or bridging multiple sectors; or
- programmes of work in one or more different regions.

An FAC-1 *Framework Alliance Contract* can support all the categories of framework listed above, fulfilling different purposes in different sectors and meeting varying national and regional needs. FAC-1 creates relationships and systems based on principles that are common to all framework types. It is designed to offer clients and industry a route through the maze that will help them to understand, identify and adopt the features of a Gold Standard framework and a Gold Standard framework contract.

Despite the potential of frameworks as vehicles for integrating teams and improving value, they are sometimes used cynically to attract lower prices by exaggerating the potential pipeline of works, services or supplies. Without confidence in a credible pipeline under a long-term relationship and clear conditions governing the award of work, the expectations of clients and industry when they create a framework can soon deteriorate into mutual disillusionment and distrust.

Gold Standard Recommendation 8. 'Avoid wasted procurement costs and improve supplier commitments by ensuring that frameworks offer sustainable pipelines of work.'

A clear pipeline of the prospective works, services or supplies comprising the *Framework Programme* should be stated in an FAC-1 *Framework Brief.* In response to industry concerns regarding the significant cost and time wasted by clients and industry in procuring speculative frameworks, and in order to optimise competitive bids and strategic commitments from prospective industry *Alliance Members*, 'Constructing the Gold Standard' recommends that the *Client/Additional Clients* should make clear in all framework procurements the pipelines of works, services and supplies to which they commit and the preconditions to implementing those commitments. More than 70% of the industry participants in 'Constructing the Gold Standard' stated that they will not bid for a framework that does not offer a clear pipeline of works, services or supplies.

Practice Note 18. Pipeline visibility.
Crown Commercial Service uses FAC-1 on all its frameworks. It states that 'the lack of pipeline visibility across the public sector reduces contractors' ability to plan and diminishes the ability of clients to collaborate'. Crown Commercial Service provides:

- 'Pipelines of registered projects, updated systematically as part of framework processes by a dedicated construction category team.'
- 'Weekly updates of projects status and procurement dates as a shared pipeline on a web platform for accessible, centralised pipeline management.'

It goes on to state that: 'This enables clients to find synergies and collaborate either through information-sharing, or at a deeper level, through multiparty integration via FAC-1.'
See also Case Studies 1, 7, 16 and 21.

An FAC-1 *Alliance* can create a sound commercial basis for the procurement of a *Framework Programme* of multiple *Projects* if it offers an attractive amount of works, services or supplies; if it sets out fair procedures governing how *Project Contracts* are awarded; if it establishes the means by which performance is expected to improve over time; and if it makes clear how *Alliance Members* will be rewarded for improved performance. An FAC-1 *Alliance* can also strengthen and integrate the systems of pre-construction phase planning for each *Project* and each group of *Projects,* and it can improve the quality of information shared and used to underpin safe and efficient design, construction and *Operation.*

In their strategy, their procurement process and their framework contract, the FAC-1 *Client/Additional Clients* and the *Alliance Manager* should identify and use every available opportunity for aggregating multiple *Projects* in ways that provide the benefits of long-term contracting for portfolios of works, services and supplies. Participants in 'Constructing the Gold Standard' emphasised the greater potential for *Improved Value* where a single framework award procedure can be aggregated to cover a programme or bundle of *Projects* with common requirements.

An FAC-1 *Alliance* provides a flexible and dynamic model that delivers the efficient and collaborative procurement of *Projects*, portfolios of *Projects* and pipelines of multiple *Projects*. For frameworks to attract innovation and investments that deliver improved productivity and efficiency savings, the *Client/Additional Clients* and the *Alliance Manager* need to provide a clear understanding to the industry *Alliance Members* as to the scope and nature of *Project* call-offs, including the *Success Measures* by which good performance will lead to longer-term *Project* awards and/or additional *Project* awards without the additional framework tender processes known as 'mini-competitions'.

Frameworks will not drive efficiency and continuous improvement if they use excessive mini-competitions to call off one *Project* at a time or if those mini-competitions give rise to disproportionate costs. More than 60% of contractor participants in 'Constructing the Gold Standard' expressed concern that the resources required to compete for individual framework *Projects* can be wasteful and can fragment the potential of frameworks to stimulate effective long-term commitments. They emphasised the greater scope for innovation and investment in new technologies, for improving value and for reducing risk where framework systems enable the award of longer-term *Project Contracts* or the award of successive *Project Contracts* on the basis of proven performance.

Case Study 14. NHS Shared Business Services health sector framework alliances and sustainability.
NHS Shared Business Services is using FAC-1 for its public sector construction frameworks, which have a projected value of up to £1.5 billion per annum over seven years and are delivered through 57 contractors in five lots:

- Lot 1 for projects of up to £2.5 million (12 regions).
- Lot 2 for projects of £2.5 million–£5 million (12 regions).
- Lot 3 for projects of £5 million–£15 million (12 regions).
- Lot 4 for projects of £15 million–£35 million (national).
- Lot 5 for projects of more than £35 million (national).

NHS Shared Business Services uses FAC-1 in conjunction with *Project Contracts* based on the JCT and NEC standard forms.

NHS Shared Business Services is also developing a new 'Sustainable Transport Framework' worth up to £300 million for use across NHS estates and the wider public sector. The framework will use FAC-1 to enable the design and build of sustainable car park structures and to deliver the infrastructure of a growing electric vehicle charging point network. FAC-1 will support the collaboration that NHS Shared Business Services wants to see across the *Supply Chain*.

Case Study 15. Glasgow Housing Association new build and refurbishment framework alliances.

Glasgow Housing Association procured FAC-1 prototype framework alliances governing a £1 billion programme of stock refurbishment for more than 40,000 properties, which required the coordination of 63 housing associations with 24 constructors and 27 framework consultants. Savills, as *Independent Adviser*, reported that 'the ability to get the constructors on board early, and to involve them in the design, programming and scoping decisions before works began, undoubtedly saved the client – and the constructors – hundreds of thousands of pounds'. The alliance contract provided for

- use of a contractual *Core Group* as 'an essential means for joint problem solving and strategic decision making' and
- an integrated *Supply Chain* structure that 'allowed [Glasgow Housing Association] to create supplier framework agreements with key components suppliers, so they had representation on *Core Groups* and were full members of the team'.

Glasgow Housing Association reported that through the alliance contract 'the support of employment and skills outputs led to an exceptional number of apprenticeships, recognised in the Scottish government's report on community benefits'.

Glasgow Housing Association used an FAC-1 prototype in conjunction with *Project Contracts* based on the PPC2000 standard form project alliance contract and went on to use the same approach for their programme of new-build projects.

CHAPTER 12

How does FAC-1 integrate the components of one or more complex projects?

F AC-1 enables and describes the integrated relationships and processes that are necessary for the success of a complex project. It connects the organisations who contribute to a complex project in ways that improve performance and results by, for example:

- integrating the work of engineering, procurement and construction (EPC) contractors and other contractors with the design/cost/time/risk data provided by and to the front-end engineering design (FEED) team and other designers;
- integrating the work of EPC contractors or other contractors with the design/cost/time/risk data provided by and to the *Alliance Manager*, the site remediation/preparation team, the *Supply Chain* specialists and manufacturers, and the operator;
- clarifying the interests of the regulators and funders, the impact of their decisions, and the work to be done to meet their requirements;
- integrating the lifecycle of a complex project; and
- creating clear *Incentives* for *Improved Value*.

FAC-1 can improve performance and results on a complex project by

- governing conditional early appointments leading up to the award of each *Project Contract*;
- describing a hybrid approach to procurement, e.g. through fees/cost reimbursement for *Project Contracts* governing engineering/other design, leading to more complete and more accurate fixed prices or target prices for *Project Contracts* governing installation, construction and operation;
- improving value by standardising *Supply Chain* contributions from consultants, specialist subcontractors and manufacturers; and

- clarifying the *Intellectual Property Rights* and other consents by which designs, innovations and lessons learned can be conveyed to future *Projects*.

Practice Note 19. FAC-1 definitions for a single complex project.
When FAC-1 is used to integrate the components of a single complex project

- the whole of the complex project is defined in FAC-1 as the *Framework Programme* and
- each contract comprising components of the complex project (e.g. each FEED contract and each EPC contract) is defined in FAC-1 as a *Project*.

An FAC-1 *Alliance* can integrate a complex project as a *Framework Programme* of related *Projects* through the creation of a multiparty FAC-1 'Sub-Alliance'. Development of the Sub-Alliance model in the UK has been led by Crown Commercial Service, whose FAC-1 framework alliances provide the option for calling-off groups of *Projects* through an FAC-1 Sub-Alliance (see Practice Note 5) in relation to

- a programme of works, services or supplies;
- a *Supply Chain Alliance*;
- a multi-client purchasing consortium;
- a *BIM Alliance*; or
- a *Project* whole-life *Alliance*.

The use of FAC-1 as a Sub-Alliance contract for a complex project has been pioneered by the UK Ministry of Justice (see Practice Note 5 and Case Study 16) and is being explored by other UK government departments. FAC-1 as a Sub-Alliance contract

- integrates multiple *Project Contracts* awarded to tier 1 industry *Alliance Members* under an overarching FAC-1 *Framework Alliance Contract*;
- stimulates collaboration among the tier 1 industry *Alliance Members* in order to drive *Improved Value*, effective *Risk Management* and strategic *Supply Chain* relationships;
- includes a *Timetable* of strategic *Supply Chain Collaboration*, describing the preconstruction processes and interfaces that govern the development of consistent design, supply, manufacture and working methods;
- motivates *Supply Chain* members to propose innovative solutions that improve value for the benefit of all *Projects* within the Sub-Alliance; and
- acts as an integrator between the *Client/Additional Clients* with the tier 1 industry *Alliance Members* and *Supply Chain* members for the efficient use

of *BIM* and related technologies to create, exchange, review, agree and implement digital information.

When a public–private partnership (PPP) is used to procure a complex project, an FAC-1 alliance can integrate the long-term relationships and can ensure that the client benefits from agreed systems that seek to achieve *Improved Value*. The need for FAC-1 as a PPP integrator is revealed by the UK 'Connect Plus' PPP trial project (see Annex F for links). The Connect Plus case study demonstrated how a PPP can deliver improved value through a strategic collaborative alliance among service providers, consultants, contractors and supply chains. However, this case study also showed how the client in an arm's-length PPP contract is left out of these benefits.

FAC-1 can ensure that the PPP *Client* participates in the processes for developing and agreeing *Improved Value* and makes clear how the PPP *Client* can benefit from the results. For example, FAC-1 is being used in conjunction with a bespoke PPP contract through which the University of Milan and Lendlease are delivering a 'design–build–operate' concession for a new university campus (see Case Study 17).

Complex projects often depend on the procurement and contracting model being aligned with a financial model that secures the required funding. Funders are increasingly interested in the potential for an FAC-1 alliance to integrate the range of *Project Contracts* that they are funding. FAC-1 can provide for a funder to be a *Stakeholder* under clause 1.10 and can state how *Alliance Members* are expected to engage with the funder in terms of reporting and consultation. FAC-1 can also provide for a duty of care to be extended by *Alliance Members* in favour of a funder in accordance with clause 10.6 (see also Chapter 35).

Through FAC-1 a funder can monitor the progress, performance and integration of the various consultants, contractors, specialist subcontractors and operators who are engaged on the *Framework Programme* comprising a complex project. For example, the European Bank for Reconstruction and Development encourages its clients to consider the creation of an FAC-1 alliance and is trialling this approach on a mining alliance in Kazakhstan (see Case Study 18).

Case Study 16. Ministry of Justice Sub-Alliance using MMC, *Supply Chain Collaboration* and *BIM*.
Under the Crown Commercial Service FAC-1 construction framework alliance, the Ministry of Justice created an FAC-1 Sub-Alliance to procure the four prisons comprising their £1.2 billion 'New Prisons Programme'. The Ministry of Justice FAC-1 Sub-Alliance integrates the work of ISG, Kier, Laing O'Rourke and Wates as contractor *Alliance Members*, with Mace as

Alliance Manager, and it supports their use of *BIM* and MMC to agree optimum designs and strategic relationships with key tier 2 *Supply Chain* members.

Engagement with tier 2 *Supply Chain* members is led jointly by the four contractor *Alliance Members* and the *Alliance Manager.* The Sub-Alliance is using FAC-1 *Supply Chain Collaboration* to agree strategic commitments with tier 2 *Supply Chain* members for each key package, bringing them into the Sub-Alliance and preserving their collaborative commitments to efficiency and *Improved Value* after the award to each contractor *Alliance Member* of an NEC4 construction phase *Project Contract.*

The FAC-1 Sub-Alliance contract also creates an Integrated Information Management Contract (IIMC), as described in Chapter 14 of this handbook, that connects the licensing of *Intellectual Property Rights* to the *BIM* contributions of the four contractors and the *Supply Chain* members across the four prison *Projects.*

The Ministry of Justice is using FAC-1 to create and implement three more Sub-Alliances:

- Womens' Estate Programme comprising five *Projects* with a combined value of approximately £140 million for which the *Alliance Manager* is Mace and the tier 1 contractor is Galliford Try;
- Accelerated Houseblocks Delivery Programme comprising six *Projects* with a combined value of approximately £500 million for which the *Alliance Manager* is Mace and the tier 1 contractors are Kier and Wates; and
- Small Secure Houseblocks (SSHB) for which details are being finalised.

The Ministry of Justice uses FAC-1 in conjunction with *Project Contracts* based on the NEC4 standard-form building contract.

Defence Infrastructure Organisation has procured two FAC-1 Sub-Alliances worth £5.1 billion. Other Crown Commercial Service FAC-1 *Alliance Members* who are considering the potential of FAC-1 Sub-Alliances include the Department for Education, the UK Parliament, the Department for Environment, Food & Rural Affairs, the Ministry of Defence, the UK Atomic Energy Authority, the Government Property Agency and the Department for Work & Pensions.

Case Study 17. University of Milan public–private partnership alliance with Lendlease.

The University of Milan is using FAC-1 as a contractual integrator for a public–private partnership with Lendlease. The university has used FAC-1 to define the legal framework for the €338 million 'design–build–operate' concession of a new university campus.

The new campus covers a total area of more than 190,000 square metres. The duration of the concession awarded to Lendlease is 30 years, including design (1 year), works (3 years) and site management (26 years, 11 months). Executive planning activities started in the first months of 2021, with the works to be completed by 2025.

The University of Milan is using FAC-1 in conjunction with *Project Contracts* that comprise a bespoke public–private partnership contract and bespoke building contracts.

Case Study 18. European Bank for Reconstruction and Development (EBRD) mining alliance in Kazakhstan.
The EBRD supports the use of FAC-1 and reported its use on a pilot project in Kazakhstan as a strategic integrator of multiple FIDIC *Project Contracts*.

The EBRD made a US$350 million loan to JSC ShalkiaZinc Ltd, a Kazakh mining company, for the expansion of the Shalkia zinc and lead mine in the Kyzlorda region of Kazakhstan and for the construction of a new processing plant on the same site. FAC-1 will provide additional visibility and controls for EBRD and for the *Client*, acting as an umbrella contract connecting the different components of the works for which EBRD is providing a loan.

The EBRD and JSC ShalkiaZinc Ltd are using FAC-1 in conjunction with *Project Contracts* that are FIDIC EPC contracts.

Case Study 19. HMP Five Wells complex project alliance.
The Ministry of Justice and Kier used a prototype for FAC-1 and a PPC2000 *Project Contract* to deliver HMP Five Wells. This project won the Constructing Excellence National Building Project of the Year award in 2022. The team included Bison Precast, Banagher Precast Concrete, ASSA ABLOY, PCE, Mace, Pick Everard, HLM Architects, Arup, Curtins and WTP. The Ministry of Justice procurement and contracting model included a range of collaborative relationships and processes, both at strategic level using the FAC-1 prototype and at project level using PPC2000. These multistage, multiparty contracts described and supported the efficient use of *BIM*, MMC, early supply chain involvement and successful joint risk management – techniques that in turn led to innovations, sustainable designs, new opportunities for local and regional businesses, new jobs and training plus cost certainty and measurable savings in time.

Constructing Excellence reported that HMP Five Wells represents a step change in the evolution of offsite manufacture and sets new standards for excellence in innovation, collaborative working and sustainability. Completed on time and to budget, the prison provides around 1,700 places and features a design that is 80% standardised. This design is the first of its kind and will be used to deliver a further five new prisons in the coming years. With repeatable, standardised components, the use of offsite manufacturing and sustainable features making it 70% more energy efficient than traditional facilities, HMP Five Wells is a brilliant example of the use of Modern Methods of Construction and provides a blueprint for infrastructure delivery for the construction industry. Its innovations will result in better outcomes both for the prison estate (faster, greener, more efficient delivery) and for prisoners. Secure barless windows and smaller wings support rehabilitation by creating more nor-malised surroundings.

- **Standardised design.** The prison design is 80% standardised and repeatable, allowing it to be used across the next 20,000 prison places.
- **Offsite manufacture.** Innovative use of offsite manufacture saved 30% in on-site resource and resulted in assembly that was 22% faster than traditional construction.
- **Social value.** The project generated a £135m social return on invest-ment. Key achievements included the creation of 227 new jobs, 27 of which were filled by ex-offenders. Over the course of the project, Kier recruited 19 ex-offenders and 8 men on ROTL (release on temporary licence), helping them to exceed the prison leaver employment target by 36%.

See also Case Studies 4 and 23.

Case Study 20. Enel Green Power windfarm complex project alliance with EPC contractors in Brazil.
The first use of FAC-1 in Brazil was on the Aroeira Windfarm Project, consisting of eight greenfield windfarms with an installed capacity of 348.3 MW located in three municipalities (Umburanas, Morro do Chapéu and Ourolândia) in Bahia State, Brazil. The Aroeira Windfarm will be con-nected to the Ourolandia II Substation (SS) (500 kV) through an 18.5 kilo-metre single circuit transmission line (TL) by means of a new step-up substation with two main transformers (34.5 kV/500 kV). The *Client*, Enel Green Power, is investing in renewable energy projects throughout the world. As part of their international strategy for innovation in project implementation, Enel decided to make use of collaborative contracting through FAC-1.

FAC-1 is being used as a contractual platform for the integration of the *Client* and five specialist contractors, each responsible for a different part of the Aroeira Windfarm Project. As a result of their collaboration, and in addition to improving project communication and joint *Risk Management,* the *Alliance Members* will work together to

- obtain early power generation and increase the expected power production of the project;
- increase the work safety standards of the professionals allocated to the project; and
- obtain cost reductions through a *Supply Chain Collaboration* strategy.

Enel Green Power is using FAC-1 in conjunction with *Project Contracts* that are bespoke EPC forms.

See also Case Study 11.

CHAPTER 13

How does FAC-1 create an action plan under existing contracts?

An FAC-1 *Framework Alliance Contract* embodies the 'Construction Playbook' requirement to 'ensure that contracts are structured to support an exchange of data, drive collaboration, improve value and manage risk' and to 'set clear expectations for continuous improvement'. It describes the incremental processes by which the *Alliance Members* work together, in parallel with and separate from the award of *Project Contracts* and the performance of their *Project Contract* obligations, to build up the additional information they need in order to achieve *Improved Value* and *Risk Management*. These incremental contractual processes enable *Alliance Members* to create, obtain, agree and act on new information while, wherever possible, avoiding negotiation.

The FAC-1 *Alliance Activities* and the *Timetable* that governs their implementation comprise an 'action plan' that converts agreed *Objectives* into specific actions. Without a contractually binding action plan there is the danger that the active pursuit of these *Objectives* will be delayed, deferred or abandoned because *Alliance Members* focus their efforts primarily on the award of *Project Contracts* and the activities governed by each *Project Contract*.

In response to the need for urgent implementation of value improvement, risk reduction and progress towards net zero in ways that achieve the ambitions of government and industry, 'Constructing the Gold Standard' recommends that the *Client/Additional Clients* and the industry *Alliance Members* create contractually binding action plans that convert improved value objectives under their existing framework contracts into shared strategic commitments.

Gold Standard Recommendation 5. 'Create contractually binding Gold Standard action plans to convert framework objectives into actions and timetables that deliver improved economic, social and environmental outcomes.'

An effective action plan requires the *Alliance Members* to create, agree and implement a shared *Timetable* of specific *Alliance Activities*. An action plan should set out

- how and when innovations and other improvements will be captured through *Alliance Activities* undertaken by the *Client/Additional Clients*, the *Alliance Manager*, the industry *Alliance Members* and the *Supply Chain* members, both preceding and in parallel with the award and delivery of individual *Project Contracts*, and how and when these innovations and other improvements will be adopted for use on framework alliance *Projects*; and
- how and when innovations and other improvements will be captured from the delivery of framework alliance *Projects*, how and when they will be shared and agreed between the *Client/Additional Clients*, the *Alliance Manager*, the industry *Alliance Members* and the *Supply Chain* members, and how and when these innovations and other improvements will be adopted for use on other framework alliance *Projects*.

An action plan can also add more detailed value improvement systems to a current contract. These value improvement systems can be expressed as supplemental contractual commitments to implement previously agreed value improvement objectives without changing the scope or terms of the current contract. The supplemental contractual commitments describe machinery for implementing previously agreed objectives and they can be set out in

- an FAC-1 'transitional' *Framework Alliance Contract* integrating the work of tier 1 industry *Alliance Members* appointed under separate pre-existing contracts, which can clarify the shape, direction and expected outcomes of joint initiatives that explore the potential of MMC, digital technologies, *Supply Chain Collaboration* and other means to deliver *Improved Value*; or
- an FAC-1 *Supply Chain Framework Alliance Contract* led by one or more tier 1 industry *Alliance Members*, which can harmonise and aggregate demand, can develop and integrate relationships with tier 2 and tier 3 *Supply Chain* members through *Supply Chain Collaboration*, and can agree new means to deliver *Improved Value*.

Case Study 21. Crown Commercial Service transitional framework alliance action plan.
An example of an action plan under an FAC-1 'transitional' *Framework Alliance Contract* is provided by Crown Commercial Service, who report how

they led and managed a multiparty FAC-1 transitional framework alliance that supplemented and integrated the previous separate consultant frameworks awarded to Aecom, AHR Architects, AMEC Foster Wheeler Environmental and Infrastructure, Arcadis, Capita, Faithful & Gould, Gleeds, Kier Business Services, Mace, McBains, Mott McDonald, Ridge, Turner & Townsend and WYG. Crown Commercial Service and these consultants entered into the transitional FAC-1 *Framework Alliance Contract* without a new public procurement exercise because it brought to life the objectives set out in their pre-existing separate frameworks and described their shared commitments 'to deliver improved value for framework clients' by

- 'sharing and monitoring best practice intelligence';
- 'sharing and monitoring learning between projects and programmes of work';
- 'establishing, agreeing and monitoring consistent and more efficient working practices';
- 'agreeing and monitoring techniques for better team integration'; and
- 'agreeing and monitoring improved procurement and delivery systems on projects and programmes of work'.

Crown Commercial Service used FAC-1 in conjunction with *Project Contracts* based on NEC3 professional service contracts.

Case Study 22. Kier Highways *Supply Chain* framework alliance action plan.
An example of an action plan under an FAC-1 *Supply Chain Framework Alliance Contract* is provided by Kier Highways (Kier) under their six-year 'TPC2005 Core Highways Maintenance Contract' with Surrey County Council (SCC), which had an option to extend by up to four years (to 2021). SCC exercised the option to extend subject to agreeing a revised commercial model that included re-procurement of the Kier *Supply Chain* for capital schemes.

FAC-1 was adopted by Kier alongside TPC2005 for its *Supply Chain* re-procurement in order to deliver the strategic goals of

- 'increasing collaboration between SCC, Kier and the *Supply Chain*';
- 'achieving the objectives of the Surrey Business Plan';
- 'demonstrating value for money, targeting a 2.5% saving off the 2015/16 capital programme expenditure'; and
- 'developing a sustainable *Supply Chain* through to 2021'.

SCC and Kier took advice to ensure that the FAC-1 *Supply Chain Framework Alliance Contract* could coexist with TPC2005 and with the back-to-back STPC2005 sub-contracts awarded by Kier to *Supply Chain* members. Kier informed the prospective *Supply Chain* members of its intention to create FAC-1 *Supply Chain Framework Alliance Contracts* with each discipline, which gained their unanimous support, and Kier provided guidance for the proposed *Supply Chain Alliance Activities*.

Kier and its *Supply Chain* members committed, through the FAC-1 *Supply Chain Framework Alliance Contract*, to

- adopt and participate in early supply chain involvement (ESI),
- share and/or improve working practices for the benefit of Surrey and the Term Programme,
- attend other framework review meetings as required in order to achieve *Improved Value*, and
- implement social value proposals.

The agreed target was that 90% of the *Projects* ordered by Surrey as capital schemes would be able to evidence the use of ESI, with a record of ESI benefits maintained by the *Alliance Manager* to demonstrate material benefits at either the feasibility stage or the construction stage.

The immediate benefit of the re-procurement exercise was a saving of approximately 8% against prices under the previous contract model. There was also social value put forward by the *Supply Chain*, which was turnover dependent and provided social value benefits by

- developing local *Supply Chains*,
- increasing spend with local suppliers,
- creating local employment/skills development opportunities, and
- encouraging local recruitment.

Kier and SCC used FAC-1 in conjunction with *Project Contracts* based on the STPC2005 standard form term alliance subcontract.

CHAPTER 14

How does FAC-1 improve digital information management and whole-life value?

FAC-1 supports digital information management and data transparency using *BIM* and related technologies through multiparty systems of information exchange. It provides agreed *BIM* deadlines, gateways and interfaces in its multiparty *Timetable*, with flexibility to bring in specific information management contributions from specialist subcontractors, suppliers, manufacturers and operators through *Supply Chain Collaboration*. FAC-1 also supports digital information management through its direct mutual licences of *Intellectual Property Rights* and provides for clash resolution through an *Early Warning* system and through the *Core Group*.

In order to improve performance, safety, *Sustainability* and value for money over the whole life of built assets, 'Constructing the Gold Standard' recommends that the *Client/Additional Clients,* the *Alliance Manager* and the consultants/contractors/suppliers engaged on a *Framework Programme* should use *BIM* and related digital technologies to standardise data generation, classification, security and exchange, and to retain and manage a golden thread of building information. It also recommends that framework alliance contracts support these actions by integrating the information management systems of the *Client,* any *Additional Clients,* the *Alliance Manager,* industry *Alliance Members* and *Supply Chain* members.

> **Gold Standard Recommendation 12.** 'Create a whole life golden thread of asset information using *BIM* and other digital technologies integrated under a framework alliance contract.'

The ISO 19650 series 'Organization and digitization of information about buildings and civil engineering works, including building information modelling' stresses that 'collaboration between the participants involved in construction projects and in asset management is pivotal to the efficient delivery and operation of assets' and that a significant outcome from collaboration is 'the potential to communicate, re-use and share information efficiently and to reduce the risk of loss, contradiction or misinterpretation'.

The FAC-1 multiparty structure and processes can be used to create an Integrated Information Management Contract ('IIMC') that complies with ISO 19650 and that overcomes the limitations of multiple traditional two-party *BIM* 'protocols'. The effect of an IIMC is illustrated in Figure 6, which shows that it

- integrates the multiple contributors to digital information management across all phases of one or more *Projects*; and
- connects digital information management with collaborative systems of strategic planning, early supply chain involvement, *Supply Chain* engagement, joint *Risk Management* and the joint finalisation of agreed costs and programmes.

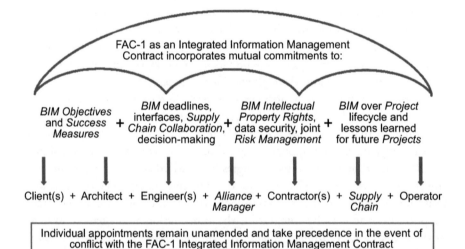

Figure 6. FAC-1 as an Integrated Information Management Contract.

The value of FAC-1 as an IIMC reflects learning from teams who have shown how the combination of digital information management with collaborative integration can improve value and reduce risks. Case studies include the UK government Trial Project team at HMP Berwyn (see Case Study 23), the Liscate School team in Milan (see Case Study 24) and the 'Construction Playbook' case study project at Five Wells (see Case Study 19). FAC-1 is also being used as an IIMC for the procurement and delivery of the £1 billion Ministry of Justice 'New Prisons Programme' (see Case Study 16).

Development of the IIMC was part of a research programme funded by Innovate UK and the Centre for Digital Built Britain, under which the King's College London Centre of Construction Law & Dispute Resolution and the University of Cambridge Laing O'Rourke Centre examined how collaborative procurement models, integrated contracts and digital information management can incentivise efficient project delivery and optimise whole-life outcomes. This research showed how FAC-1 as an IIMC fulfils the following requirements described in ISO 19650.

- Obligations relating to the management or production of information, including the use of a 'common data environment':
  - the multiparty structure of FAC-1 ensures that *Alliance Members* share transparently their agreed specific obligations at framework level and at *Project* level under the FAC-1 *Framework Brief, Framework Proposals, Project Briefs* and *Project Proposals*;
  - FAC-1 clause 10.3 states that the *Alliance Members* owe a duty of care in respect of their *Framework Proposals* and *Project Proposals* only to the *Client* and not to each other.

- Warranties or liabilities associated with the 'project information model':
  - FAC-1 clause 1.4 states the responsibility of each *Alliance Member* for the consequences of any error or omission in, or any discrepancy between, the documents that it prepares or contributes to, except to the extent of its stated reliance on any information provided by any one or more other *Alliance Members*;
  - FAC-1 clause 10.1 states that, unless agreed otherwise, the *Alliance Members* owe a duty of reasonable skill and care appropriate to their agreed respective roles, expertise and responsibilities;
  - the duty of care of the *Alliance Members* under their respective *Project Contracts* is stated in those *Project Contracts*, the terms of which are shared in FAC-1 Schedule 5 in order to ensure transparency and consistency.

- Treatment of 'background' and 'foreground' intellectual property rights of information:
  - the multiparty structure of FAC-1 ensures that the *Intellectual Property Rights* stated in FAC-1 clause 11 are agreed and enforceable directly between *Alliance Members* rather than only via the *Client*.

- Treatment of existing asset information:
  - the multiparty structure of FAC-1 ensures that *Alliance Members* agree transparently the arrangements stated in the *Framework Brief* and each *Project Brief* for the use of existing asset information.

- Use of shared resources:
  - o the multiparty structure of FAC-1 ensures that *Alliance Members* agree transparently the arrangements stated in the *Framework Brief* and each *Project Brief* for the use of shared resources.

- Use of information during the project, including any associated licensing terms:
  - o the multiparty structure of FAC-1 ensures that *Alliance Members* agree transparently the arrangements stated in the *Framework Brief* and each *Project Brief* for the use of information during each *Project*;
  - o FAC-1 clause 11.3 creates mutual licences to copy and use documents prepared by each *Alliance Member* and limits these licences to the agreed *Alliance Activities*.

- Reuse of information following appointment or in the event of termination:
  - o the multiparty structure of FAC-1 ensures that *Alliance Members* agree transparently the arrangements stated in the *Framework Brief* and each *Project Brief* for the reuse of information following appointment or in the event of termination;
  - o FAC-1 clause 11.3 creates mutual licences to copy and use documents prepared by each *Alliance Member* and limits these licences to the agreed *Alliance Activities*.

FAC-1 as an IIMC creates a multiparty collaborative integrator for the management of digital information over the whole lifecycle of any *Project*. It supports the key interfaces between the capital works team and the *Operation* team that are essential to the success of whole-life procurement through, for example,

- licences of *Intellectual Property Rights* in respect of *BIM* models and other design documents by the design and construction *Alliance Members* so that the *Operation* team can access and use all available asset information;
- interfaces between the defects liability obligations of the design and construction *Alliance Members* and commencement of the obligations of the *Operation* team that make clear who responds to notification of a problem and at whose expense;
- an understanding of all exclusions and limitations in the liability of the design and construction industry *Alliance Members*, including their *Supply Chain* members, so that it is clear where the *Operation* team must step in to avoid leaving any gaps in the service;
- availability of information regarding plant and equipment warranties to the *Operation* team, including the terms and conditions of those warranties,

so that the *Operation* team does not invalidate them through any act or omission;

- a clear understanding of the specific obligations of the *Operation* team in relation to warranted plant and equipment; and
- clarity as to the liability of the design and construction industry *Alliance Members*, including their *Supply Chain* members, in the event of an error or omission by the *Operation* team.

Practice Note 20. Whole-life procurement.
NHS Shared Business Services shows commitment to whole-life procurement in its FAC-1 construction framework alliance, which it reports 'offers extended support for Contracting Authorities and End Users in the operation and maintenance of the building with FM-aligned and integrated information and data protocols plus integrated supply chains'.
See also Case Study 14.

FAC-1 establishes and sustains a collaborative approach to digital information management and whole-life procurement through the following multiparty systems, which can improve value and manage risks.

- Optimising and integrating digital information management contributions from all *Alliance Members* through data transparency in the multiparty structure and the Schedule 1 *Objectives* and *Success Measures*.
- Agreeing and integrating deadlines, gateways and interfaces between *Alliance Members* for each stage of digital information management exchanges, reviews and approvals over the whole life of one or more *Projects* in the Schedule 2 *Timetable* and the clause 6 *Alliance Activities*.
- Optimising and integrating any combination of digital information management and whole-life contributions through the multiparty structure and under clause 1.11 and the Appendix 2 *Joining Agreements*.
- Supporting early *Supply Chain* involvement in digital information management activities with flexibility to bring in contributions from specialist subcontractors, sub-consultants, suppliers, manufacturers and operators, through clause 6.3 *Supply Chain Collaboration* and clause 7 *Orders*.
- Creating a transparent decision-making forum through the clause 1 *Core Group* so that *Alliance Members* can consider and agree whole-life proposals for *Improved Value* emerging from information management.
- Enabling joint *Risk Management* and agreed actions to resolve problems such as clashes between digital information management contributions and whole-life proposals by addressing these clashes through the clause 1 *Core Group* and *Early Warning* provisions and the clause 5 *Alliance Manager* role.

- Integrating digital information exchanges over the life cycle of each *Project*, including the digital information required for safety and quality in the design, construction and operational phases of a built asset with flexibility to obtain contributions from additional *Alliance Members* involved in the *Operation* of a completed *Project*, under the clause 1.11 and Appendix 2 *Joining Agreements* and in the definition of *Operation* as a feature of *Improved Value*.
- Optimising the potential for *Alliance Members* to learn from each *Project* and to improve digital information management and whole-life value from *Project* to *Project* (under the Schedule 1 *Success Measures* and *Targets* and under the clause 5 and Schedule 4 *Direct Award Procedure* and *Competitive Award Procedure*).

Case Study 23. HMP Berwyn *BIM* framework alliance and project alliance.
Digital information management was a central feature of the £157 million HMP Berwyn project, one of the largest prisons in Europe. The Ministry of Justice team used an FAC-1 prototype framework alliance to create a team that included Lendlease, AECOM, Sweett Group, WYG, Capita Symonds, TPC Consulting, Hoare Lea and Crown House. The team worked together using digital technologies during a 38-week preconstruction period to develop the *Alliance Members'* and *Supply Chain* members' contributions to designs, to risk management and to finalisation of agreed costs. The *Client* applied the lessons learned from the previous Cookham Wood *Alliance Project*, which enabled additional benefits from an information management perspective and greater contributions from tier 2 and tier 3 *Supply Chain* members, including a specific focus on local and regional SMEs. From a *Budget* of £212 million, the team agreed innovations and efficiency improvements that led to a fixed price of £157 million without eroding the quality or function of the *Project*. The savings included

- reducing cost and time on site using MMC standardised pre-cast provided by a range of European suppliers;
- reducing the footprint for the entry building/energy centre, using lessons learned from the Ministry of Justice framework's Oakwood Prison *Project* and from consultation with operational colleagues;
- incorporating an open swale to create a new environment for wildlife while also reducing construction costs; and
- overcoming significant environmental challenges caused by asbestos, soft ground conditions and the remains of an old munitions factory.

Use of digital information management combined with access to lessons learned on previous *Alliance Projects* enabled agreement of innovations proposed by Lend Lease and Crown House, such as value engineered lighting, improved building footprints, environmental benefits, and reprogramming to make up for a delayed start on site. Collaboration through the FAC-1 prototype *Alliance* also increased social value, e.g. through the appointment of SMEs on £30 million of the work packages and through the engagement on site of a workforce drawn mostly (77%) from local people.

The Ministry of Justice team used an FAC-1 prototype in conjunction with *Project Contracts* based on the PPC2000 standard form project alliance contract.

See also Case Studies 4 and 19.

Case Study 24. Liscate school and civic centre Italian *BIM Alliance*.
The Liscate team in Italy, advised by Professor Sara Valaguzza, used FAC-1 to integrate *BIM* contributions by the consultants, contractor and specialist suppliers engaged on a £5 million new build school and civic centre. The Liscate team reported how the use of FAC-1 led to 6.8% cost savings and 48% time savings, plus design innovations and improved health and safety.

The Milan Union of Municipalities Adda Martesana created the first FAC-1 contract in Italy, governing the integration of *BIM* contributions to the design and construction of a high school and a civic centre. The FAC-1 *Alliance Members* were the client, the contractor, the design team, the construction manager, the safety coordinator and the subcontractors, and the *Alliance Activities* included data sharing, *BIM* model management and maximum *Supply Chain* involvement.

FAC-1 enabled effective joint *Risk Management* on site. Further details appear in a Youtube video titled 'Delivering a *BIM* Alliance in Milan' (see https://bit.ly/3FGTUyg).

The Liscate team used FAC-1 in conjunction with *Project Contracts* that were bespoke building contracts.

CHAPTER 15

How does FAC-1 support manufacture and offsite construction?

FAC-1 framework alliances can provide consistent pipelines of work that support the planning and investment required to develop manufacturing and offsite manufacturing technologies, and they can enable delivery of *Improved Value* by the strategic application of manufacturing technologies and offsite construction, including the optimum use of standard products and components.

In order to obtain *Improved Value* from industry organisations by planning, investing in and delivering MMC through manufacturing and offsite construction, 'Constructing the Gold Standard' recommends that *Client/ Additional Clients* and the *Alliance Manager* use their framework strategies, procurements and contracts to explore and agree the benefits of MMC and offsite manufacturing technologies and the additional MMC benefits of the *Client/Additional Clients* calling off aggregated portfolios of work.

Longer-term call-off commitments enable *Alliance Members* to agree plans for delivering work linked to plans for *Improved Value* so that they can jointly monitor delivery, review performance, provide feedback, take corrective actions, measure effectiveness and implement a process of continuous improvement.

Gold Standard Recommendation 11. 'Improve supplier investments in MMC and other offsite technologies by awarding framework call-off contracts for portfolios of work.'

An FAC-1 *Alliance* can provide the long-term commitments that enable balanced and thorough assessment of potential MMC solutions. It can also provide the systems for longer-term, larger-scale appointments of tier 2 and tier 3 *Supply Chain* members who have MMC production facilities and expertise.

The 'Construction Playbook' proposes harmonising, digitising and rationalising demand across multiple clients under longer-term contracts in order to

- accelerate the development and use of standard products and components;
- transform the market's ability to plan, invest and deliver digital and offsite manufacturing technologies; and
- fulfil the potential for greener solutions as a result of an increase in manufacturing approaches.

An FAC-1 *Framework Alliance Contract* can provide for the award of long-term MMC *Project Contracts*, e.g. under the TAC-1 Term Alliance Contract. These long-term *Project Contracts* can govern the issue of multiple *Orders* for successive *Projects*, which is a more efficient way to sustain an MMC production line than creating multiple, separate *Project Contracts*. Long-term *Project Contracts* are used, for example, by the clients of Crown Commercial Service under their FAC-1 £1.2 billion Modular Building Solutions framework alliance, which comprises

- the supply, design, delivery and construction/installation of a range of modular buildings for education and healthcare purposes; and
- the hire or purchase of education, healthcare and other modular buildings.

Practice Note 21. Integration with manufacturers.
The September 2020 report 'Build Homes, Build Jobs, Build Innovation – A Blueprint for a Housing Industrial Strategy' explains how 'more innovative and progressive contracts reflect earlier and closer engagement with manufacturers, for instance the ACA *Framework Alliance Contract* (FAC-1) for long-term strategic relationships enabling one or more clients to integrate housing programmes that are delivered through smart construction linked to separate design, construction and operation contracts'.

Crown Commercial Service is using FAC-1 to procure its £10 billion 2023 'Offsite Construction Solutions' framework alliance, appointing 29 manufacturers who offer a range of MMC solutions and making these available to all government departments.

The Offsite Homes Alliance led by Great Places Housing Group is using FAC-1 to procure and deliver its £2 billion MMC Framework, through which 23 registered housing providers work with selected industry partners to deliver affordable homes across the North of England using MMC and offsite technologies.

FAC-1 enables the *Client/Additional Clients* to plan their *Framework Programme* together, collaborating at an early stage to consider the best ways in which MMC can be applied consistently across multiple *Projects*. It provides the system through which to explore how consistent workflow across successive *Projects* can help to sustain MMC production lines. This active collaboration among multiple clients can create an environment in which it is possible to improve value by harmonising, digitising and rationalising MMC solutions that deliver the required and desired *Project* outcomes.

The 'Construction Playbook' recommends that 'contracting authorities should collaborate to find opportunities not only for their own platform solutions but also for ways in which cross-sector platform solutions can be applied'. It states that 'future procurements and frameworks should support this with the development of a market that can develop and deliver designs based on these platform approaches, manufacture and supply components, and innovate to improve and develop these over time'.

The provisions governing a portfolio approach in an FAC-1 *Alliance*, and in its *Project Contract* call-off and feedback procedures, can include clear contractual obligations to drive continuous improvement in safety, time, cost and quality. These obligations help to sustain a competitive market through *Success Measures* and *Incentives* that are linked to *Project* outcomes. For example, where MMC *Project Contracts* comprise a *Framework Programme* of works, services or supplies shared among multiple industry *Alliance Members*, the agreed *Success Measures* for continuous improvement can be taken into account when calculating possible increases or decreases in the scope of the *Project Contracts* awarded to each industry *Alliance Member*.

Case Study 25. Football Foundation MMC framework alliances.
The UK Football Foundation (with involvement from the Football Association and Sport England) used FAC-1 to procure two national programmes worth £150 million and £60 million. Their drivers were the Football Association chairman's report of 2014, which stated that 'players and coaches repeatedly tell us that the quality of pitches (and their associated facilities) is a barrier to both recruiting and retaining players' and which sought 'wider social and community benefits from increased physical activity including the fight against preventable diseases, improving cohesion and personal development for young people'.

The first Football Foundation programme combined FAC-1 with JCT building contracts for modular build changing rooms using

- £150 million of investment and
- match funding from applicants.

The FAC-1 framework alliance was created between the Football Foundation and

- Gleeds and QMP in the role of framework managing consultant;
- Western Building Systems, Integra Buildings, Extraspace Solutions, Ashley House and Portakabin as the modular suppliers; and
- Cameron Consulting as the *Independent Adviser*.

The second FAC-1 procurement was for a Mini-Pitch Programme, using

- £60 million of investment and
- integrating mini-pitches with changing room facilities through an interface protocol.

The FAC-1 framework alliance was created between the Football Foundation and

- Labosport in the role of framework managing consultant;
- Support in Sport (SIS Pitches) as the 3G pitch supplier; and
- Cameron Consulting as the *Independent Adviser*.

The Football Foundation used FAC-1

- to integrate specialists and consultants rather than depend on main contractors;
- to create flexibility through *Joining Agreements* for *Additional Clients* who are primarily applicants for funding from the Football Foundation; and
- to develop common supply chains and integrated processes and to participate in value-engineering exercises, all designed to improve the way in which changing rooms and pitches are delivered.

The Football Foundation used FAC-1 in conjunction with *Project Contracts* based on the JCT 2016 standard form building contract.

Case Study 26. Building Better MMC framework alliances.
Building Better and Procurement for Housing are using FAC-1 to deliver a programme of 800 homes worth £600 million over five years, creating collaborative relationships with three selected manufacturers: Top Hat, Ilke Homes and Impact Modular. Lawyers from Trowers & Hamlins advised on this procurement and noted that: 'FAC-1 was the right choice for Building

Better since it underpins the alliance that the registered providers want to create to aggregate demand across their development programmes and provide a guaranteed pipeline for the manufacturers to improve process and delivery. FAC-1 focusses on supply chain collaboration, which is essential in standardising product development and design and building safer and sustainable homes.' Building Better added that 'sharing information and learning together are critical to improving the take up of MMC and overcoming traditional barriers'.

Building Better used FAC-1 in conjunction with *Project Contracts* based on a range of JCT, NEC and PPC standard forms.

PART III

HOW DOES FAC-1 WORK CLAUSE BY CLAUSE?

CHAPTER 16

Who are the *Alliance Members*?

The parties who sign FAC-1 are known as the *Alliance Members* and they comprise 'the *Client*, the *Alliance Manager*, all other parties who execute the *Framework Alliance Agreement* and any *Additional Clients* and other *Additional Alliance Members* who execute *Joining Agreements*' (see Appendix A). The FAC-1 provisions relating to the roles, expertise and responsibilities of the *Alliance Members* and *Additional Alliance Members* are summarised in Checklist 5.

FAC-1 makes direct connections between *Alliance Members* through multi-party relationships and related two-party relationships (see Chapter 19). Clause 1.1 of FAC-1 states that the *Alliance Members* 'will work together and individually for the benefit of the *Framework Programme*, within the scope of their agreed roles, expertise and responsibilities as stated in the *Framework Documents*'.

In addition to the *Client/Additional Clients* and the *Alliance Manager*, the *Alliance Members* may include one or more consultants, main contractors, subcontractors, suppliers, manufacturers, operators and other industry organisations in any combination.

The *Framework Alliance Agreement* provides space on page (i) for insertion of the names of the *Client* and the other *Alliance Members*, plus their agreed roles, expertise and responsibilities, and it provides space on signature pages (vi) and (vii) for insertion of their postal and email addresses.

FAC-1 clause 1.11 states that the *Alliance Members* may agree that *Additional Clients* and other *Additional Alliance Members* will join the *Alliance* by entering into *Joining Agreements* in the form set out in Appendix 2, and the *Framework Alliance Agreement* provides space on page (ii) for insertion of a list of *Additional Clients* and other *Additional Alliance Members* if these are agreed in advance.

Page (i) — The *Alliance Members* are the *Client*, any *Additional Clients, the Alliance Manager* and the industry *Alliance Members* who all sign the *Framework Alliance Agreement*

1.1 — The roles, expertise and responsibilities of the *Alliance Members* are described in the *Framework Documents*

1.11 — *Additional Clients* and other *Additional Alliance Members* may be listed in the *Framework Alliace Agreement* or agreed by the current *Alliance Members*

1.11.1 — The current *Alliance Members* sign a *Joining Agreement* with an *Additional Client* or other *Additional Alliance Member* who it is agreed joins the *Alliance*

1.11.2 — Following execution of a *Joining Agreement* an *Additional Client* or other *Additional Alliance Member* is bound by the *Framework Alliance Contract*

1.11.4 — Additional and amended *Framework Documents* in a *Joining Agreement* can describe the role, expertise and responsibilities of an *Additional Alliance Member*

1.11.4 — An *Additional Alliance Member* has no rights or obligations in relation to any matter arising before the effective date of its *Joining Agreement* unless so agreed

14.6 — If the *Alliance Manager*'s appointment is terminated, the *Client/Additional Clients* identify a replacement and all *Alliance Members* enter into a *Joining Agreement*

Note — Some FAC-1 *Clients* use an exchange of notices creating third party rights to agree *Additional Alliance Members* without the formalities of a *Joining Agreement*

Checklist 5. FAC-1 *Alliance Members* and *Additional Alliance Members*.

Practice Note 22. *Additional Alliance Members.*
Crown Commercial Service reports that: 'By adopting the FAC-1 as the centre point of our framework agreement structure, this enables CCS to establish closer relations with the additional clients and supplier alliance members, focus on collaborative opportunities, drive best practice, improve framework performance and outputs across our frameworks.'
See also Case Studies 1, 7, 16 and 21.

Additional and amended *Framework Documents* can be included in a *Joining Agreement* in order 'to describe the role, expertise and responsibilities of each *Additional Client* or other *Additional Alliance Member*' (clause 1.11.4). Following completion of a *Joining Agreement*,

- clause 1.11.2 states that 'all the provisions of the *Framework Alliance Contract* shall apply to the *Additional Client* or other *Additional Alliance Member* as if it were separately identified in the *Framework Alliance Contract*'; and

- clause 1.11.5 states that 'unless otherwise agreed, an *Additional Client* or other *Additional Alliance Member* shall have no rights or obligations under the *Framework Alliance Contract* in relation to any matter arising before the effective date of its *Joining Agreement*'.

Some FAC-1 users streamline the joining process by agreeing that *Additional Clients* and other *Additional Alliance Members* can join the *Alliance* through an exchange of standard-form notices rather than by all *Alliance Members* signing a *Joining Agreement*. Where the applicable law allows an exchange of notices to create third-party rights, the agreement and use of these notices avoids the need to arrange for all *Alliance Members* to sign each *Joining Agreement,* as illustrated in Practice Note 23.

Practice Note 23. Reduced administration for *Additional Alliance Members*.
In order to avoid the additional administration burden of all *Alliance Members* having to sign each *Joining Agreement*, some FAC-1 users such as Crown Commercial Service and LHC have provided for a *Joining Agreement* to be created through a system of notices. This approach uses FAC-1 clause 10.6 governing the extension of contractual duties to third parties. FAC-1 clause 10.6 is completed in the *Framework Alliance Agreement* to describe the process and authority by which

- a notice is issued to the *Client* by a party applying to become an *Additional Client* or other *Additional Alliance Member*; the notice includes a commitment to all other *Alliance Members* to comply with the provisions of the *Framework Alliance Contract*; and
- a notice is issued by the *Client* approving an application to become an *Additional Client* or other *Additional Alliance Member*; this notice includes a commitment on behalf of all other *Alliance Members*, which the other *Alliance Members* authorise the *Client* to make, that all the provisions of the *Framework Alliance Contract* shall apply to the *Additional Client* or other *Additional Alliance Member* as if it were separately identified in the *Framework Alliance Contract*.

See also Case Studies 1 and 2.

FAC-1 distinguishes between the commitments made by all *Alliance Members* and certain commitments made between only two or more specific *Alliance Members*. The FAC-1 commitments between two or more specific *Alliance Members* cover processes, duties of care, confidentiality and

Intellectual Property Rights, and they are described in Chapters 19, 35 and 36 of this handbook.

As regards the rights of an *Additional Client*, clause 1.11.3 states that each *Additional Client* may implement the following processes independently and that only the *Client* or *Additional Client* implementing these processes shall be liable to the other *Alliance Members*:

- the *Direct Award Procedure* and the *Competitive Award Procedure* under clause 5;
- the award of *Project Contract*s under clause 5;
- the creation of *Orders* under clause 7; and
- payment of agreed amounts under clause 8.

FAC-1 governs how *Alliance Members* work with parties outside the *Alliance*, e.g. by engagement with any range and types of *Supply Chain* members through the system of *Supply Chain Collaboration* described in clause 6.3 (see Chapter 30).

FAC-1 also recognises the interests of *Stakeholders*, which are defined in Appendix 1 as 'any one or more organisations or groups of individuals, as stated in the *Framework Alliance Agreement* by reference to clause 1.10, who are not *Alliance Members* and who have an interest relating to the *Framework Programme*'. Clause 1.10 states: 'The *Alliance Members* shall engage with the *Stakeholders* as stated in the *Framework Alliance Agreement*, but no *Alliance Member* shall owe a *Stakeholder* a duty of care unless agreed in accordance with clause 10.6.'

As regards the interests of *Stakeholders* and the use of clause 10.6 to extend a duty of care to *Stakeholders*, see for example Chapter 12 regarding the interests of the funder of a complex project.

CHAPTER 17

What are the *Framework Programme* and *Projects*?

[FAC-1 clauses 1.1, 5.6 and 5.7 and the *Framework Brief*]

The scope of an FAC-1 *Alliance* comprises the known *Projects* or prospective *Projects*, or the components of a complex project, that form part of a *Framework Programme* of 'works and/or services and/or supplies governed by the *Framework Alliance Contract*, as described in the *Framework Documents*' (Appendix 1).

An FAC-1 *Project* is 'a project forming part of the *Framework Programme* as described in the *Framework Brief* and in a *Project Brief* issued pursuant to a *Direct Award Procedure* or *Competitive Award Procedure*' (Appendix 1).

The first entry in the *Framework Alliance Agreement* is the title of the *Framework Programme*. Details of the *Framework Programme* and the *Projects* comprising the *Framework Programme* are set out in

- the *Framework Brief,*
- the Schedule 1 *Objectives* and
- the Schedule 5 *Template Project Documents.*

These details reflect what is known at the time of entering into FAC-1, although for certain *Framework Programmes* it may be that no specific *Projects* have been identified at that time.

FAC-1 governs the integration of the *Projects* as part of the *Framework Programme* and it describes the collaboration between *Alliance Members* through agreed *Alliance Activities* and *Risk Management* actions designed to achieve agreed *Objectives, Success Measures, Targets* and *Incentives*. It also governs the award of *Project Contracts*, although it is the relevant *Project Contracts* that govern the delivery of each *Project*.

FAC-1 *Projects* can take many different forms, for example:

- *Projects* that comprise a *Framework Programme* of similar *Projects*;
- *Projects* that comprise a *Framework Programme* of unrelated *Projects*; and
- *Projects* that comprise the components of a *Framework Programme* that is itself a single complex project.

FAC-1 states whether there is a minimum value or type in respect of the *Project Contracts* that will be awarded to any one or more *Alliance Members* so that, if possible, they have a clear picture as to the level of certainty in the flow of work (clause 5.6). It also states whether there is any exclusivity granted to *Alliance Members* in relation to all or part of the *Framework Programme* (clause 5.7) and whether there is any adjustment of that exclusivity according to achievement of agreed *Targets* (Schedule 1, Part 2).

It is not necessary to make unconditional promises in respect of the award of the *Projects* that comprise an FAC-1 *Framework Programme*, but it is essential to the credibility of an *Alliance* that the *Framework Brief* provides as much information as the *Client/Additional Clients* have available at each stage when procuring and delivering the *Framework Programme*. Industry *Alliance Members* understand and accept the constraints on certainty that are created by funding cycles, regulatory consents and intervening changes in *Client* circumstances, and they can still invest in framework alliances that identify these matters as preconditions to the award of *Project Contracts*. However, industry *Alliance Members* need the *Client/Additional Clients* to share as much as possible of the following information:

- in the *Framework Brief*, the planned pipelines of works, services and supplies comprising the FAC-1 *Framework Programme*;
- also in the *Framework Brief*, the known funding cycles, regulatory consents and other preconditions that could affect all or part of each pipeline of works, services and supplies comprising the FAC-1 *Framework Programme*;
- in clause 5.6, any minimum values and types of works, services and supplies that are committed to the FAC-1 *Framework Programme* and the procedures governing those commitments; and
- in clause 5.7, any exclusivity created by the award of *Projects* and the procedures governing any adjustments to that exclusivity.

The confidence shown by the *Client/Additional Clients* in providing clarity on these matters in turn creates industry confidence and attracts increased industry interest, commitment and investment.

The scoping of an FAC-1 *Alliance*, and of the *Projects* within the scope of the *Framework Programme*, should be based on strategies that consider the best means for delivering the required and desired outcomes of the *Client/Additional Clients*. The assessment of the best delivery model for each FAC-1 *Project* is an early strategic decision for the *Client/Additional Clients* and the *Alliance Manager*, and ongoing assessments can also form part of the *Alliance Activities* undertaken with other *Alliance Members*.

It is likely that different delivery models will be adopted on different *Projects* forming part of the *Framework Programme*, and the *Alliance Manager* should provide the guidance that the *Client/Additional Clients* need when assessing the best delivery model for each *Project*. These skills enable an *Alliance Manager* and the *Client/Additional Clients* to work together, taking into account the relevant value profile, strategic risks and other factors.

CHAPTER 18

What are the *Framework Brief* and the *Framework Proposals*?

[FAC-1 clauses 1.3, 1.4 and 1.5]

The FAC-1 *Framework Brief* describes 'the scope and nature of the *Alliance* and of the *Projects* comprising the *Framework Programme*' (Appendix 1). It is signed separately by all *Alliance Members* for identification.

The FAC-1 *Framework Proposals* comprise each of the documents 'describing the proposals of an *Alliance Member* in response to the *Framework Brief,* agreed confidentially between that *Alliance Member*, the *Client,* any *Additional Clients* and the *Alliance Manager*' (Appendix 1). FAC-1 clause 13.3.2 makes clear that 'the *Framework Prices* and *Framework Proposals* of an *Alliance Member* are confidential as between that *Alliance Member*, the *Client,* any *Additional Clients* and the *Alliance Manager*'.

FAC-1 clause 10.3 protects the commercial sensitivity of the *Framework Proposals* and other documents created by an industry *Alliance Member*, stating that 'an *Alliance Member* shall owe a duty of care in respect of its *Framework Proposals, Framework Prices, Project Proposals* and *Agreed Prices* only to the *Client,* any *Additional Clients* and the *Alliance Manager* and not to the remaining *Alliance Members*'.

The FAC-1 *Framework Brief* is provided to all prospective industry *Alliance Members* as the basis for their selection to join the *Alliance* and it sets out

- all technical, management and commercial requirements in relation to the *Framework Programme*;
- the required approaches to design, *Supply Chain* engagement, costing, *Risk Management* and programming;
- all other relevant procedures and expected outcomes; and
- where appropriate, the required approach to *BIM*.

In order to identify and incentivise improved *Project* outcomes through a mutually beneficial approach to sharing ideas and innovative solutions, 'Constructing the Gold Standard' recommends that the *Client/Additional Clients* and the *Alliance Manager* use specifications that focus on required *Client* outcomes, that they include a whole-life carbon assessment that minimises GHG emissions, that they use a 'Project Outcome Profile' linking performance criteria to *Incentives*, and that they clarify which *Intellectual Property Rights* are relevant to the needs of the *Client/Additional Clients* and to the needs of the industry *Alliance Members*.

> **Gold Standard Recommendation 14.** 'Incentivise innovative solutions by creating specifications for frameworks and call-offs that focus on required client outcomes.'

The *Framework Brief* should focus on *Objectives* and *Success Measures* linked to the outcomes that the *Client/Additional Clients* need to achieve, and it should encourage prospective industry *Alliance Members* to demonstrate their capabilities in the *Framework Proposals* that they submit. In order to attract strong *Framework Proposals*, the *Framework Brief* should make clear

- how the *Framework Proposals* submitted by prospective industry *Alliance Members* form part of the quality criteria that shift the evaluation focus away from lowest price and towards a deeper understanding of capabilities;
- the purpose of seeking competitive *Framework Proposals* from prospective industry *Alliance Members*, including the processes by which these proposals are reviewed, developed and adopted once *Alliance Members* are selected and appointed, and the basis on which these proposals will then be used to deliver improved *Client* outcomes;
- by what process the *Client/Additional Clients* and the *Alliance Manager* will seek agreement to share with other *Alliance Members* the *Framework Proposals* submitted by a selected industry *Alliance Member*; and
- how the evaluation and recognition of *Framework Proposals* submitted by a selected industry *Alliance Member*, and the success of those *Framework Proposals* in delivering *Improved Value* and *Risk Management*, will affect *Incentives* such as the award of future *Projects*.

When FAC-1 governs a *Framework Programme* of multiple *Projects*, it requires suitably generic, outcome-based approach specifications in the *Framework Brief* that in turn enable an outcome-based approach to evaluating *Framework Proposals* submitted by a prospective industry *Alliance*

Member. The solutions put forward in response to outcome-based specifications should form a significant part of the qualitative evaluation criteria for selecting *Alliance Members.* This approach should then be followed through in an outcome-based approach to specifications and evaluation when calling-off specific *Projects* forming part of the *Framework Programme* (see Chapter 28).

It is important to distinguish between the information set out in the *Framework Brief* and the information set out in

- the *Direct Award Procedure* and/or *Competitive Award Procedure* as regards the procurement model for individual *Projects*; and
- the *Template Project Documents* as regards the structure, components and requirements for each *Project Brief.*

It is important to also state in the *Framework Brief* whether any of the *Framework Proposals* are already approved for use on any *Project* at the point when the *FAC-1 Framework Alliance Contract* is entered into and whether others may be accepted at a later stage, either in accordance with agreed procedures or at the option of the *Client*, and either in relation to all *Projects* or in relation to any particular *Projects*.

The *Framework Proposals* can include

- proposals for complying with the *Framework Brief*;
- proposals for achieving the stated *Objectives, Success Measures* and *Targets*;
- drawings, specifications and other proposals in respect of standard *Project* components and/or model *Projects*;
- procedures and working practices for implementing *Projects*;
- proposed approaches to *Risk Management*;
- proposals for ESI, *Supply Chain Collaboration, BIM* and MMC;
- proposals for achieving net zero carbon *Targets* and other measures of improved *Sustainability*;
- proposals for working with SMEs, including local and regional *Supply Chain* members; and
- proposals for training and employment, community benefits and other measures of social value.

CHAPTER 19

How does FAC-1 align a multiparty structure with two-party relationships?

[FAC-1 clauses 1.3–1.5, 10.3–10.5, 11.2 and 13.3]

FAC-1 is a multiparty contract that creates direct relationships between *Alliance Members*; that integrates their shared *Objectives, Success Measures* and *Targets;* and that integrates their mutual commitments to systems such as *Supply Chain Collaboration,* other *Alliance Activities, Risk Management,* a common *Timetable* and *Core Group* decision-making. FAC-1 is designed to overcome the limitations of two-party framework contracts and to avoid the divisions and misunderstandings that arise where *Alliance Members* do not have the benefit of direct mutual commitments on consistent contract terms. The multiparty structure of FAC-1 is summarised in Figure 7.

> **Practice Note 24. Limitations of two-party framework contracts.**
> 'Constructing the Gold Standard' found that: 'Separate two-party framework contracts make it difficult to align the objectives, success measures, targets and incentives of framework providers, clients, managers, suppliers and supply chain members. The two-party framework contracts created with each supplier are not visible to other suppliers, and this lack of transparency is unnecessary and inefficient. It contributes to an atmosphere of mutual distrust and limits the collaboration through which shared experiences, ideas and innovations can improve outcomes, improve value and manage risks.'

FAC-1 also recognises and distinguishes the need for specific relationships between two or more *Alliance Members,* for agreed limits on who owes a duty of care to whom, and for agreed limits on who has access to commercially sensitive information. For example, FAC-1 states certain matters where a duty of care is owed only between specific *Alliance Members* (clauses 1.11.3, 10.3–10.5 and 11.2), and also states that these restrictions can only be amended by agreement (clause 10.2) (see also Chapter 35).

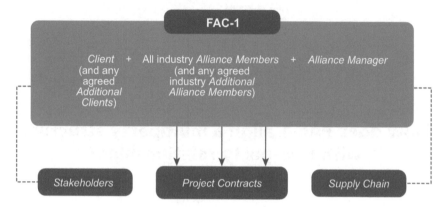

Figure 7. FAC-1 multiparty structure.

FAC-1 clause 1.3 states that 'any *Framework Document* created or amended in accordance with these *Contract Terms* is binding on all *Alliance Members*' except that:

- 'unless otherwise agreed in the *Contract Terms*, no *Framework Document* added or amended after the date of the *Framework Alliance Agreement* shall add to or amend the role, expertise, responsibilities or other obligations of any *Alliance Member* who does not agree it' (clause 1.3.1);
- 'the *Alliance Manager Payment Terms* shall bind only the *Client*, any *Additional Clients* and the *Alliance Manager*' (clause 1.3.2); and
- 'the *Framework Prices* and *Framework Proposals* of an *Alliance Member* shall bind only the *Client*, any *Additional Clients*, the *Alliance Manager* and that *Alliance Member*' (clause 1.3.3).

FAC-1 clause 1.4 states: 'Each *Alliance Member* who prepares any one or more *Framework Documents* shall be responsible for the consequences of any error or omission in, or any discrepancy between, those *Framework Documents* or its contributions to them, except to the extent of its reliance (if stated in those *Framework Documents*) on any information provided by any one or more other *Alliance Members*.'

Clause 1.5 states that the *Framework Documents* are complementary, and that

- an *Alliance Member* shall give *Early Warning* in accordance with clause 1.8 as soon as it becomes aware of any error, omission or discrepancy in or between the *Framework Documents* (clause 1.5.1);

- if any error, omission or discrepancy cannot be resolved under clause 1.5.1, the priority between *Framework Documents* shall follow the sequence set out in the *Framework Alliance Agreement* in descending order except that the *Contract Terms* shall have priority over Schedules 1–5 to the *Framework Alliance Agreement* and except where the *Alliance Members* otherwise agree (clause 1.5.2); and
- if there is any discrepancy between the *Framework Documents* and any *Project Contract*, then the *Project Contract* shall take precedence (clause 1.5.3).

FAC-1 provides commercial protections for *Alliance Members* in respect of their exchanges of information by means of

- the clause 11 provisions governing mutual *Intellectual Property Rights* (see Chapter 36); and
- the clause 13.3 provisions for *Framework Prices* and other *Framework Proposals* to be confidential between the *Client/Additional Clients,* the *Alliance Manager* and the other *Alliance Member* who provides them, and for any amended confidentiality provisions to be stated in the *Framework Alliance Agreement* (see Chapters 18, 35 and 36).

These commercial protections ensure that there is clear understanding as to which information is the exclusive property of one specific *Alliance Member*, e.g. because it represents the results of research and development intended to create a competitive advantage. Where a *Client* using FAC-1 wishes to ensure that information is not retained confidentially by one *Alliance Member*, and is instead shared with other *Alliance Members* for specific purposes related to seeking *Improved Value* across the *Framework Programme*, then this should be stated in the *Framework Brief* by reference to

- specific requested *Framework Proposals*,
- expected outputs from *Supply Chain Collaboration* and other *Alliance Activities*, and
- potential lessons learned on individual *Projects*.

CHAPTER 20

What are the FAC-1 *Project Contracts* and *Template Project Documents*?

[FAC-1 clauses 1.5.3 and 5.3, and the Schedule 5 *Template Project Documents*]

FAC-1 integrates the work of the *Alliance Members* while acknowledging their separate appointments under *Project Contracts*. It is designed for use in conjunction with any one or more *Project* procurement models, with any form of building or engineering contract, with any form of consultant appointment, and with any form of supply contract or service contract.

These *Project Contract Conditions* can cover any combination of responsibilities for design, supply, manufacture, construction, facilities management and *Operation*. FAC-1 defines *Operation* as the 'use, occupation, operation, maintenance, repair, alteration and demolition of a *Project*'.

FAC-1 is not itself a *Project Contract*. It is designed for use with any one or more forms of *Project Contract Conditions* entered into in accordance with clause 5 and included in the *Template Project Documents* at Schedule 5. FAC-1 is compatible with all and any combination of the *Project Contract Conditions* such as the published FIDIC, ICC, JCT, NEC, PPC, RIBA, RICS and TAC-1 forms and any combination of standard or bespoke forms.

All FAC-1 *Framework Documents* are 'treated as complementary' but, in the event of any 'error, discrepancy or omission' that cannot be resolved by agreement of *Alliance Members* following an *Early Warning*, the order of priority is set out in the *Framework Alliance Agreement* and a *Project Contract* takes precedence over the *Framework Documents* (clause 1.5).

The *Project Contract Conditions* form part of the FAC-1 *Template Project Documents* that govern the award of *Project Contracts* in accordance with the *Direct Award Procedure* and the *Competitive Award Procedure* (see Chapter 28).

The *Template Project Documents* are described in FAC-1 Schedule 5 as including

- the *Project Contract Conditions* to be used for each *Project Contract*, comprising the applicable standard forms of contract and any amendments;
- the structure and standard components of the *Project Brief* that forms part of each *Project Contract* describing the scope and nature of a *Project*, setting out the *Client's/Additional Clients'* technical, management and commercial requirements and expected outcomes in respect of the *Project*, and including all required quality standards and warranties;
- all standard requirements in each *Project Brief* in respect of insurances and securities, and all standard processes and procedures in each *Project Brief* for the management of communication, performance, quality, design, *Supply Chain* engagement, cost, payment, time, change, risk, health and safety, and all other project management processes and procedures, in each case including the required approach to *BIM* as appropriate;
- any standard requirements in each *Project Brief* in respect of *Sustainability*, *Operation* and engagement with *Stakeholders* and *Users*; and
- the required structure and content of the *Agreed Prices* and other *Project Proposals* forming part of each *Project Contract*.

FAC-1 clause 7 states an option for the *Client* or an *Additional Client* to issue *Orders* for *Pre-Contract Activities* in advance of a *Project Contract*. The *Pre-Contract Activities* governed by an *Order* should be incorporated into the *Project Contract* if and when it is awarded (see Chapter 31).

Practice Note 25. *Framework Documents* for a complex project.
Where FAC-1 is used to integrate the roles, expertise and responsibilities of *Alliance Members* who undertake a complex project that comprises the FAC-1 *Framework Programme*, and where the components of that complex project are the FAC-1 *Projects*, then all or some of the *Project Contracts* may be awarded simultaneously with, or if necesssary in advance of, the creation of the FAC-1 *Alliance*.

In these circumstances,

- the Schedule 4 *Direct Award Procedure* and/or *Competitive Award Procedure* can state in simple terms the separate arrangements outside the FAC-1 procedures for the award of *Project Contracts*; and
- the *Template Project Documents* can state relevant details of the *Project Contracts* that are awarded outside the FAC-1 procedures.

CHAPTER 21

What is the role of the *Core Group*?

[FAC-1 clauses 1.6–1.8 and 15.1]

To drive improved framework outcomes, 'Constructing the Gold Standard' recommends collaborative systems for managing framework relationships and strategic supply chain relationships that include a *Core Group* or an equivalent joint decision-making group through which to manage strategic planning, value improvement, risk reduction and dispute avoidance.

FAC-1 provides for consensus-based decision-making by a *Core Group* of named individuals or agreed alternates representing each *Alliance Member* in support of their agreed mutual commitments. The FAC-1 *Core Group* makes its decisions by *Consensus* (defined in Appendix 1 as 'unanimous agreement following reasoned discussion') reached by a quorum of all those members who are present, so that there is no risk of one or more *Core Group* members being overruled by a majority and so that individual *Core Group* members cannot frustrate the work of the entire *Core Group* by failing to attend a meeting (clauses 1.6 and 1.7). The *Core Group* provisions are distinct from the FAC-1 options for appointment of an *Independent Adviser* (clause 3.3) and/or a *Dispute Board* (clause 15.2), which are considered in Chapters 25 and 40.

The FAC-1 provisions governing membership and meetings of the *Core Group* are summarised in Checklist 6. The names of the *Core Group* members and any alternates are inserted in the *Framework Alliance Agreement* (page ii). The *Core Group* functions are set out in the FAC-1 *Contract Terms*, and other functions can be stated in the *Framework Documents* or can be agreed by *Alliance Members* (clause 1.6).

The work of an equivalent *Core Group* under the PPC2000 form of project alliance contract has agreed *Risk Management* solutions and has resolved prospective disputes, as a result of which the teams working on PPC2000 projects have been involved in only two reported cases over the last 22 years.

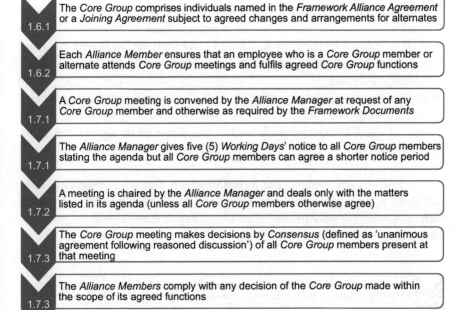

Checklist 6. *Core Group* members and meetings.

FAC-1 clause 1.6 states: 'The *Core Group* shall review and support the implementation of the *Framework Alliance Contract* and shall fulfil the other functions stated in the *Framework Documents* or agreed by the *Alliance Members*.' It requires that

- the *Core Group* comprises the individuals named in the *Framework Alliance Agreement* or in any *Joining Agreement* subject to changes and arrangements for alternates agreed by the *Alliance Members* (clause 1.6.1); and
- each *Alliance Member* shall ensure at its own cost that any employee who is a *Core Group* member or an agreed alternate shall attend *Core Group* meetings and fulfil the agreed functions of a *Core Group* member in accordance with the *Framework Documents* (clause 1.6.2).

FAC-1 clause 1.7 states that each *Core Group* meeting

- shall be convened by the *Alliance Manager* at the request of any *Core Group* member and otherwise as required by the *Framework Documents* at not less than five *Working Days*' notice (unless all *Core Group* members agree a shorter period), and that this notice shall be issued to all *Core Group* members stating the agenda for the meeting (clause 1.7.1);

- shall be chaired by the *Alliance Manager* and shall deal only with the matters listed in its agenda (unless all *Core Group* members otherwise agree) (clause 1.7.2); and
- shall make decisions by *Consensus* of all *Core Group* members present at that meeting, and that the *Alliance Members* shall comply with any decision of the *Core Group* made within the scope of its agreed functions (clause 1.7.3).

The FAC-1 *Core Group* is the forum in which *Alliance Members* consider and agree proposals for *Improved Value*, and in which they can raise issues with each other in order to resolve problems before they become disputes. Its functions are summarised in Checklist 7.

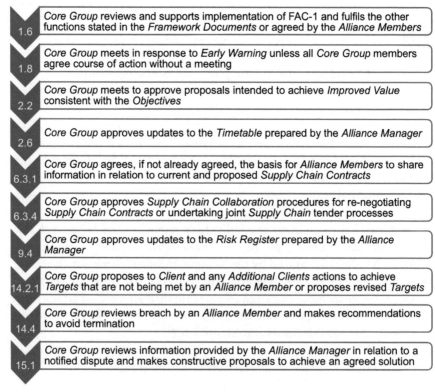

1.6 *Core Group* reviews and supports implementation of FAC-1 and fulfils the other functions stated in the *Framework Documents* or agreed by the *Alliance Members*

1.8 *Core Group* meets in response to *Early Warning* unless all *Core Group* members agree course of action without a meeting

2.2 *Core Group* meets to approve proposals intended to achieve *Improved Value* consistent with the *Objectives*

2.6 *Core Group* approves updates to the *Timetable* prepared by the *Alliance Manager*

6.3.1 *Core Group* agrees, if not already agreed, the basis for *Alliance Members* to share information in relation to current and proposed *Supply Chain Contracts*

6.3.4 *Core Group* approves *Supply Chain Collaboration* procedures for re-negotiating *Supply Chain Contracts* or undertaking joint *Supply Chain* tender processes

9.4 *Core Group* approves updates to the *Risk Register* prepared by the *Alliance Manager*

14.2.1 *Core Group* proposes to *Client* and any *Additional Clients* actions to achieve *Targets* that are not being met by an *Alliance Member* or proposes revised *Targets*

14.4 *Core Group* reviews breach by an *Alliance Member* and makes recommendations to avoid termination

15.1 *Core Group* reviews information provided by the *Alliance Manager* in relation to a notified dispute and makes constructive proposals to achieve an agreed solution

Checklist 7. *Core Group* functions.

FAC-1 provides for the *Core Group* to

- review and support the implementation of the *Framework Alliance Contract* (clause 1.6);
- review *Early Warning* notices (clause 1.8);
- review proposals for *Supply Chain Collaboration* and other *Alliance Activities* intended to achieve *Improved Value* (clause 2.2);
- approve updates to the *Timetable* (clause 2.6);
- agree the basis for *Alliance Members* to share information in order to enable *Supply Chain Collaboration* (clause 6.3.1);
- agree procedures for *Alliance Members* to jointly re-negotiate or tender *Supply Chain Contracts* in order to enable *Supply Chain Collaboration* (clause 6.3.4);
- approve updates to the *Risk Register* (clause 9.4);
- propose actions necessary for *Alliance Members* to achieve agreed *Targets* or revised *Targets* (clause 14.2.1);
- make recommendations in the event of notified breach (clause 14.4); and
- seek resolution of a notified dispute (clause 15.1).

The *Core Group* should be active from the inception of the FAC-1 *Alliance* so that *Core Group* members can develop mutual trust and exchange all relevant information, both of which are necessary for the *Core Group* to make decisions that are both informed and based on consensus. A problem experienced on some collaborative projects has been a failure to hold any *Core Group* meetings until a problem arises. If a *Core Group* only meets to consider potential disputes, it cannot actively contribute to the success of collaborative procurement.

The *Core Group* is less effective if the *Client* member does not attend meetings, particularly where there is a likelihood of conflicting views. For example, a *Client/Additional Client* might seek to delegate difficult decisions to the *Alliance Manager* and it might expect a consultant to attend a *Core Group* meeting on its behalf, but this does not create or sustain a credible commitment to seeking agreed solutions. By contrast, the track record of problem-solving and dispute avoidance under PPC2000 illustrates what can be achieved under FAC-1 when the *Client/Additional Clients* take an active role in the work of the *Core Group*.

Practice Note 26. *Core Group* relationships.
In relation to their FAC-1 'New Prisons Programme', the Ministry of Justice report that

- 'alliancing is both a relationship and a contract form';
- 'this approach helped to embed the collaborative relationship early, from the alliance launch to transition through the different phases';
- 'each of the four alliance members nominated representatives from their organisation, both at Board and operational levels, to sit alongside representatives from the Ministry of Justice and its delivery partners (Mace Limited, WT Partnership and Perfect Circle)'; and
- 'together, they formed the "Core Group", establishing strong leadership and trust from the outset'.

See also Case Study 16.

CHAPTER 22

What are the *Objectives, Success Measures* and *Targets*?

**[FAC-1 clauses 2.1–2.3 and the Schedule 1
Objectives, Success Measures and *Targets*]**

The success of a framework alliance needs to be measured in a way that is open, fair and constructive. FAC-1 states agreed *Objectives* that make clear the purposes of the procurement strategy that underpins the *Framework Programme*, and it provides flexible foundations that the *Client/Additional Clients* and their advisers can use when developing this procurement strategy. Its multiparty structure links the agreed *Objectives* to the agreed *Success Measures* and *Targets* through a shared system of transparent performance measurement and related *Incentives* agreed by all *Alliance Members*.

FAC-1 states that – within the scope of their agreed roles, expertise and responsibilities – each of the *Alliance Members*

- shall seek to achieve the *Objectives* set out in Part 1 of Schedule 1 to the *Framework Alliance Agreement* (clause 2.1); and
- shall investigate and submit for *Core Group* approval proposals for *Supply Chain Collaboration* and/or other *Alliance Activities* intended to achieve *Improved Value* consistent with the *Objectives* (clause 2.2).

The FAC-1 *Objectives* state the agreed overall objectives of the *Alliance* and the *Framework Programme*, and they can also state the individual objectives of each of the *Alliance Members*. These *Objectives* form the basis for the *Success Measures* and *Targets* that determine the success of the *Alliance* and the *Framework Programme* and that are used to measure the performance of the *Alliance Members*.

Practice Note 27. *Objectives* **(1).**

Crown Commercial Service report that: 'The FAC-1 *Framework Alliance Contract* enables the government to align its strategies in construction with the key objective policies outlined in the "Construction Playbook". The benefits of this drive improvements across the construction industry.'

The Crown Commercial Service FAC-1 *Objectives* comprise the creation and implementation of an effective framework that

- 'has a demonstrable business need';
- 'has effective governance processes, active *Stakeholder* engagement and *Client* leadership';
- 'actively supports *Additional Clients* throughout the *Project* lifecycle, ensuring that *Additional Clients, Supplier Alliance Members* and their *Supply Chain* members receive a legacy of improvement';
- 'is driven by aggregated demand to create volume and generate efficiencies, and provides sufficient work opportunities to cover *Supplier Alliance Members*' investment';
- 'maintains competitive tension in terms of value, quality and performance during its life';
- 'is designed and managed to deliver the required outcomes and continuously improve upon them';
- 'can demonstrate greater value for money for the taxpayer';
- 'pays fairly for the work done and the risks taken';
- 'contributes to the development of an effective and efficient construction market';
- 'harnesses the power of public sector procurement to provide jobs and skills, local employment and enables SMEs to prosper';
- 'ensures *Supply Chain* members are engaged from the earliest stages of a *Project*'; and
- 'ensures transparency and collaborative values flow down the *Supply Chain* to produce *Supply Chain* members that *Additional Clients* can have confidence in'.

In order to achieve the Crown Commercial Service *Objectives*, the *Objectives* of all *Alliance Members* are

- 'to operate the *Framework Alliance Contract* in a way that is accessible to a wide range of *Additional Clients* covering a broad *Framework Programme*';
- 'to deliver the *Framework Programme* in order to achieve *Improved Value* for the *Client* and *Additional Clients*';

- 'to undertake *Supply Chain Collaboration* and other *Supply Chain* development, including subcontracting opportunities for SMEs';
- 'to generate employment and training opportunities';
- 'to maximise the safe and efficient occupation and *Operation* of completed *Projects*';
- 'to maximise *Sustainability* and social value and to minimise negative environmental impacts'; and
- 'to undertake *Alliance Activities* that include

  o sharing and monitoring best practice intelligence,
  o sharing and monitoring learning between *Projects* and programmes of *Projects*,
  o establishing, agreeing and monitoring consistent and more efficient working practices'.

See also Case Study 1.

Practice Note 28. *Objectives* (2).
LHC and the Scottish Procurement Alliance used FAC-1 to procure

- £1.5 billion of housing and development projects including sheltered accommodation, care homes and student accommodation plus associated works including land purchases; and
- £150 million of professional services that include project management, cost consultancy, architecture, structural engineering and building services engineering.

The agreed FAC-1 *Objectives* were

- for LHC as a central purchasing body to operate the *Framework Alliance Contract* in a way that is accessible to a wide range of *Additional Clients* covering a broad *Framework Programme*;
- to deliver the *Framework Programme* in order to achieve *Improved Value* for LHC and *Additional Clients* on the terms agreed with all other *Alliance Members*;
- to generate employment and training opportunities for priority groups;
- to upskill the existing workforce;
- to make subcontracting opportunities available to SMEs, the third sector and supported businesses;
- to work with schools, colleges and universities to offer work experience; and

- to minimise negative environmental impacts, e.g. impacts associated with vehicle movements and/or associated emissions and impacts on protected areas, buildings or sites.

See also Case Study 2.

Practice Note 29. *Objectives* (3).
The *Objectives* of the Epping Forest District Council FAC-1 framework alliance – created to deliver a £22 million house building programme of new homes and integrating a multidisciplinary team that comprised the design consultants, a cost consultant and a group of four main contractors – comprised commitments

- 'to deliver high levels of *User* satisfaction that improve and enhance the lives of those living in their new homes';
- 'to deliver homes that are sustainable for the *Client* and *Users*';
- 'to demonstrate value for money through both capital investment and whole life costs'; and
- 'to learn from shared experiences on the *Alliance* and to adapt, develop and improve the quality of new homes over the life of the *Framework Alliance Contract*'.

The *Success Measures* and *Targets* should be transparent and objectively measurable, stating

- the method of recording relevant performance information,
- the *Alliance Members* who are responsible for measuring that information, and
- the agreed systems for reporting to the *Client/Additional Clients* and to the other *Alliance Members*.

Each *Alliance Member* needs to understand how the agreed *Objectives*, *Success Measures* and *Targets* may affect

- the future award of *Projects*,
- the continuation of its role as an *Alliance Member* and
- the continuation of the *Alliance* as a whole.

FAC-1 clause 14.2 describes a procedure for the *Core Group* to propose actions to achieve the agreed *Targets* or revised *Targets* in the event of a failure by an *Alliance Member* to achieve its agreed *Targets* stated in Schedule 1,

Part 2. It states that any proposed actions are subject to approval by the *Client* and any *Additional Clients* and, if approved, shall be signed by all *Alliance Members* as a supplement to the Schedule 2 *Timetable*.

FAC-1 clause 14.2.2 states the rights of termination arising if the *Client* or any *Additional Client* gives notice that it does not approve actions proposed under clause 14.2.1 or if any approved actions are not implemented (see Chapter 39). Exercising a right of termination under clause 14.2.2 is stated to be 'a last resort' in Schedule 1, Part 2, which also states

- the agreed limitations as to which *Success Measures* and *Targets* may justify the exercise of a right of termination under clause 14.2.2 and
- any additional procedures that precede the exercise of that right.

CHAPTER 23

How do the *Incentives* work?

[FAC-1 clause 2.4 and the Schedule 1 *Incentives*]

FAC-1 links success in meeting agreed *Targets* to rewards for *Alliance Members* by means of a range of agreed *Incentives*. For example, the prospect of being awarded additional or expanded *Projects* forming part of the *Framework Programme* and the potential for extending the scope of the *Framework Programme* or the duration of the *Alliance* are major *Incentives* if they are based on a fair and transparent system of performance measurement. The FAC-1 *Framework Brief* should clarify the links between *Objectives, Success Measures, Targets* and *Incentives*.

Practice Note 30. *Success Measures.*
Gold Standard participants expressed concern that value improvement opportunities can be missed where framework performance measures

- 'are not outcome-based',
- 'are not applied transparently',
- 'are inconsistent or subjective',
- 'are used primarily to penalise suppliers rather than reward them',
- 'are not used as a basis to award further work',
- 'are not relevant to the client's required or desired outcomes',
- 'are not used for feedback to suppliers', or
- 'are not used to drive continuous improvement'.

The FAC-1 *Success Measures* should state how performance measurement recognises achievement of required and desired outcomes, including

- who evaluates the performance,
- how feedback is shared in order to drive continuous improvement, and
- how *Incentives* are used to reward and incentivise excellence.

The required outcomes in the *Success Measures* should be objectively measurable, and mutual trust between the *Client/Additional Clients* and the other *Alliance Members* can be damaged where measurement is conducted privately or subjectively.

Practice Note 31. *Incentives.*
In relation to their FAC-1 'New Prisons Programme', the Ministry of Justice report that

- 'it was essential to ensure the FAC-1 alliance was incentivised to continue to leverage the benefits of early engagement as it moved into individual project delivery (governed by its own set of NEC4 ECC terms) and achieved (or where possible exceeded) a set of stretching additional targets, beyond that of a standard new prison build';
- 'to support this, the alliance approach included an incentivisation sum for targets over and above the "core" key performance indicators, and key performance indicators that focused on early supply chain involvement';
- 'the overarching FAC-1 alliancing terms still applied throughout the new prison build'; and
- 'delivery of each individual prison build was closely monitored through 34 key performance indicators, including incentivisation of early supply chain involvement'.

The decision to incentivise the *Alliance* was based on

- 'additional encouragement for alliance members to work together to achieve better outcomes for the HM Prison and Probation Service, Ministry of Justice, and the construction sector'; and
- 'promotion and incentivisation of activities that provide significant and long-term value to the project, department and beyond'.

The *Success Measures* were developed to incentivise 'over-performance', i.e. the incentivisation pot could not be accessed through business-as-usual performance. This was due to the structure of the *Success Measures*, split into three 'tiers' of core, stretch, and performance. The *Alliance Members* needed to achieve all core *Success Measures* and green status on 12 of 16 stretch *Success Measures* in each month to be considered for incentivisation. In creating the *Alliance*, the Ministry of Justice used incentivisation to drive continued benefits following the initial collaboration phase, getting the most out of bringing the four tier 1 contractor *Alliance Members* together over the longer term.
See also Case Study 16.

The FAC-1 *Incentives* stated in FAC-1 Schedule 1, Part 3 can include

- additional payments, including shares of savings achieved through *Supply Chain Collaboration* and other *Alliance Activities*;
- adjustment of any exclusivity in the award of *Project Contracts*; and
- extension of the scope of the *Framework Programme* and/or the duration of the *Framework Alliance Contract*.

'Constructing the Gold Standard' highlights the importance of *Incentives* that offer the prospect of additional work. It recommends that, as part of their framework strategy, the *Client/Additional Clients* establish the optimum duration, scope and continuity of framework call-offs, including the potential benefits of awarding long-term *Project Contracts* or additional *Project Contracts* without additional mini-competitions. It also recommends that the *Client/ Additional Clients* seek clarification in the *Framework Proposals* submitted by prospective industry *Alliance Members* as to how the award of long-term *Project Contracts* or additional *Project Contracts* without additional mini-competitions will lead to innovations and investments that deliver improved productivity and efficiency savings.

> **Gold Standard Recommendation 10.** 'Reduce procurement costs and improve value through the award of longer-term call-off contracts and the incentive of additional work.'

A powerful but less visible *Incentive* is for the *Client/Additional Clients* and the *Alliance Manager* to provide constructive responses to problems that any other *Alliance Member* encounters in achieving the agreed *Targets*. For example, a *Core Group* review under FAC-1 clause 14.2 can

- recognise where performance against agreed *Targets* is impaired by limited capacity or temporary resource issues or other matters that can be discussed and resolved by agreed actions; and
- lead to agreed adjustment in the number or size or type of *Projects* awarded to a particular *Alliance Member* until its capacity or resources or other declared problems are dealt with.

Adjusting the amount of work awarded to *Alliance Members* was an *Incentive* adopted by the SCMG and Land Securities FAC-1 prototype alliances (see Case Studies 12 and 28), whose framework alliance contracts stated the process by which performance against agreed *Success Measures* and *Targets* could determine variations in the award of future *Project Contracts*.

Case Study 27. Erimus Housing framework alliance incentives
Erimus Housing procured a £105 million five-year housing improvement framework alliance using an FAC-1 prototype to upgrade 11,000 houses, working with ROK, Dunelm Property Services and Erimus Building Services. All contractors committed to a multiparty framework alliance contract that allowed benchmarking of performance and promoted exchange of best practice. The programme showed a high degree of cooperation between the strategic partners, e.g. when one contractor had short-term personnel difficulties and the other two stepped in to assist. Initially each contract was an annual schedule of rates.

By year two, all parties agreed to an open-book costing approach and, by convergence of best practice and supply chains, the partners moved towards adopting common rates. A pain–gain formula shared cost overruns and savings 50/50 up to 10% over or under the budget. The contractors retained or paid any more than the 10% variances, and actual cost outturns were the basis for the next budget.

Residents were involved by consultation and choice through the use of a mobile exhibition unit. The average resident satisfaction score was 9/10.

Erimus Housing used an FAC-1 prototype in conjunction with *Project Contracts* based on the PPC2000 standard form project alliance contract.

CHAPTER 24

How does the *Timetable* work?

[FAC-1 clauses 2.5, 2.6 and 6.1 and the Schedule 2 *Timetable*]

The achievement of agreed *Objectives* and *Success Measures* depends not only on the award of *Project Contracts* and the successful delivery of *Projects* but also on a clear understanding of what else the *Alliance Members* will do 'together and individually in the spirit of trust, fairness and collaboration for the benefit of the *Framework Programme*' (clause 1.1).

Many frameworks state ambitious objectives and detailed success measures but fail to make significant progress because they lack clarity as to the scope and timing of the activities through which these objectives and success measures will be achieved. FAC-1 links the pursuit of *Objectives* and *Success Measures* to a stated range of *Alliance Activities* and makes clear in a shared *Timetable* which of the *Alliance Members* will undertake these *Alliance Activities* and within what agreed deadlines, gateways and milestones.

As set out in Annex D, FAC-1 states

- the principle that 'in all matters governed by the *Framework Alliance Contract* the *Alliance Members* shall act reasonably and without delay' (clause 1.1);
- the clarification of this principle through time limits stated in the FAC-1 *Contract Terms*; and
- a commitment by *Alliance Members* to specific deadlines, gateways, milestones and other timescales stated in the Schedule 2 *Timetable* and, where appropriate, in the Schedule 3 *Risk Register*.

Practice Note 32. *Timetable* deliverables and milestones.
The Ministry of Justice reported on its FAC-1 New Prisons alliance that 'the deliverables and milestones were measured at regular intervals, monitored

weekly through face-to-face core groups, and challenged in monthly steering groups'. Those 'deliverables and milestones' included

- 'reviewing and improving the building reference design';
- 'contributing to the development of site-specific design for the first new prison at Full Sutton';
- 'supporting and developing a common supply chain';
- 'standardising the supply chain, building components, and building engineering systems';
- 'providing a clear commercial pipeline to the supply chain to secure and smooth market capacity';
- 'realising economies of scale across the supply market';
- 'delivering cost certainty sooner in the delivery process';
- 'providing early works and services (as required)';
- 'improving enabling and main works programme integration through early engagement and collaboration';
- 'improving shared learning across projects';
- 'providing resource efficiencies and optimising resource profiling'; and
- 'understanding and mitigating, eliminating, or reducing the risk to the New Prisons Project with the aim of bringing forward prisoner-in dates'.

See also Case Study 16.

The development of the FAC-1 Schedule 2 *Timetable* is illustrated in Figure 8, and it provides the spine of a successful framework alliance. The *Timetable* can govern the timing of

- agreed deadlines, gateways and milestones in respect of the *Framework Programme* and achievement of the *Objectives*;
- the timescales for *Supply Chain Collaboration* and other *Alliance Activities*, including the nature, sequence and duration of the agreed actions of each *Alliance Member* and any consents or approvals (whether required from *Alliance Members* or third parties) that are preconditions to subsequent actions;
- the selection of team members for a specific *Project* under the *Project Contract* award procedures;
- cycles of *Core Group* meetings;
- engagement with *Stakeholders*, *Users* and other parties outside the *Alliance*;
- performance reviews by reference to *Success Measures* and *Targets*;
- activities required for the implementation of *BIM* and related technologies; and

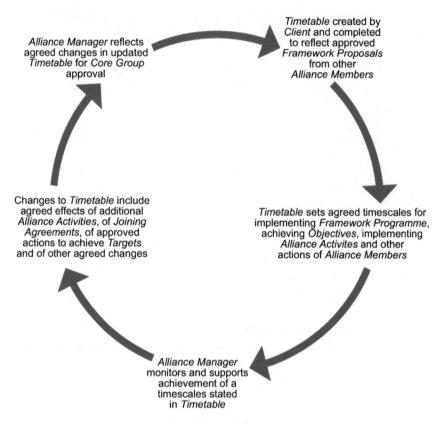

Figure 8. Development of the FAC-1 *Timetable*.

- recognition of where actions, decisions and information are dependent on parties or events outside the control of the *Alliance Members*.

FAC-1 reflects the ISO 44001 recommendations that 'the collaborative partners shall agree on plans for delivery and performance based on the objectives' and that 'joint management shall'

- 'monitor delivery against mutually agreed plans and performance criteria';
- 'regularly review performance at both executive and operation levels';
- 'where appropriate, take corrective action to ensure performance is maintained';
- 'establish, implement and maintain procedures for monitoring and measuring the effectiveness of its collaborative business relationship arrangement'; and

- 'establish a process of continual improvement to enhance the effectiveness of its collaborative business relationship management'.

The FAC-1 *Timetable* sets out the deadlines for each stage of each *Alliance Member*'s work that affects or is affected by another *Alliance Member* or a third party. It should state each activity that is time-critical, the relevant deadline, the *Alliance Member* responsible and the preconditions on which it is dependent.

The FAC-1 *Timetable* should be used to describe action plans for converting agreed *Objectives* into specific *Alliance Activities* in accordance with agreed deadlines, including the development, agreement and implementation of the *Framework Proposals* that are submitted by consultant/contractor/supplier *Alliance Members* and that are reserved by the *Client/Additional Clients* for later review and adoption.

The FAC-1 *Timetable* can be linked to *Targets* for achievement of *Success Measures*. Improved 'time certainty' and 'time savings' are included in the FAC-1 definition of *Improved Value* (Appendix 1).

Practice Note 33. Time savings.
The SCMG FAC-1 prototype used a shared *Timetable* to underpin 'programmed design, risk management, costing and progressing activities undertaken during the early conditional appointment of an integrated team to seek additional savings and improved value'.

As a result, the SCMG *Alliance Members* achieved 'time savings, such as through quicker build-up of prices leading to earlier start on site and reduced client/consultant time/costs'.

An SCMG subcontractor reported: 'I don't know any other London borough that has managed to carry out so much work in so short a time.'

See also Case Study 12.

CHAPTER 25

What are the roles of the *Alliance Manager* and the *Independent Adviser?*

[FAC-1 clause 3 and *Alliance Manager Services Schedule* and *Alliance Manager Payment Terms*]

Important opportunities are missed if framework management, as distinct from the management of individual *Projects*, is limited to project award procedures and performance measurement. Leadership and professional framework management are essential to creating and maintaining a collaborative framework alliance culture and to achieving successful outcomes.

In response to industry concerns regarding varying levels of framework leadership and management, 'Constructing the Gold Standard' recommends that the *Client/Additional Clients* invest in framework management that demonstrates value for money for all *Alliance Members* and that includes

- integration of strategic interests,
- support for collaborative joint working and
- assurance that framework commitments and opportunities are understood and implemented.

Gold Standard Recommendation 6. 'Invest in framework management that demonstrates value for money for clients and suppliers.'

The role, expertise and responsibilities of an *Alliance Manager* should include the fair and constructive exercise of any discretion as well as an active approach towards leading and coordinating the implementation of

- outcome-based strategies, procurement and incentivisation;
- strategic value improvement and risk management processes;
- consistent, proportionate and relevant performance measurement; and
- collaborative decision-making and dispute avoidance.

FAC-1 clause 3 provides for the appointment of an in-house or external *Alliance Manager* who integrates the work of the *Alliance Members*, 'exercising any discretion fairly and constructively'. The role of the *Alliance Manager* is summarised in Checklist 8.

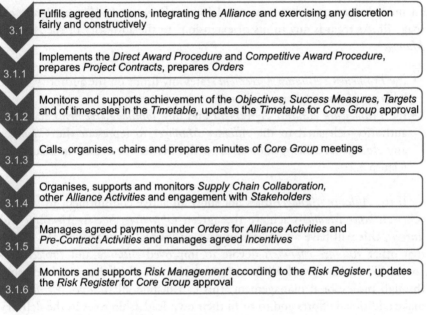

3.1 Fulfils agreed functions, integrating the *Alliance* and exercising any discretion fairly and constructively

3.1.1 Implements the *Direct Award Procedure* and *Competitive Award Procedure*, prepares *Project Contracts*, prepares *Orders*

3.1.2 Monitors and supports achievement of the *Objectives, Success Measures, Targets* and of timescales in the *Timetable*, updates the *Timetable* for *Core Group* approval

3.1.3 Calls, organises, chairs and prepares minutes of *Core Group* meetings

3.1.4 Organises, supports and monitors *Supply Chain Collaboration*, other *Alliance Activities* and engagement with *Stakeholders*

3.1.5 Manages agreed payments under *Orders* for *Alliance Activities* and *Pre-Contract Activities* and manages agreed *Incentives*

3.1.6 Monitors and supports *Risk Management* according to the *Risk Register*, updates the *Risk Register* for *Core Group* approval

Checklist 8. FAC-1 *Alliance Manager.*

FAC-1 clause 3.1 states that, subject to any agreed restrictions in the FAC-1 *Framework Alliance Agreement*, the *Alliance Manager* shall

- Implement *Direct Award Procedures* and *Competitive Award Procedures* under clause 5, prepare *Project Contracts* under clause 5, and prepare *Orders* under clause 7;
- monitor and support achievement of the *Objectives, Success Measures* and *Targets*, monitor and support achievement of deadlines, gateways and milestones in the *Timetable*, and prepare updates of the *Timetable* for *Core Group* approval in accordance with clause 2.6;
- call, organise, chair and minute *Core Group* meetings under clauses 1.7 and 15.1;
- organise, support and monitor *Supply Chain Collaboration* and other *Alliance Activities* under clause 6 and engagement with *Stakeholders* under clause 1.10;
- manage payments under clause 8 and *Incentives* under clause 2.4; and

- monitor and support *Risk Management* in accordance with the *Risk Register* set out in Schedule 3 to the *Framework Alliance Agreement*, and prepare updates of the *Risk Register* for *Core Group* approval in accordance with clause 9.4.

The name of the *Alliance Manager*, who may be a *Client* employee or an independent consultant, is stated in the *Framework Alliance Agreement* (page ii). As regards any limits or extensions to the authority of the *Alliance Manager*:

- the *Framework Alliance Agreement* states any limits on the authority of the *Alliance Manager* (clause 3.1); and
- the *Framework Alliance Agreement* and any *Joining Agreements* state any authority delegated to the *Alliance Manager* to represent the *Client* or any *Additional Client*, additional to the matters described in clause 3.1 (clause 3.2).

If the *Alliance Manager* does not show an active commitment to helping other *Alliance Members* achieve the agreed *Objectives*, *Success Measures* and *Targets*, this will have an adverse impact on mutual trust and on the efforts that other *Alliance Members* devote to improved *Alliance* and *Project* outcomes. Where framework alliances have the benefit of collaborative leadership through professional management, this can inspire all *Alliance Members* to make additional efforts and to fulfil their own leadership roles in the delivery of the *Projects* comprising the *Framework Programme*.

> **Practice Note 34. Leadership.**
> The Project Horizon FAC-1 prototype benefited from 'personal leadership and the recognition of different stakeholder interests in client and contractor organisations who need to be identified, consulted and persuaded to adopt a new and bolder approach'.
> See also Case Study 5.

Where FAC-1 is adopted as an integrator of a complex project, the *Alliance Manager* may also be responsible for managing the delivery of individual *Projects*. On other FAC-1 *Framework Programmes* it is likely that other parties will be appointed by the *Client* or an *Additional Client* to manage the delivery of each *Project*.

In all cases the *Alliance Manager* needs to monitor *Project*-level management and collaborate with the managers of each *Project* so that:

- the management of individual *Projects* is consistent with the agreed FAC-1 *Objectives* and *Success Measures*;
- the managers of each *Project* understand and contribute to the wider *Objectives* and *Success Measures* of the *Alliance*;
- the managers of each *Project* ensure that their teams benefit from the innovations and other improved practices gained from other *Projects* that have been assessed and adopted by *Alliance Members*;
- the managers of each *Project* share with *Alliance Members* the *Project*-level information necessary for *Alliance Members* to assess and adopt learning on other *Projects*; and
- the management of individual *Projects* does not undermine the collaborative culture created by the *Alliance* at a strategic level.

Practice Note 35. Consistent management.
Gold Standard participants expressed concern that a collaborative framework culture can be compromised if clients do not take framework objectives and commitments into account when managing call-off projects, e.g. when a client uses a contractor framework but appoints a project consultant who is not connected with or interested in the contractor framework.

If the *Alliance Manager* is appointed as an independent consultant, then their agreed services are set out in the *Alliance Manager Services Schedule*. This schedule clarifies the role, expertise and responsibilities of the *Alliance Manager* as an *Alliance Member*. The *Alliance Manager Services Schedule* is signed by the *Alliance Members* separately for identification and should include

- the individuals comprising the *Alliance Manager*'s team and any agreed constraints on their removal or replacement,
- the resources and expertise committed by the *Alliance Manager*, and
- the *Alliance Manager*'s agreed approach to their functions.

If the *Alliance Manager* is paid as a consultant, then their fees and expenses and any fluctuation provisions are set out in the *Alliance Manager Payment Terms* so as to enable payment under FAC-1 clauses 8.2–8.11. FAC-1 clause 13.3.1 states that 'the *Alliance Manager Payment Terms* are confidential as between the *Alliance Manager*, the *Client* and any *Additional Clients*'. The *Alliance Manager Payment Terms* are signed separately by the *Alliance Manager*, the *Client* and any *Additional Clients* for identification.

The expertise of the FAC-1 *Alliance Manager* should include the collaborative skills needed to draw together the *Client*, any *Additional Clients* and the other *Alliance Members,* to integrate and motivate their joint working and to help them align their different commercial interests. The *Alliance Manager* is supported by a contractual decision-making process that gives appropriate collective authority to the *Client,* any *Additional Clients* and the other *Alliance Members* through the *Core Group* (see Chapter 21).

The FAC-1 *Alliance Manager* should, as an integrator, help the *Client,* any *Additional Clients* and the other *Alliance Members* to

- integrate commitments to the agreed *Objectives* and *Success Measures*;
- integrate consistent approaches to the call-off and delivery of *Projects* forming part of the *Framework Programme*;
- integrate participation in joint activities seeking to achieve *Improved Value* and successful *Risk Management*;
- integrate agreed *Alliance* commitments with the agreed roles, expertise and contributions of *Supply Chain* members; and
- integrate consistent and transparent performance measurement based on achieving agreed *Alliance* and *Project* outcomes and *Improved Value.*

In addition to and separate from the *Alliance Manager,* FAC-1 provides for the role of an *Independent Adviser* as an optional source of fair and constructive advice to *Alliance Members* on implementation of the *Framework Alliance Contract,* including the avoidance or resolution of disputes. FAC-1 clause 3.3 states: 'If stated in the *Framework Alliance Agreement,* the *Alliance Members* may appoint an *Independent Adviser* to provide impartial and constructive advice and support to the *Core Group.*'

An *Independent Adviser* should be appointed as early as possible, preferably before the FAC-1 *Framework Alliance Contract* is entered into, so that they can become familiar with the *Alliance* and be available to provide advice and support at any time. If an *Independent Adviser* is appointed at a later date, it may be harder for the *Alliance Members* to agree who is suitable, and doubts may arise on matters such as the neutrality of an *Independent Adviser* recommended by the *Client* or by another *Alliance Member.*

The decision as to who pays the *Independent Adviser* is an important practical issue that can be made clear in the FAC-1 *Framework Alliance Agreement* by reference to clause 3.3. Payment arrangements should not affect how the *Independent Adviser* performs their role, but shared payment can underline their independence and neutrality. For example, the effective resolution of disputes by the SCMG *Core Group* was supported by an *Independent Adviser* who was asked to advise on a prospective dispute and who was paid in equal shares by the *Client* and the relevant contractor *Alliance Member* (see also Case Study 12 and Practice Note 45).

CHAPTER 26

How does FAC-1 manage costs and prices?

[FAC-1 clause 4 and the *Framework Prices*]

The FAC-1 *Framework Prices* are submitted by prospective consultant/ contractor/supplier *Alliance Members* in response to the *Framework Brief*. They are binding only between the *Client/Additional Clients*, the *Alliance Manager* and the selected *Alliance Member* who submits them (clause 1.3.3).

The *Framework Prices* are agreed confidentially between the *Alliance Member* who submits them and the *Client/Additional Clients* and *Alliance Manager* (clause 13.3.2), and each set of *Framework Prices* is signed separately by those parties for identification. The *Framework Brief* or the *Template Project Documents* state any provision for fluctuation in the *Framework Prices* (clause 4.2).

The FAC-1 *Framework Prices* are defined as describing 'the prices of an *Alliance Member* in response to the *Framework Brief*, agreed confidentially between that *Alliance Member*, the *Client*, any *Additional Clients* and the *Alliance Manager*'. Their content and structure vary according to the selected procurement and delivery model(s) for the *Framework Programme* and *Projects* and according to the roles and disciplines governed by the *Framework Alliance Contract*.

Improved cost certainty and cost savings are included in the FAC-1 definition of *Improved Value,* and the *Alliance Members* commit to investigate and submit proposals for improved cost certainty and cost savings as part of their commitment to *Improved Value* under clause 2.2 if this is consistent with the agreed *Objectives*. The *Alliance Members* should agree how improved cost certainty and cost savings are linked to the Schedule 1, Part 2 *Success Measures* and *Targets* and to the Schedule 1, Part 3 *Incentives*.

Cost savings that can be obtained through FAC-1 include

- savings established as part of the competitive process by which industry *Alliance Members* are selected, by reason of the FAC-1 *Framework Alliance*

Contract setting out clear *Objectives, Success Measures, Targets* and *Incentives* that are attractive to prospective industry *Alliance Members*;

- savings that reflect reduced costs quoted by prospective industry *Alliance Members* by reason of FAC-1 offering an established standard form that can be accepted with less legal advice and without price contingencies in respect of concerns as to hidden risks;
- savings that are established by *Alliance Members* through agreed *Supply Chain Collaboration* and other *Alliance Activities* and that are adopted in the *Agreed Prices* of future *Projects*;
- savings established as part of the *Direct Award Procedure* and *Competitive Award Procedure* in respect of *Project Contracts*; and
- savings established through lessons learned from current and completed *Projects* that are adopted in the *Agreed Prices* of future *Projects*.

A collaborative approach to costing an FAC-1 *Framework Programme* and its *Projects* is not dependent on adopting a particular cost model. Different approaches to pricing will be appropriate according to the nature of the *Framework Programme* and each *Project*. These approaches could include

- the early involvement of *Alliance Members* and *Supply Chain* members to identify fixed costs for tier 2 and tier 3 *Supply Chain* work/service/supply packages and to examine the scope for efficiency savings in each work/service/supply package, leading to the build-up and agreement of fixed *Agreed Prices* for a *Project* that comprise the approved package costs and separately agreed *Profit* and *Overheads*;
- the combination of separately agreed *Profit* and *Overheads* with a schedule of rates for predictable and repetitive work/service/supply types that is reviewed through *Supply Chain Collaboration* in order to seek and agree efficiency savings in tier 2 and tier 3 *Supply Chain* costs;
- the use of benchmarks to establish maximum costs and the combination of early involvement of *Alliance Members* and *Supply Chain* members, with *Incentives* for industry *Alliance Members* to achieve efficiency savings against those maximum costs;
- the payment of actual costs expended on a *Framework Programme* of numerous similar *Projects*, with cost savings against benchmarks used as one of the measures that determine the allocation of additional *Projects* among multiple industry *Alliance Members*; or
- the payment of *Alliance Members* according to the delivery of required outcomes across the whole *Framework Programme*, with *Incentives* for delivering improvements against historic baseline performance.

In order to drive *Improved Value* and fair treatment, 'Constructing the Gold Standard' recommends that the *Client/Additional Clients* and the *Alliance Manager* should create payment and pricing mechanisms for *Framework Programmes* and *Projects* that maximise cost certainty; that identify agreed fees, profit and overheads separately from other costs; that incentivise desired outcomes; that require the *Client/Additional Clients* to always pay other *Alliance Members* promptly; and that require industry *Alliance Members* to always pay *Supply Chain* members promptly.

> **Gold Standard Recommendation 19.** 'Create transparent pricing mechanisms for frameworks and call-offs that maximise cost certainty and ensure prompt payment.'

The FAC-1 definition of *Improved Value* includes 'improved profitability', and FAC-1 provides the option for *Framework Prices* to identify the *Profit* and *Overheads* of an *Alliance Member* separately from net costs in its *Framework Prices* and in its *Agreed Prices* for each *Project* (clause 4.3). This enables *Alliance Members* to identify savings arising from *Supply Chain Collaboration* and other *Alliance Activities*, and to ensure that agreed savings do not erode the margins of *Alliance Members* (see Chapters 27, 29 and 30). Identifying and ringfencing *Profit* and *Overheads* stabilises and justifies fair returns and expectations for industry *Alliance Members*, it aligns the commercial interests of all *Alliance Members,* and it motivates all *Alliance Members* to work together on agreed *Alliance Activities* that improve value and reduce risks.

Successful identification and agreement of cost savings depends on the chosen cost model identifying separately the *Profit* and *Overheads* payable to tier 1 industry *Alliance Members*. This enables the objective calculation, review and agreement of all other costs on a net basis, e.g. the costs payable to tier 2 and tier 3 *Supply Chain* members. Under FAC-1 clause 13.3.2, the agreement of *Profit* and *Overheads* as part of the *Framework Prices* is confidential between the tier 1 industry *Alliance Member* who notifies them, the *Client/Additional Clients* and the *Alliance Manager*.

Where *Profit* and *Overheads* are distinguished from other costs, the *Client/Additional Clients* and the *Alliance Manager* have greater control over the otherwise-invisible benefits that some industry *Alliance Members* might expect to obtain through practices such as *Supply Chain* rebates and prompt payment discounts on amounts that are in any event contractually due to tier 2 and tier 3 *Supply Chain* members. Hidden discounts and rebates agreed with subcontractors and suppliers are an obstacle to accurate costing. Any discount or rebate in the *Framework Prices* and *Agreed Prices* should only be permissible if agreed by the *Client/Additional Clients* in advance.

Profit and *Overheads* are set in accordance with the *Framework Prices* and/ or in accordance with a *Direct Award Procedure* or *Competitive Award Procedure* (see Chapter 28). *Profit* and *Overheads* can be percentages of *Agreed Prices* or agreed lump sums, and it is preferable to agree them as lump sums so that *Alliance Members* do not receive less *Profit* and *Overheads* as a result of other costs being reduced.

Many of the framework contracts reviewed in 'Constructing the Gold Standard' expressed *Profit* and *Overheads* as percentages rather than lump sums, and some also stated that the rates of *Profit* and *Overheads* quoted at framework level are maximums that can be reduced in call-off competitions for the award of *Project Contracts*. These approaches give rise to two risks.

- Firstly, there is a risk that percentage *Profit* and *Overheads* rise in step with increased costs and therefore do not incentivise efficiency savings. To tackle this, it is preferable for *Profit* and *Overheads* to be quoted as lump sums, or to be converted into lump sums at an early stage, so that they do not rise in step with increased costs and so that cost savings can be linked more easily to *Incentives* based on achievement of agreed targets.
- Secondly, the discounting of maximum *Profit* and *Overheads* in mini-competitions can perpetuate a race to the bottom. To tackle this risk, call-off processes and evaluation criteria should not encourage industry *Alliance Members* to quote the lowest *Profit* and *Overheads* but should instead require them to demonstrate how they will earn these amounts through the delivery of required and desired *Client/Additional Client* outcomes and through innovations, efficiencies and other benefits.

The agreement of accurate costs is dependent on the transparent sharing of available information. For example, the *Client/Additional Clients* should not withhold information about known obstacles on *Project* sites, and industry *Alliance Members* should not withhold information relating to the basis for calculating financial allowances such as risk contingencies.

> **Practice Note 36. Avoiding a race to the bottom.**
> The Housing Forum report 'Stopping Building Failures' recognises how building safety is jeopardised by the lowest-price 'race to the bottom', and considered the following evaluation models that could reduce the risks of unrealistic pricing.
>
> - 'The "optimum pricing model" in which the contracting authority sets out the optimum price which it considers appropriate for the contract, based on market research. The tenderer is then incentivised to make the

effort to reach the optimum price without undercutting it. The tenderer closest to the optimum price receives the highest mark. This should protect against abnormally low bids but arguably curbs the potential for truly innovative approaches.'

- 'The "fixed price model" where the contracting authority fixes the price for the contract and then undertakes a value for money evaluation on the non-price element of the contract's delivery, such as the quality and experience of the team, choice of materials, health and safety standards, liaison with residents, or environmental and social aspects of the project. By fixing the price and considering alternative value for money proposals, the contracting authority will again be neutralising the effect of any abnormally low bids on the overall evaluation.'

FAC-1 *Alliance Members* can agree any cost model according to the features and circumstances of the *Projects* and prospective *Projects* comprising the *Framework Programme*. While some FAC-1 *Alliance* models are based on cost reimbursement linked to shared risk and reward incentives (see, for example, Case Studies 27 and 28), other FAC-1 *Alliance* models provide for agreement of fixed costs following conclusion of agreed pre-construction phase activities. In all cases the *Alliance Members* should make clear in the *Framework Prices*

- the extent to which elements of a *Project* can or should be sufficiently designed at the point of selection of prospective industry *Alliance Members* to be costed as part of their evaluation, and/or so as to enable the provisional selection of preferred *Supply Chain* members at the point of selection of industry *Alliance Members*;
- the extent, where appropriate, to which certain work/service/supply packages can or should be suitable for prospective industry *Alliance Members* to develop a business case for self-delivery;
- the breakdown of *Profit* and *Overheads* at the point of selection of prospective industry *Alliance Members* so as to provide evidence of the value attributable to those *Profit* and *Overheads* and so as to enable the finalisation of *Overheads* on each *Project* to reflect new information emerging from design development, from the selection of subcontracted *Supply Chain* members and from lessons learned on other *Projects*;
- the basis for subdividing work/service/supply packages and the extent to which it is valuable to agree the *Profit* and *Overheads* payable to subcontracted *Supply Chain* members;
- the extent to which subcontracted *Supply Chain* members can provisionally be approved in line with the recommendations of prospective industry *Alliance Members*, and the activities required to create a business case that

finalises accurate and competitive costs for their respective work/service/ supply packages during the preconstruction phase of a *Project*;
- the timing for obtaining prices for all other work/service/supply packages from prospective *Supply Chain* members, and the basis for establishing accurate and competitive costs; and
- the extent, where appropriate, to which the costs of certain work/service/ supply packages should be treated as provisional sums and should be finalised by the relevant industry *Alliance Member* obtaining prices from prospective *Supply Chain* members after commencement of the construction phase of a *Project*.

The procurement of a public sector framework alliance can breach public procurement regulations if it does not involve sufficient comparative cost information at the point of selection of prospective industry *Alliance Members* or if it does not include sufficient comparative cost information as part of the selection process for specific *Projects*.. The *Client/Additional Clients* may obtain, as part of an FAC-1 procurement process, the costing of initial rates or a sample *Project* in order to test the costs and other proposals of prospective industry *Alliance Members* in greater detail. This approach was adopted in, for example, the procurement of the Ministry of Justice FAC-1 prototype framework alliance (see Case Study 4).

CHAPTER 27

How does FAC-1 establish *Agreed Prices* for each *Project*?

[FAC-1 clause 4 and the *Framework Prices*]

F AC-1 describes the processes by which *Framework Prices* are developed into the *Agreed Prices* payable for the delivery of each *Project*. FAC-1 clause 4.1 states that the *Agreed Prices* for each *Project* are developed and agreed

- in accordance with the *Direct Award Procedure* or *Competitive Award Procedure* (clauses 4.1.2 and 5),
- using *Framework Prices* as agreed (clause 4.1.3), and
- within any stated *Budget* (clause 4.1.4).

The FAC-1 *Alliance Members* build up the costs for each *Project* through the *Project Contract* award processes (see Chapter 28), and they can establish *Agreed Prices* for each *Project* using all or any of the following approaches:

- a fixed-price or target price, and/or
- rates for units of work, and/or
- categories of actual cost incurred.

No specific collaborative cost model is compulsory, and FAC-1 *Clients* have adopted a range of different commercial models according to their needs, priorities and preferences.

The *Agreed Prices* payable for each *Project* are paid under each *Project Contract* and not under FAC-1 unless otherwise agreed (clause 8.1).

FAC-1 clauses 4.3 and 4.4 require that:

- 'If stated in the *Framework Alliance Agreement*, the *Agreed Prices* shall state separately an *Alliance Member*'s *Profit* and *Overheads* set in accordance with *Framework Prices* and the *Direct Award Procedure* or *Competitive Award Procedure* applicable to each *Project*.'

- 'If stated in the *Framework Alliance Agreement*, the *Agreed Prices* shall include costs approved by the *Client* and any *Additional Clients* as a result of *Supply Chain Collaboration* or other *Alliance Activities* under clause 6.'

The FAC-1 provisions for establishing *Agreed Prices* are summarised in Checklist 9. Many FAC-1 teams use separately agreed *Profit* and *Overheads* plus costs established through *Supply Chain Collaboration* to build up and agree more accurate and complete fixed *Agreed Prices* for each *Project*, while others use this approach to build up and agree *Agreed Prices* that comprise target costs or cost reimbursement as described below.

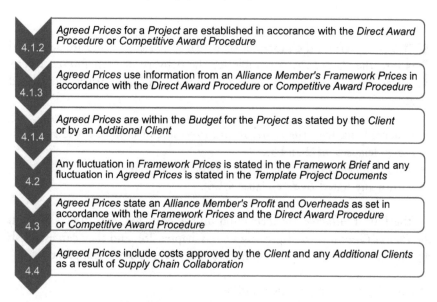

4.1.2	*Agreed Prices* for a *Project* are established in accorance with the *Direct Award Procedure* or *Competitive Award Procedure*
4.1.3	*Agreed Prices* use information from an *Alliance Member's Framework Prices* in accordance with the *Direct Award Procedure* or *Competitive Award Procedure*
4.1.4	*Agreed Prices* are within the *Budget* for the *Project* as stated by the *Client* or by an *Additional Client*
4.2	Any fluctuation in *Framework Prices* is stated in the *Framework Brief* and any fluctuation in *Agreed Prices* is stated in the *Template Project Documents*
4.3	*Agreed Prices* state an *Alliance Member's Profit* and *Overheads* as set in accordance with the *Framework Prices* and the *Direct Award Procedure* or *Competitive Award Procedure*
4.4	*Agreed Prices* include costs approved by the *Client* and any *Additional Clients* as a result of *Supply Chain Collaboration*

Checklist 9. FAC-1 *Agreed Prices*.

The use of FAC-1 *Alliance* systems to build up agreed costs with a common understanding of the factors affecting those costs is a significant improvement on the risks and uncertainties inherent in single-stage arm's-length tenders. For collaborative procurement, establishing a point in time at which accurate costs can be translated into a fixed price for a specific *Project* makes FAC-1 *Alliances* attractive to a much wider range of *Clients*. If fixed prices are established through the collaborative development of cost information and supported by suitable *Incentives*, the agreement of the costs that comprise those fixed prices can build trust, can help to overcome an adversarial approach to construction and can enable agreed conflict resolution. A well-informed fixed price also creates a reasonable commercial *Incentive* to complete a *Project* as efficiently as possible with high productivity.

FAC-1 describes the establishment of *Agreed Prices* for each *Project* through costed submissions by industry *Alliance Members* as part of the *Direct Award Procedure* and the *Competitive Award Procedure* combined with the cost savings achieved through *Supply Chain Collaboration* and other *Alliance Activities*. The *Agreed Prices* for each *Project* can comprise

- the *Profit* and *Overheads* of industry *Alliance Members*, preferably agreed as lump sums subject to increase according to the achievement of agreed *Targets*;
- cost components priced by industry *Alliance Members* at the point of their selection as *Alliance Members*;
- cost components priced by industry *Alliance Members* during or after their selection for each *Project*, using agreed processes that maximise the contributions of industry *Alliance Members* and *Supply Chain* members; and
- adjustments to reflect cost savings established on previous *Projects* and to reflect cost savings established through *Supply Chain Collaboration* and other agreed *Alliance Activities*.

Practice Note 37. Costing and value for money.
In relation to their New Prisons FAC-1 alliance, the Ministry of Justice report that tendered prices submitted by prospective industry *Alliance Members* during the initial call-off/tender stage from Crown Commercial Service provided cost certainty in the following ways:

- Fees for the pre-construction collaboration phase (Phase 1A) were finalised at tender stage.
- Direct fees (overhead and profit) were fixed at tender stage.
- Staff preliminary rates were fixed at tender stage.
- Programme duration and contract value were assumed at tender stage, based on the ongoing prison builds at HMP Five Wells and Glen Parva.

During the pre-construction collaboration stage (Phase 1A) for the four new prisons, cost certainty was built upon by transparent *Supply Chain* engagement for key or critical packages, i.e. mechanical, electrical and plumbing engineering, pre-cast concrete, and cell windows and doors. Following the pre-construction collaboration stage (Phase 1A), industry *Alliance Members* prepared their proposed *Agreed Prices* for the first new prison at Full Sutton (Phase 1B). These were based upon a completed design and the *Alliance* package procurement strategy, allowing the Ministry of Justice to have cost certainty in the form of an agreed lump sum contract value for the first new prison. The proposed *Agreed Prices* for the first new prison at Full Sutton submitted by each industry *Alliance Member* (made up of the transparently tendered packages plus rates agreed at tender stage) then formed the basis for pricing for prison sites 2, 3 and 4, allowing for adjustment for site-specifics only. Whilst the *Alliance Members* were already in contract, value for money was driven during Phase 1B in several ways:

- Competitive rates set at framework level could not be exceeded
- Call-off competition to form the *Alliance* provided additional competitive tension on these rates.
- Key *Supply Chain* packages were subject to procurement mapping by the *Alliance Members* during the pre-construction collaboration (Phase 1A) to build a common *Supply Chain*, driving value through collective buying power
- Circa 80% of the total value of each of the four new prisons would be competed transparently, competitively tendered on Ministry of Justice's sourcing portal, enabling additional reviews and benchmarking of costs
- The second, third, and fourth of the four new prisons would be priced on the same basis as the first at Full Sutton, with the only permitted adjustments being for site-specific differences (cost data from the Full Sutton prices will be used to build up these adjustments to ensure competitive prices are maintained).
- The ongoing prison builds at HMP Five Wells and Glen Parva provided valuable cost and benchmark data, particularly in the second stage without further tender.

See also Case Study 16.

If the preconstruction phase costing processes for each *Project* are not made clear in the FAC-1 *Framework Prices* and *Template Project Documents*, and if they are not supported by clear timeframes set out in the FAC-1 *Timetable*, there is the risk that industry *Alliance Members* will not allocate the time needed for seeking savings against their *Framework Prices* when developing their costed *Project Proposals*. The *Alliance Manager* should actively monitor and support the implementation of these preconstruction phase processes because, if proposed *Project* costs are not jointly examined by the relevant *Alliance Members*,

- the *Client* or an *Additional Client* may take an overly optimistic view of costs and related risks,

- industry *Alliance Members* may add contingencies in order to cover their perceived financial risks, and
- the interests of *Alliance Members* will not be fully aligned.

It is not always possible for *Alliance Members* to establish fixed *Agreed Prices* for a *Project*, e.g. where

- the extent of the materials and works required to complete the *Project* cannot be calculated with precision, or
- extensive works need to be undertaken underground in conditions that cannot be fully investigated in advance of starting on site.

In these circumstances an FAC-1 *Alliance* can adopt a 'target cost' model for a *Project* that establishes *Agreed Prices* combining agreed rates or agreed categories of cost with the sharing of savings and overruns, so as to align the commercial interests of *Alliance Members* if and to the extent that fixed *Agreed Prices* cannot be calculated accurately in advance. Target cost *Agreed Prices* may reflect a lack of detailed knowledge as to the extent and design of relevant works, services or supplies at the time of entering into the *Project Contract*. Target costs can be combined with *Incentives* that share overruns and savings in order to motivate reductions in adjustable costs.

A further alternative approach to *Agreed Prices* is 'cost reimbursement', which can be adopted where the nature or extent of the required works/services/supplies comprising a *Project* is not clear at the inception of the *Project Contract* and cannot be priced accurately. The calculation of what is payable pursuant to a cost reimbursement model requires regular analysis of industry *Alliance Members*' records in order to establish the extent of 'allowed' and 'disallowed' costs. It is usual for cost reimbursement payment applications to be supported by evidence of actual costs incurred to demonstrate that the activities undertaken were appropriate and that the costs were properly and reasonably incurred. The accuracy of cost reimbursement is linked to the amount of detailed cost analysis that precedes approval of payments.

Agreement to use cost reimbursement for *Agreed Prices* under FAC-1 should be combined with *Incentives* that motivate *Alliance Members* to minimise expenditure. For example, savings through cost reimbursement can be motivated by including those savings in the criteria that determine the award of further work under FAC-1 (see, for example, Case Studies 27 and 28).

Whether the costs of a *Project* are based on fixed *Agreed Prices* or target *Agreed Prices,* on rates for units of work, or on categories of actual cost incurred, it is important for the *Client/Additional Client* to establish an appropriate *Budget* as a cost ceiling for each *Project*, taking into account current market factors such as the impact of inflation. In creating a *Budget*, benchmarks can enable a *Client* or *Additional Client* to identify, by reference to its *Project Brief*, what a *Project* should cost and whether it is reasonable to expect the procurement and delivery of that *Project* within the *Budget* as a cost ceiling.

In order to assess framework deliverables in respect of cost, schedule, GHG emissions and other expected outcomes, and in order to maintain cost controls that support call-off, ESI, performance measurement, value improvement and other framework processes, 'Constructing the Gold Standard' recommends that the *Client/Additional Clients* and the *Alliance Manager* use benchmarks based on information from past projects and programmes and that they create 'Should Cost Models' in order to forecast what each *Framework Programme* or *Project* should cost over its whole life.

> **Gold Standard Recommendation 16.** 'Assess and control the costs of framework deliverables through the use of evidence-based benchmarks and whole-life Should Cost Models.'

Stating a *Budget* under FAC-1 clause 4.1.4 for each *Project* and monitoring *Project* costs through the FAC-1 processes for call-off, preconstruction phase ESI and strategic *Supply Chain Collaboration*, and through the *Project Contract* processes for cost control and transparency, enable the *Client/Additional Clients* and the *Alliance Manager* to

- create and apply evidence-based cost benchmarks as part of the *Success Measures* and *Targets*,
- create and apply accurate *Budgets* as 'Should Cost Models' in accordance with 'Constructing the Gold Standard', and
- assess and control the costs of framework deliverables.

Stating a *Budget* under FAC-1 clause 4.1.4 for each *Project* also enables prospective industry *Alliance Members* to calculate

- their expected *Profit* and *Overheads* by reference to that *Budget*,
- evidence of their ability to deliver the *Project* within that *Budget*,
- their *Project Proposals* for achieving *Improved Value* within that *Budget*, and
- their *Project Proposals* for seeking cost savings that could establish *Agreed Prices* lower than that *Budget*.

The FAC-1 *Framework Brief* and *Project Briefs* should state how the *Budget* for each *Project* is to be developed in further detail in order to create the *Agreed Prices* for that *Project*, including the systems and gateways for early involvement of *Alliance Members* and *Supply Chain* members and in agreed activities designed to ensure that the *Profit, Overheads* and costs of industry *Alliance Members* and the costs of *Supply Chain* members comprise *Agreed Prices* that remain within each *Budget*.

In order to address concerns that a selected industry *Alliance Member* could quote *Agreed Prices* that exceed the agreed *Budget*, the systems set out in the FAC-1 *Framework Brief* and *Project Briefs* can include

- early involvement processes for *Alliance Members* and *Supply Chain* members that allow time for review of the relevant *Alliance Members'* and *Supply Chain* members' proposed costs, requiring that these costs remain within the *Budget* as a precondition to granting authority for the construction phase of each *Project* to proceed;
- close monitoring by the *Alliance Manager* of the *Supply Chain Collaboration*, tendering and appointment procedures operated by industry *Alliance Members*, ensuring that these procedures do not impose excessive demands on *Supply Chain* members or inflate *Supply Chain* prices; and
- transparency at each stage of costing each *Project*, requiring that the *Alliance Manager* receives all *Project* documentation prepared and issued by industry *Alliance Members*, receives all tender returns and proposals submitted by prospective *Supply Chain* members, and is invited to attend all relevant meetings.

Case Study 28. Land Securities framework alliance procured using cost reimbursement
Land Securities (LandSec) and the Department for Work & Pensions (DWP) used cost reimbursement to deliver significant savings on their Job Centre Plus programme, where an FAC-1 prototype governed a large number of similar *Projects*. These *Projects* were awarded successively to fourteen contractors under a multiparty framework alliance, subject to measurement of their performance on previous *Projects* according to criteria that included minimising the costs expended.

A fast-track programme of office adaptations was undertaken through a framework alliance set up jointly by LandSec and DWP, using standard designs, materials and equipment adapted to a wide variety of different buildings. The *Objectives* included an efficient contract structure that would enable a quick start on site, utilising model processes and contract documents to streamline a nationwide programme.

The *Framework Programme* subdivided England, Wales and Scotland into multiple districts, and a tier 1 contractor was appointed to undertake works in each district. LandSec and DWP wanted to ensure cross-pollination between districts, and this was achieved through a single multiparty framework alliance contract entered into between all fourteen tier 1 contractors and the two clients. LandSec and DWP also wanted to create a fully integrated *Supply Chain* to support the roll-out programme, and specialist framework agreements were negotiated in parallel with key subcontractors and suppliers.

Strict *Timetables* were agreed to govern both the preconstruction and construction phases of each *Project*. The framework alliance used cost reimbursement combined with *Incentives* that linked cost savings to the future award of work, and the final cost of the *Framework Programme* was £737 million against a forecast of £981 million, achieving cost savings of 24.8%.

LandSec and DWP used an FAC-1 prototype in conjunction with *Project Contracts* based on the PPC2000 standard form project alliance contract.

CHAPTER 28

How are *Project Contracts* awarded?

**[FAC-1 clause 5 and the Schedule 4 *Direct Award*
Procedure and *Competitive Award Procedure*]**

It is fundamental to successful *Alliance* relationships that *Alliance Members* understand not only the prospective scope and nature of the works/ services/supplies comprising the *Framework Programme* but also how the *Project Contracts* for those works/services/supplies will be awarded.

FAC-1 sets out the following two procedures by which the *Client* or any *Additional Client* may award *Project Contracts* for works/services/supplies.

- The Schedule 4, Part 1 *Direct Award Procedure* governing direct allocation of the works/services/supplies described in a *Project Brief* to any one or more *Alliance Members* who submit *Project Proposals* and proposed *Agreed Prices* according to agreed rules (clause 5.1).
- The Schedule 4, Part 2 *Competitive Award Procedure* governing a competition for the works/services/supplies described in a *Project Brief* in which two or more *Alliance Members* submit *Project Proposals* and proposed *Agreed Prices* according to agreed rules and evaluation criteria (clause 5.2).

The FAC-1 provisions governing the award of *Project Contracts* are summarised in Checklist 10, and the Schedule 4 *Direct Award Procedure* and *Competitive Award Procedure*

- state the agreed procedure and timescales for the issue of each *Project Brief,* for the submission of proposed *Agreed Prices* and other *Project Proposals*, and for all steps leading to award of *Project Contracts*, including the method, rules and criteria for evaluation of proposed *Agreed Prices* and other *Project Proposals* and the required format for proposed *Agreed Prices* and other *Project Proposals*;

- explain how the *Template Project Documents* will be applied to each *Project*;
- explain the procurement model for each *Project*, including the sources and timing of all contributions to design, *Supply Chain* engagement, costing, programming and *Risk Management*, and incorporating the required approach to *BIM* as appropriate;
- explain all procedures relating to the conditional and/or unconditional award of *Project Contracts*, including any intended *Orders* for *Pre-Contract Activities*; and
- explain how it will be decided when the *Direct Award Procedure* or the *Competitive Award Procedure* will be used.

An FAC-1 *Client* and any *Additional Clients* should use consistent, proportionate and relevant processes for evaluation in any *Direct Award Procedure* or *Competitive Award Procedure*. The evaluation criteria should also be consistent with the evaluation criteria used for selecting the industry *Alliance Members* when the *Alliance* was created, and they should make clear how *Project Contract* evaluation criteria are linked to *Alliance Objectives* and *Success Measures*.

Sch.5	*Projects* may be awarded using the *Direct Award Procedure* and/or *Competitive Award Procedure* if and as set out in Schedule 5
5.1	*Direct Award Procedure*: the *Alliance Manager* issues a *Project Brief* to one *Alliance Member* who submits *Project Proposals*/proposed *Agreed Prices*
5.2	*Competitive Award Procedure*: the *Alliance Manager* issues a *Project Brief* to multiple *Alliance Members* who submit *Project Proposals*/proposed *Agreed Prices*
5.3	*Direct Award Procedure* and *Competitive Award Procedure* use Schedule 5 *Template Project Documents* completed with *Project* details
5.3	Schedule 5 *Template Project Documents* include *Project Contract Conditions*
5.4	*Alliance Manager* issues *Project Contract* to successful *Alliance Member*, incorporating *Agreed Prices* and other approved *Project Proposals*
5.5	*Alliance Member* executes and returns to *Alliance Manager* a *Project Contract* that complies with the *Framework Documents* within ten *Working Days* from receipt
5.6	No minimum value or type of *Project Contracts* is guaranteed except as stated in the *Framework Alliance Agreement*
5.6	No liability for expenditure incurred by *Alliance Members* in expectation of a *Project Contract* except as stated in the *Framework Alliance Agreement* or an *Order*
5.7	Any exclusivity in award of *Project Contracts* is stated in the *Framework Alliance Agreement* and subject to adjustments set out in the *Success Measures* and *Targets*

Checklist 10. FAC-1 award of *Project Contracts*.

A persistent industry concern is that financial criteria inevitably dominate an evaluation procedure and tempt bidders to undercut each other's prices regardless of other criteria. Overcoming this concern requires the FAC-1 *Client/Additional Clients* to ensure that their *Direct Award Procedure* and/or *Competitive Award Procedure* for each *Project* will make clear their expected outcomes, their priorities and their definition of value in ways that contractor/ consultant/supplier *Alliance Members* can respond to in their qualitative *Project Proposals*. This requires sufficient weighting to be given to qualitative criteria, and it necessitates careful analysis of how to avoid unrealistic responses to cost criteria.

The FAC-1 *Template Project Documents* used in any *Direct Award Procedure* or *Competitive Award Procedure* are listed in Schedule 5 to the *Framework Alliance Agreement*. They include

- the *Project Contract Conditions* to be used for each *Project Contract*, comprising the applicable standard forms of contract and any amendments;
- the structure and standard components of the *Project Brief* that forms part of each *Project Contract* describing the scope and nature of a *Project*, setting out the *Client's* technical, management and commercial requirements and expected outcomes in respect of the *Project*, and including all required standards and warranties;
- all standard requirements in each *Project Brief* in respect of insurances and securities, and all standard processes and procedures in each *Project Brief* for the management of communication, performance, quality, design, *Supply Chain* engagement, cost, payment, time, change, risk, health and safety, and all other project management processes and procedures, in each case including the required approach to *BIM* as appropriate;
- any standard requirements in each *Project Brief* in respect of *Sustainability*, *Operation* of the completed *Project*, and engagement with *Stakeholders* and with *Users*; and
- the required structure and content of the *Agreed Prices* and other *Project Proposals* forming part of each *Project Contract*.

FAC-1 defines the *Project Brief* as including

- all required quality standards and warranties, including all requirements in respect of insurances and securities;
- all processes and procedures for management of communication, performance, quality, design, *Supply Chain* engagement, cost, payment, time, change, risk, health and safety, and all other project management processes and procedures;

- the required approach to *BIM* as appropriate; and
- all requirements in respect of *Sustainability, Operation* and engagement with *Stakeholders* and *Users*.

Please see also Chapter 20 in relation to the *Project Contracts* and *Template Project Documents*, and Chapter 27 in relation to the *Agreed Prices* for each *Project*.

When the *Project Proposals* and proposed *Agreed Prices* of an *Alliance Member* are approved in accordance with a *Direct Award Procedure* or a *Competitive Award Procedure*, the *Alliance Manager* issues a *Project Contract* to that *Alliance Member* incorporating the relevant *Project Proposals* and *Agreed Prices* (FAC-1 clause 5.4). Within ten *Working Days* from the date of its receipt, the *Alliance Member* then executes and returns the *Project Contract* to the *Alliance Manager* if it is in accordance with the *Framework Documents* (FAC-1 clause 5.5).

The only minimum value or type of *Project Contracts* to be awarded to any *Alliance Member* is stated in the *Framework Alliance Agreement*, and neither the *Client* nor any *Additional Client* guarantees any awards in excess of that minimum or shall have any liability for expenditure incurred by other *Alliance Members* in expectation of a *Project Contract* except as stated in the *Framework Alliance Agreement* or an *Order* (FAC-1 clause 5.6).

Subject to FAC-1 clause 5.6, any exclusivity in the award of *Project Contracts* is stated in the *Framework Alliance Agreement*, and any agreed exclusivity is subject to any adjustments set out in the *Success Measures* and *Targets* (FAC-1 clause 5.7 and Schedule 1, Part 2).

CHAPTER 29

What are the *Alliance Activities*?

For an *Alliance* to fulfil its agreed *Objectives* and *Targets*, the *Alliance Members* must undertake specific activities that are designed to achieve *Improved Value* and successful *Risk Management*. These activities go beyond winning *Project Contracts* and delivering *Projects*: they require a clear understanding of what the *Alliance Members* will do 'together and individually in the spirit of trust, fairness and collaboration for the benefit of the *Framework Programme*' (clause 1.1).

At the point when a framework alliance is created, the *Alliance Members* do not know everything they need to know about what each can offer the others, about the *Projects* to be awarded, about the teams who will deliver each *Project*, or about the *Alliance Activities* that will improve value and reduce risks. FAC-1 embodies the 'Construction Playbook' requirement for *Clients* to 'ensure that contracts are structured to support an exchange of data, drive collaboration, improve value and manage risk' and to 'set clear expectations for continuous improvement and be consistent with the principles in this Playbook'.

The development and implementation of FAC-1 *Alliance Activities* are illustrated in Figure 9. The FAC-1 *Framework Brief* and *Framework Proposals* should describe the incremental processes by which the *Alliance Members* work together – in parallel with and separate from the award of *Project Contracts* and separate from the performance of their *Project Contract* obligations – to build up the additional information they need for collaborative value improvement and risk management. These incremental contractual processes enable *Alliance Members* to create, obtain, agree and act on new information while, wherever possible, avoiding negotiation.

FAC-1 links the pursuit of *Objectives* and *Success Measures* to a stated range of *Alliance Activities*, and it makes clear in the shared *Timetable* which of the *Alliance Members* will undertake these *Alliance Activities* and within what agreed deadlines and with what gateways and milestones (see Chapter 24).

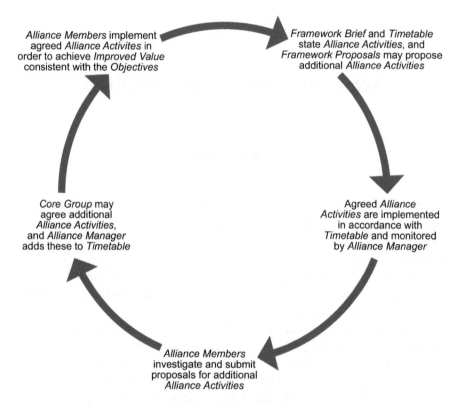

Alliance Members implement agreed *Alliance Activites* in order to achieve *Improved Value* consistent with the *Objectives*

Framework Brief and *Timetable* state *Alliance Activities*, and *Framework Proposals* may propose additional *Alliance Activities*

Core Group may agree additional *Alliance Activities*, and *Alliance Manager* adds these to *Timetable*

Agreed *Alliance Activities* are implemented in accordance with *Timetable* and monitored by *Alliance Manager*

Alliance Members investigate and submit proposals for additional *Alliance Activities*

Figure 9. Development and Implementation of
FAC-1 *Alliance Activities.*

FAC-1 Appendix 1 defines *Alliance Activities* as 'any activities agreed to be performed by *Alliance Members* under clause 6 in order to achieve *Improved Value* consistent with the *Objectives*', including

- agreed *Supply Chain Collaboration*;
- agreed innovation and education;
- agreed exchanges of information; and
- agreed integration, adaptation and standardisation of roles, expertise and responsibilities.

FAC-1 clause 6.1 states: 'The *Alliance Members* shall implement the *Alliance Activities* described in the *Framework Alliance Agreement* and the *Framework Brief* and otherwise agreed by *Alliance Members*, working within the timescales stated in the *Timetable* and other timescales agreed by *Alliance Members*, in order to create *Improved Value* consistent with the *Objectives*.'

The *Alliance Manager* is responsible for organising, supporting and monitoring the *Alliance Activities* (clause 3.1.4) by reference to the deadlines, gateways and milestones set out in the Schedule 2 *Timetable*. The *Alliance Manager* is also responsible for updating the *Timetable* if and when additional *Alliance Activities* are agreed by the *Alliance Members*, subject to the *Core Group* approving updates to the *Timetable* (clauses 2.6, 3.1.2 and 6.1).

Alliance Activities can be undertaken in advance of and in parallel with the award of *Project Contracts* and the delivery of *Projects*. The agreed outputs from *Alliance Activities* should form part of the proposals 'intended to achieve *Improved Value* consistent with the *Objectives*' that are submitted for *Core Group* approval (clause 2.2).

Alliance Activities are undertaken separately from the award of *Project Contracts* and the delivery of *Projects* and may not attract any additional payment by the *Client/Additional Clients*. As a result, certain *Alliance Members* may wish to defer or minimise their commitment of resources to these *Alliance Activities*. To overcome this potential problem, the *Alliance Manager* should make clear when organising, supporting and monitoring the *Alliance Activities*

- the links between the *Alliance Activities* and the success of the *Alliance* in achieving *Improved Value* and *Risk Management* and
- the links between the *Alliance Activities* and the agreed *Objectives*, *Success Measures*, *Targets* and *Incentives*.

If costs are payable to an *Alliance Member* in respect of its work on *Alliance Activities*, these costs should be authorised by the *Client/Additional Clients* and set out in an *Order* pursuant to clause 7 (see Chapter 31). Where the *Alliance Members* agree additional *Alliance Activities* beyond those described in the *Framework Alliance Agreement* and the *Framework Brief*, they also need to agree whether any *Alliance Member* should be paid for its contribution to those additional *Alliance Activities*.

Practice Note 38. Impact of *Alliance Activities*.
The SCMG FAC-1 prototype reported how *Alliance Activities* led to

- 'reduced risks, cost savings and time savings through accelerated constructor/supply chain briefing' and
- 'time savings, such as through quicker build-up of prices leading to earlier start on site and reduced client/consultant time/costs'.

See also Case Study 12.

CHAPTER 30

How does *Supply Chain Collaboration* work?

[FAC-1 clauses 6 and 13.2]

The UK 'Construction Playbook' requires that 'all public works projects should contract for early supply chain involvement (ESI)', which it defines as extending 'the principle of early contractor involvement by formally engaging the tier 1 contractor alongside the tier 2 and tier 3 subcontractors and suppliers in the pre-construction phase to input into the design (including the use of standards for products and interfaces), costing, risk management and structuring of a project or programme'. This mandate represents an important step towards more integrated construction procurement, but ESI opportunities for tier 2 and tier 3 *Supply Chain* members are limited if they are asked to contribute only to a single project in isolation. These opportunities and contributions are far more likely to offer *Improved Value* and effective *Risk Management* if ESI is undertaken on *Projects* forming part of a *Framework Programme*, and this strategic ESI is brought to life through FAC-1 *Supply Chain Collaboration*.

The FAC-1 *Alliance Activities* include *Supply Chain Collaboration* under clause 6.3, which enables *Alliance Members* to harmonise and share *Supply Chains* and create *Improved Value* by

- reviewing and comparing the value offered by *Supply Chain* members;
- reviewing the potential for more consistent, longer-term, larger-scale *Supply Chain* contracts and for other improved *Supply Chain* commitments and working practices;
- jointly renegotiating or retendering *Supply Chain* contracts; and
- agreeing more consistent, longer-term, larger-scale *Supply Chain* contracts and other improved *Supply Chain* commitments and working practices.

In order to maximise the *Improved Value* demonstrated by early supply chain involvement in collaborative framework case studies – including efficiency savings, improved quality and safety, improved social value, and reduced GHG emissions – 'Constructing the Gold Standard' recommends that the *Client/Additional Clients* and the *Alliance Manager* should use framework-level ESI to obtain and evaluate industry insights, innovations and proposals, including a contractual *Supply Chain Collaboration* system through which to create strategic *Supply Chain* relationships that improve *Project* outcomes.

Gold Standard Recommendation 13. 'Improve economic, social and environmental outcomes through framework early supply chain involvement (ESI), using Supply Chain Collaboration systems in all framework contracts.'

FAC-1 Appendix 1 defines *Supply Chain Collaboration* as 'any activities agreed to be performed by *Alliance Members* under clause 6.3 in order to achieve *Improved Value* through more consistent, longer term, larger scale *Supply Chain Contracts* and through other improved *Supply Chain* commitments and working practices'. The three main stages of *Supply Chain Collaboration* are summarised in Figure 10.

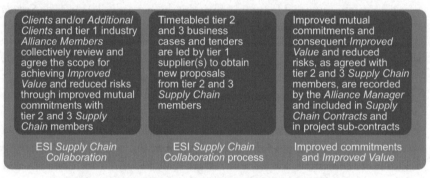

Figure 10. Stages of *Supply Chain Collaboration*.

FAC-1 clause 6.3 describes how, 'If stated in the *Framework Alliance Agreement* or the *Framework Brief* or otherwise agreed by *Alliance Members*, the *Alliance Activities* shall include *Supply Chain Collaboration* in order to achieve *Improved Value* consistent with the *Objectives* through more consistent, longer term, larger scale *Supply Chain Contracts* and through other improved *Supply Chain* commitments.'

Unlocking the potential of *Supply Chain Collaboration* requires a well-planned approach, using techniques that connect the *Alliance Members* with the specialist *Supply Chain* members who undertake crucial aspects of works, services, supplies and *Operation*. This goes much further than leaving each industry *Alliance Member* to renegotiate privately with its prospective *Supply Chain* members.

Commitments to undertake *Supply Chain Collaboration* are inserted in the *Framework Alliance Agreement* by reference to FAC-1 clause 6 (page iii), and details of the agreed scope of *Supply Chain Collaboration* are stated in the *Framework Brief*. Additional *Supply Chain Collaboration* may be agreed by *Alliance Members* at any time.

Any other arrangements for assigning or subcontracting the rights or obligations of any *Alliance Member* are inserted in the *Framework Alliance Agreement* by reference to FAC-1 clause 13.2 (page iv).

FAC-1 clause 6.3 describes *Supply Chain Collaboration* as working practices that comprise

- agreeing through the *Core Group*, if not already set out in the *Framework Brief*, the basis for sharing information between *Alliance Members* in relation to their current and proposed *Supply Chain Contracts* and, if not already set out in the *Timetable*, the timescales for each stage of *Supply Chain Collaboration*;
- reviewing and comparing the value offered by each *Alliance Member*'s current and proposed *Supply Chain*;
- reviewing the potential for more consistent, longer-term, larger-scale *Supply Chain Contracts* and for other improved *Supply Chain* commitments and working practices;
- jointly renegotiating *Supply Chain Contracts* or undertaking joint *Supply Chain* tender processes, in each case through procedures to be approved by the *Core Group*, to be led by one or more agreed *Alliance Members*, and to be organised, monitored and supported by the *Alliance Manager*; and
- subject to approval by the *Client* and any *Additional Clients* of the *Improved Value* resulting from *Supply Chain Collaboration*, agreeing and entering into more consistent, longer-term, larger-scale *Supply Chain Contracts* and other improved *Supply Chain* commitments and working practices.

The FAC-1 cycle of *Supply Chain Collaboration* is illustrated in Figure 11 and it should be subdivided into a series of activities to be undertaken by *Alliance Members* that are identified in the FAC-1 *Timetable*. For example, in order for the *Alliance Manger* to organise, monitor and support a *Supply Chain Collaboration* joint tender process, the activities and deadlines can be broken down into the following stages for each work/service/supply package:

- Agreement of work/service/supply specifications in sufficient detail for pricing.

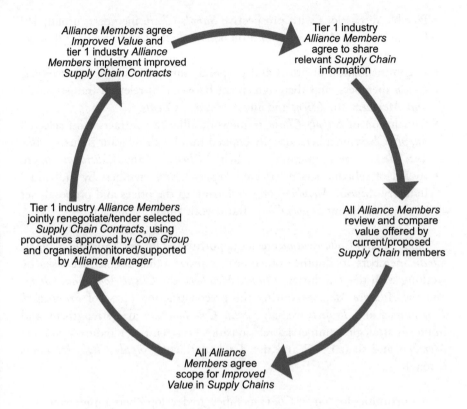

Figure 11. FAC-1 cycle of *Supply Chain Collaboration.*

- Agreement of 'invitations to tender' governing the process for submission of *Supply Chain* prices and proposals to the industry *Alliance Members*, and a form of *Supply Chain* framework alliance contract that the industry *Alliance Members* will enter into with the successful *Supply Chain* bidders, preferably using FAC-1.
- Agreement of a list of *Supply Chain* bidders from whom submissions will be invited by the industry *Alliance Members*.
- Issue of invitations to tender to prospective *Supply Chain* members, usually by one industry *Alliance Member* on behalf of all relevant industry *Alliance Members*.
- Return of tenders from prospective *Supply Chain* members.
- Review of *Supply Chain* prices and proposals by one or more industry *Alliance Members* with other *Alliance Members*.

- Possible discussions with prospective *Supply Chain* members, usually led by one industry *Alliance Member* on behalf of all relevant industry *Alliance Members*.
- Recommendation of prices and proposals submitted by preferred *Supply Chain* members, and their agreement between all relevant industry *Alliance Members*, the *Client* and any *Additional Clients*.
- Conclusion of *Supply Chain* framework alliance contracts with selected *Supply Chain* members, usually entered into by all relevant industry *Alliance Members* and sometimes also by the *Client* and any *Additional Clients*.
- Award of subcontracts to selected *Supply Chain* members by individual industry *Alliance Members*, cross-referring to the prices and proposals set out in the relevant *Supply Chain* framework alliance contract.

Supply Chain Collaboration creates opportunities for tier 2 and tier 3 *Supply Chain* members to improve outcomes, improve value and reduce risks by working with tier 1 industry *Alliance Members*, the *Client/Additional Clients* and the *Alliance Manager* during the preconstruction phase of *Framework Programmes* and *Projects*. *Supply Chain Collaboration* also strengthens and improves strategic commercial relationships between tier 1 industry *Alliance Members* and their tier 2 and tier 3 subcontracted *Supply Chain* members through

- opportunities for *Supply Chain* members to develop a better understanding of the *Framework Programme* and *Projects* through direct dialogue with the *Client/Additional Clients*, the *Alliance Manager* and the other *Alliance Members*;
- opportunities for *Supply Chain* members to win more work for longer periods by demonstrating proposals for efficiency savings, other *Improved Value*, risk reduction, extended warranties, employment and skills commitments, and innovations that improve the *Sustainability* of the *Framework Programme* and *Projects*;
- opportunities for *Supply Chain* members to influence the approach taken by the *Client/Additional Clients*, the *Alliance Manager* and the other *Alliance Members* in calling off *Projects* so as to improve efficiency and reduce risks in the delivery of specialist works, services and supplies; and
- where appropriate, opportunities for *Supply Chain* members to become *Alliance Members*.

Clients can use *Supply Chain Collaboration* to enhance the opportunities for local and regional SMEs to win additional work, by exploring with tier 1 industry *Alliance Members* the extent to which local or regional businesses offer better value than the tier 1 industry *Alliance Members'* usual *Supply Chain* members. This system enables the FAC-1 *Client* and any *Additional Clients* to influence improved tier 2 and tier 3 relationships and contributions as part of transparent, strategic subcontract procurements that are led by tier 1 industry *Alliance Members* and do not require a new public procurement process.

Supply Chain Collaboration can also enable *Alliance Members* to earn greater rewards because

- contractor/consultant/supplier *Alliance Members* are incentivised by the prospect of a continued pipeline of work;
- *Clients* can expect and measure continuous improvement;
- *Alliance Members* can capture lessons learned and pass them on from *Project* to *Project*; and
- joint commitment to the new processes is replicated and can become standard business practice.

Obstacles to *Supply Chain Collaboration* may arise where

- industry *Alliance Members* do not see the benefits of reviewing what is offered by their current *Supply Chain* members;
- industry *Alliance Members* suspect that the *Client/Additional Clients* are not committed to a transparent, collaborative approach; or
- prospective *Supply Chain* members suspect that industry *Alliance Members* are not committed to a transparent, collaborative approach.

FAC-1 describes the process of *Supply Chain Collaboration* in sufficient detail to ensure that the *Alliance Members*

- create a clear contractual path through any perceived obstacles;
- comply with public procurement regulations;
- implement clear, transparent processes, which are key to avoiding the risk of anti-competitive behaviour; and
- avoid interfering in the subcontracts through which industry *Alliance Members* manage their appointed *Supply Chain* members when delivering *Projects*.

Practice Note 39. *Supply Chain Collaboration.*
Supply Chain Collaboration under the FAC-1 prototype between Surrey County Council, Kier, Aggregate Industries and Marshall Surfacing was motivated by the prospect of a contract extension, plus a client offer of £100 million of additional work subject to demonstrable delivery of

£120 million of value. It led to the tier 2/tier 3 subcontractors/suppliers offering the following cost savings against the previously quoted rates in return for

- greater involvement in planning work and developing continuity of work (saving: 2%);
- agreed minimum annual volume of work (saving: 5%);
- agreed minimum size of individual works orders (saving: 2%);
- prompt(er) payment by the tier 1 contractor (saving: 1%); and
- storage facilities in available space at the client's depot (saving: 2%).

Supply Chain Collaboration under this FAC-1 prototype also enabled other *Improved Value* comprising

- 'improved whole life value, including 10 year warranties for 76% of schemes and 5–8 year warranties for 22% of schemes';
- 'improved quality control through joint risk management';,
- 'improved apprentice commitments by tier 2 and 3 supply chain members';
- 'time savings through lean programming';
- 'innovations that increased recycling, reduced landfill and reduced cost for treating tarbound roads from £140 per tonne to £60 per tonne';
- 'no major remedial work required and no health and safety incidents'; and
- 'over 100 complimentary letters from residents and Council members'.

See also Case Study 5. Kier then led *Supply Chain Collaboration* with its wider *Supply Chain*, using the published version of FAC-1, and achieved 8% savings, ESI and a range of social value as described in Case Study 22.

CHAPTER 31

What are *Orders* and *Pre-Contract Activities*?

[FAC-1 clause 7 and the Appendix 3 form of *Order*]

FAC-1 clause 7 creates flexibility for *Alliance Members* to agree *Orders* in respect of *Alliance Activities* or *Pre-Contract Activities*. These *Orders* can be used to clarify the scope, value and duration of *Alliance Activities,* e.g. if and when it is agreed that *Alliance Members* will be paid for these *Alliance Activities.*

Orders can also be used to avoid the uncertainty and complexity of creating a bespoke 'letter of intent' where the *Client* or any *Additional Client* wishes to authorise certain limited works, services or supplies in advance of the award of a *Project Contract.*

FAC-1 clause 7 states: 'The *Client* or any *Additional Client* and any other *Alliance Member* may sign an *Order* in the form set out in Appendix 3 describing any payment to be made for *Alliance Activities* or describing any *Pre-Contract Activities* to be undertaken by an *Alliance Member* in advance of entering into a *Project Contract.*'

A form of *Order* is set out in Appendix 3 to the *Contract Terms,* and each *Order* states the scope of the agreed *Alliance Activities* or *Pre-Contract Activities,* the dates for their completion and the amounts payable for the relevant works, services or supplies (clause 7.3). The FAC-1 provisions governing each *Order* are summarised in Checklist 11.

FAC-1 clause 7.2 states that each *Order* shall be subject to the *Contract Terms* unless stated to be subject to the *Project Contract Conditions,* and clause 7.4 states that no *Order* shall be a *Project Contract* or give rise to any rights or obligations beyond its stated scope.

The form of *Order* states at paragraph 5 (unless that paragraph is deleted) that *Pre-Contract Activities* shall be treated as part of the relevant *Project* and shall be governed by the relevant *Project Contract Conditions* if and when a *Project Contract* is entered into.

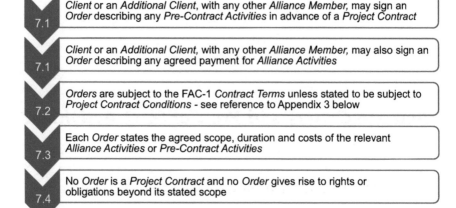

7.1   Client or an Additional Client, with any other Alliance Member, may sign an Order describing any Pre-Contract Activities in advance of a Project Contract

7.1   Client or an Additional Client, with any other Alliance Member, may also sign an Order describing any agreed payment for Alliance Activities

7.2   Orders are subject to the FAC-1 Contract Terms unless stated to be subject to Project Contract Conditions - see reference to Appendix 3 below

7.3   Each Order states the agreed scope, duration and costs of the relevant Alliance Activities or Pre-Contract Activities

7.4   No Order is a Project Contract and no Order gives rise to rights or obligations beyond its stated scope

7.5   The issuing Client/Additional Client or the Alliance Manager may terminate an Order by not less than ten Working Days' notice at any time

App.3   The Appendix 3 Order Form states details of the Order and also states that, if and when a Project Contract is entered into, the Pre-Contract Activities are governed by the applicable Project Contract Conditions

Checklist 11. FAC-1 *Orders* and *Pre-Contract Activities.*

FAC-1 clause 7.5 states that the *Client* or any *Additional Client* that signs an *Order*, or the *Alliance Manager*, shall be entitled to terminate that *Order* by not less than ten *Working Days'* notice at any time.

FAC-1 provides for agreed payment under *Orders* issued in respect of *Alliance Activities* and *Pre-Contract Activities* (clauses 8.2–8.11), and the *Framework Brief* and *Framework Prices* state the basis for agreeing these payments.

FAC-1 clause 10.5 states that under an *Order* for *Pre-Contract Activities* only the *Client* or *Additional Client* who issues it, the other *Alliance Member* who signs it and the *Alliance Manager* shall owe each other a duty of care.

Insurances under FAC-1 clause 12 cover the *Alliance Activities* or *Pre-Contract Activities* governed by an *Order* (see Chapter 37).

CHAPTER 32

How does FAC-1 manage payment?

[FAC-1 clause 8]

The success of a framework alliance depends on prompt payment of *Alliance Members* under *Project Contracts* and prompt payment of *Supply Chain* members under *Supply Chain Contracts*. Prompt payment enables *Alliance Members* and *Supply Chain* members to concentrate their efforts on the best interests of the *Projects*, and it reduces unproductive time spent in devising tactics for claims.

The only amounts payable under FAC-1 comprise payments by the *Client* or any *Additional Client* of

- agreed amounts due to the *Alliance Manager* under the *Alliance Manager Payment Terms* and
- agreed amounts due to each *Alliance Member* under any *Order*.

The FAC-1 payment process and periods are summarised in Checklist 12. They make no reference to English law but are drafted to comply with the UK Housing Grants, Construction and Regeneration Act 1996 as amended.

FAC-1 clause 8.1 states that, except as otherwise agreed, payment of *Agreed Prices* in respect of *Projects* shall be made under each *Project Contract* and not under the *Framework Alliance Contract*.

The amounts payable under FAC-1 are 'in each case subject only to any fluctuation provisions stated in the *Alliance Manager Payment Terms* or the *Framework Brief* and subject to adjustment in accordance with these *Contract Terms*' (clause 8.2).

A payment under an *Order* can relate to any amount agreed to be payable for *Alliance Activities* or for *Pre-Contract Activities* undertaken by an *Alliance Member* in advance of the conclusion of a *Project Contract*. The relevant amount needs to be stated in clause 4 of an *Order* completed in accordance with clause 7 and Appendix 3.

Any amended payment periods are inserted in the *Framework Alliance Agreement* by reference to clause 8.6 (page iii).

The agreed rate of interest on late payment is inserted in the *Framework Alliance Agreement* by reference to clause 8.11 (page iii).

Some frameworks reviewed in 'Constructing the Gold Standard' support payment of *Supply Chain* members through the use of 'project bank accounts', and many include the prompt payment of *Supply Chain* members in their *Success Measures*.

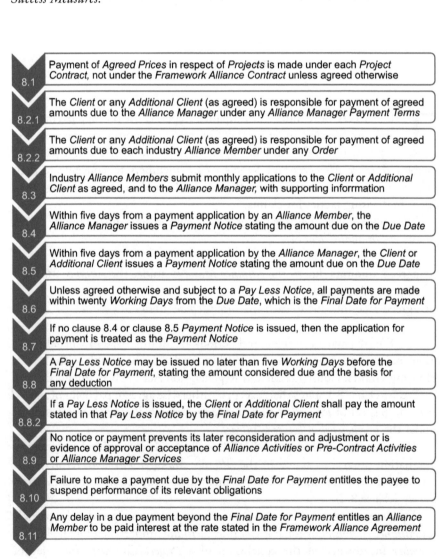

8.1 — Payment of *Agreed Prices* in respect of *Projects* is made under each *Project Contract*, not under the *Framework Alliance Contract* unless agreed otherwise

8.2.1 — The *Client* or any *Additional Client* (as agreed) is responsible for payment of agreed amounts due to the *Alliance Manager* under any *Alliance Manager Payment Terms*

8.2.2 — The *Client* or any *Additional Client* (as agreed) is responsible for payment of agreed amounts due to each industry *Alliance Member* under any *Order*

8.3 — Industry *Alliance Members* submit monthly applications to the *Client* or *Additional Client* as agreed, and to the *Alliance Manager*, with supporting inforrmation

8.4 — Within five days from a payment application by an *Alliance Member*, the *Alliance Manager* issues a *Payment Notice* stating the amount due on the *Due Date*

8.5 — Within five days from a payment application by the *Alliance Manager*, the *Client* or *Additional Client* issues a *Payment Notice* stating the amount due on the *Due Date*

8.6 — Unless agreed otherwise and subject to a *Pay Less Notice*, all payments are made within twenty *Working Days* from the *Due Date*, which is the *Final Date for Payment*

8.7 — If no clause 8.4 or clause 8.5 *Payment Notice* is issued, then the application for payment is treated as the *Payment Notice*

8.8 — A *Pay Less Notice* may be issued no later than five *Working Days* before the *Final Date for Payment*, stating the amount considered due and the basis for any deduction

8.8.2 — If a *Pay Less Notice* is issued, the *Client* or *Additional Client* shall pay the amount stated in that *Pay Less Notice* by the *Final Date for Payment*

8.9 — No notice or payment prevents its later reconsideration and adjustment or is evidence of approval or acceptance of *Alliance Activities* or *Pre-Contract Activities* or *Alliance Manager Services*

8.10 — Failure to make a payment due by the *Final Date for Payment* entitles the payee to suspend performance of its relevant obligations

8.11 — Any delay in a due payment beyond the *Final Date for Payment* entitles an *Alliance Member* to be paid interest at the rate stated in the *Framework Alliance Agreement*

Checklist 12. FAC-1 payment.

Some frameworks also exclude the use of 'retentions' by reference to defects rectification under *Project Contracts* on the basis that the long-term framework relationships provide a more effective motivator for defects rectification through the *Incentive* of prospective additional work. Early payment of *Supply Chain* members can also be a factor in calculating the efficiency savings that accrue through *Supply Chain Collaboration* (see, for example, Case Study 5).

CHAPTER 33

How does FAC-1 manage change?

[FAC-1 clauses 1.5, 2.6, 9.1 and 9.6]

A framework alliance is not frozen in time at the point when *Alliance Members* are selected and appointed, and it needs to provide for changes that may arise, for example, through the development of *Improved Value* and *Risk Management* solutions, through improved practices and other lessons learned from feedback on *Projects*, or through the agreement of new *Alliance Activities*. Change mechanisms in the FAC-1 *Contract Terms* are summarised in Checklist 13.

FAC-1 clause 9.1 states that any change to the scope or nature of the *Framework Programme* or to any other aspect of the *Framework Alliance Contract* shall be by agreement of all *Alliance Members* unless stated otherwise in the *Framework Documents*. The FAC-1 changes that require agreement by the *Alliance Members* include

- changes to the priority of *Framework Documents* (clause 1.5.2),
- joining arrangements for *Additional Clients* and other *Additional Alliance Members* not listed in the *Framework Alliance Agreement* (clause 1.11),
- fluctuation in *Framework Prices* or *Agreed Prices* (clause 4.2),
- additional *Alliance Activities* beyond those described in the *Framework Alliance Agreement* and the *Framework Brief* (clause 6.1),
- timescales for *Alliance Activities* beyond those stated in the *Timetable* (clause 6.1),
- additional *Supply Chain Collaboration* beyond that described in the *Framework Alliance Agreement* and the *Framework Brief* (clause 6.3),
- periods of time for *Alliance Members* to undertake *Risk Management* actions where not stated in the *Risk Register* (clause 9.3),
- extension of the duration of the *Framework Alliance Contract* or its early termination (clause 14.1), and

- approval of proposed actions to achieve the Schedule 1, Part 2 *Targets* or proposed amendments to those *Targets* (clause 14.2.1).

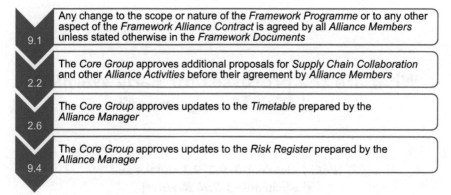

Checklist 13. FAC-1 change management.

The FAC-1 changes that require agreement by the *Core Group* rather than by the *Alliance Members* include

- a change to the notice period for a *Core Group* meeting or its agenda (clauses 1.7.1, 1.7.2 and 1.8.2);
- a course of action in response to an *Early Warning* without a *Core Group* meeting (clause 1.8.2);
- approval of proposals for *Supply Chain Collaboration* and other *Alliance Activities*, submitted by any *Alliance Member* and not already described in the *Framework Alliance Agreement* or the *Framework Brief*, before these proposals are then agreed by *Alliance Members* in accordance with clauses 6.2 and 6.3 (clause 2.2);
- the basis for sharing information in relation to the *Supply Chains* of *Alliance Members* for the purposes of *Supply Chain Collaboration*, if not stated in the *Framework Brief* (clause 6.3.1); and
- procedures for renegotiating or tendering *Supply Chain* contracts for the purposes of *Supply Chain Collaboration* (clause 6.3.4).

The FAC-1 changes that require agreement by the *Core Group* based on the advice of the *Alliance Manager* include

- approving updates proposed by the *Alliance Manager* to the Schedule 2 *Timetable* (clause 2.6) and
- approving updates proposed by the *Alliance Manager* to the Schedule 3 *Risk Register* (clause 9.4).

CHAPTER 34

What are the processes for *Early Warning* and *Risk Management*?

[FAC-1 clauses 1.8, 9.2, 9.3 and 9.4 and
the Schedule 3 *Risk Register*]

ramework Programmes and *Projects* are likely to encounter risks that cannot be fully assessed and dealt with in advance. These can range from unpredictable site conditions to an *Alliance Member* or *Supply Chain* insolvency, and the Covid-19 pandemic has shown how *Clients* and industry can respond rapidly to unforeseeable events using collaborative framework relationships.

A successful framework alliance requires agreed processes through which the *Alliance Members* exchange information in relation to the risks they face and agree what actions they need to take. Shared processes of *Early Warning* and joint *Risk Management* are crucial to effective collaboration.

FAC-1 includes open and transparent *Early Warning* and *Risk Management* systems that include commitments by all *Alliance Members* to

- create and update a shared *Risk Register* and participate in joint *Risk Management*,
- give *Early Warning* of a problem,
- participate in a *Core Group* to consider the impact of a problem and the potential for mitigating actions, and
- implement a shared plan with agreed periods and deadlines for mitigating actions.

Risk Management is defined in FAC-1 as 'a structured approach to ensure that risks are identified at the earliest opportunity, that their potential impacts are allowed for and that by agreed actions those risks and/or their impacts are eliminated, reduced, insured, shared or apportioned' (Appendix 1).

The FAC-1 cycle of *Risk Management* is set out in Figure 12 and it embodies the ISO 44001 approach to joint risk management, by which

- 'the joint risk management team shall establish and record the process to be used for joint risk management within the relationship, recognising the links into each organisations' existing risk management processes';
- 'the joint risk register shall be reviewed at planned intervals as defined under the governance structure and appropriate actions addressed';
- 'the term "joint" implies that each partner makes a contribution to all of the risk management activities'; and
- 'an effective collaboration is one where the parties share responsibility as far as is practical in supporting the individual risk of the partners'.

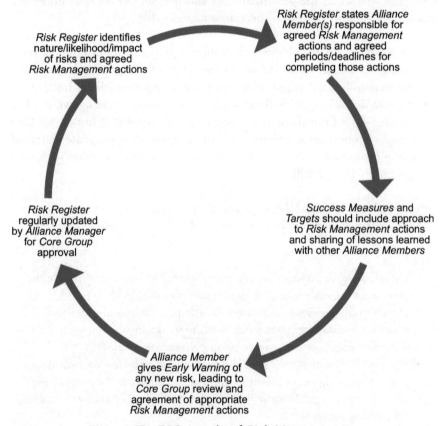

Risk Register identifies nature/likelihood/impact of risks and agreed *Risk Management* actions

Risk Register states *Alliance Member(s)* responsible for agreed *Risk Management* actions and agreed periods/deadlines for completing those actions

Risk Register regularly updated by *Alliance Manager* for *Core Group* approval

Success Measures and *Targets* should include approach to *Risk Management* actions and sharing of lessons learned with other *Alliance Members*

Alliance Member gives *Early Warning* of any new risk, leading to *Core Group* review and agreement of appropriate *Risk Management* actions

Figure 12. FAC-1 cycle of *Risk Management*.

The FAC-1 *Early Warning* system requires notification of risk issues and exploration of the reasons behind them. If an *Early Warning* notice in relation to an emerging problem is issued as soon as the problem arises, this enables timely decisions to be taken jointly and it helps to resolve a problem before it becomes a dispute. *Early Warning* combined with *Core Group* reviews

- require the *Alliance Members* to review risk issues quickly and openly,
- encourage *Alliance Members* to disclose important information and to agree mitigating actions, and
- support agreed resolution of problems and avoidance of disputes.

FAC-1 clause 1.8 states that each *Alliance Member* shall give *Early Warning* to the other *Alliance Members* as soon as it is aware of any matter adversely affecting or threatening the *Alliance* or the *Framework Programme* or its own performance or the performance of another *Alliance Member* under the *Framework Alliance Contract*. This clause requires that

- the notifying *Alliance Member* shall submit proposals for avoiding or remedying the matter notified (within the scope of its agreed role, expertise and responsibilities) as part of its *Early Warning* notice (clause 1.8.1); and
- the *Alliance Manager* shall convene a *Core Group* meeting within five *Working Days* from the date of the *Early Warning* notice (unless all *Core Group* members agree a shorter period) to agree an appropriate course of action (unless all *Core Group* members agree a course of action without a meeting) (clause 1.8.2).

Practice Note 40. *Risk Management.*
The Ministry of Justice report on their FAC-1 New Prisons alliance states that

- 'the alliance delivered tangible and significant benefits through their input into the early works, logistics, and planning process';
- 'the deep dive reviews carried out by the programme and design workstreams identified opportunities to bring works forward, overlap activities, or re-sequence to improve upon delivery timescales';
- 'this provided valuable mitigation at an earlier stage by testing and, in some cases, disproving assumptions in previous iterations of the programme';
- 'the benefits ranged from reviewing alternative access routes to ecological interventions';
- 'the alliance also input into and supported the development of scoping documents';
- 'four organisations working alongside the Ministry of Justice enabled accelerated reviews and deep dives into each project, programme and critical path, delivering maximum value in a short period'; and

> • 'despite many challenges on builds of this size, the alliance drove identification of risks at the earliest opportunity, bringing together the expertise of multiple organisations to assess options in achieving the best outcomes for the programme'.
>
> See also Case Study 16.

FAC-1 clause 9 and Schedule 3 record the commitment of *Alliance Members* to undertake *Risk Management* in accordance with a shared *Risk Register*. FAC-1 clause 9.2 states that the *Alliance Members* recognise the risks involved in the *Framework Programme* and shall undertake *Risk Management* together and individually in accordance with the *Framework Documents* in order to analyse and manage those risks using the most effective methods. The agreed approaches to *Risk Management* are set out in the FAC-1 *Framework Brief, Framework Proposals* and *Risk Register*.

FAC-1 clause 9.3 states that the *Alliance Members* shall undertake the *Risk Management* actions described in the Schedule 3 *Risk Register* within the periods stated in the *Risk Register* and as otherwise agreed by the *Alliance Members*. The commitment of *Alliance Members* to undertake agreed *Risk Management* actions includes

- 'the nature of each risk, its likelihood and impact on the *Framework Programme* and/or achievement of the agreed *Objectives* and/or agreed *Alliance Activities*, including any anticipated financial impact';
- 'the *Alliance Members* responsible for each *Risk Management* action';
- 'the agreed *Risk Management* actions, including actions to reduce the likelihood of each risk and to reduce its financial and other impact'; and
- 'the agreed periods or deadlines for completing those actions'.

The *Risk Register* is updated by the *Alliance Manager* for *Core Group* approval at the intervals stated in the *Timetable* (clause 9.4).

In order to address industry concerns regarding costly and unsustainable risk transfer, 'Constructing the Gold Standard' recommends that the *Client/ Additional Clients* and the *Alliance Manager*

- implement risk allocation informed by market engagement;
- create and update a shared contractual *Risk Register* with all other *Alliance Members* through which to jointly manage risks at framework level and help eliminate, reduce and mitigate potential risks on *Framework Programmes* and *Projects*; and
- respond efficiently to framework risk events through a framework-level *Early Warning* system and a framework-level *Core Group* or equivalent joint decision-making group.

Gold Standard Recommendation 18. 'Allocate risks based on framework market engagement and use joint framework systems for early risk mitigation and efficient responses to risk events.'

So that the *Client/Additional Clients,* the *Alliance Manager* and the industry *Alliance Members* use the stability of their long-term framework relationships to manage the financial distress of an industry *Alliance Member* and to mitigate the repercussions of that distress, 'Constructing the Gold Standard' recommends that the *Client/Additional Clients* and the *Alliance Manager* establish flexible and transparent systems for resolution planning in their framework contracts, including rapid response to any *Early Warning.* For this purpose, the FAC-1 joint *Risk Management* commitments in the *Framework Brief, Framework Proposals* and *Risk Register* can include the review and agreement of actions that manage and mitigate the risk of potential insolvency of an *Alliance Member.*

Gold Standard Recommendation 22. 'Establish shared and transparent framework systems through which to manage and mitigate the risks of a supplier's financial distress.'

FAC-1 *Risk Management* provides opportunities to reduce risks and to mitigate their potential effects. The scope to agree joint and individual *Risk Management* actions enables *Alliance Members* to reduce risks; to share risks as agreed; to insure risks if appropriate; and to price risks more accurately in the *Direct Award Procedure* and the *Competitive Award Procedure.*

Practice Note 41. *Risk Registers.*
NHS Shared Business Services report that

- 'at an overarching framework level, we chose to utilise the FAC-1 form of contract due to the prominence it gives to having a framework level *Risk Register* and also its core focus on collaboration'; and that
- 'the collaborative nature of the FAC-1 helps us as it contains mechanisms within it that lean heavily towards a decision-making process that is embarked upon by all parties working together towards a common unified goal'.

See also Case Study 14.

Practice Note 42. FAC-1 and building safety.
The UK government's 2022 'Collaborative procurement guidance for design and construction to support building safety' is recognised in the

2022 'Construction Playbook'. It describes how framework alliance contracts such as FAC-1 can use strategic collaboration to embed improved building safety. The government guidance focuses on four key aspects of collaboration that are covered by FAC-1:

- a procurement process that avoids a 'race to the bottom' (see, for example, Chapters 5 and 28);
- early supply chain involvement (see, for example, Chapter 30);
- integrated commitments and resident involvement (see, for example, Chapter 6); and
- a digital 'golden thread' to integrate design, construction and *Operation* (see, for example, Chapter 14).

As regards resident involvement, it is important to include resident groups as FAC-1 *Stakeholders* and for the *Framework Alliance Agreement* to describe, by reference to clause 1.10, how *Alliance Members* agree to engage with them.

It is also relevant to note, when exploring FAC-1 proposals for *Improved Value*, that this defined term includes benefits to *Users*, namely 'any person or party using a *Project*'.

See also Practice Note 14.

The FAC-1 *Core Group* is the *Risk Management* forum through which *Alliance Members* can raise issues with each other in order to resolve problems before they become disputes (see Chapter 21). Where problems arise that might otherwise escalate into disputes, the additional information shared among *Alliance Members* through FAC-1 *Risk Management* provides a stable basis for non-adversarial dispute resolution (see Chapter 40).

Case Study 29. Harrow schools framework alliance risk management.
A £70 million schools programme was procured by London Borough of Harrow with Kier, using an FAC-1 prototype, where the client reported that 'the complete programme has been delivered on time to provide a great boost to education in Harrow', and added that 'relations between team members and the schools' head teachers have remained positive in what could have been stressful circumstances'.

The multiparty integration of full design services at 'day one' reduced the preconstruction programme by an estimated nine months, facilitated planning applications and secured agreement to the scope of schemes with schools recognised as 'interested parties'.

When one school caught fire during the school holidays in August, joint *Risk Management* enabled the team to agree how renovation work could be started immediately, with installation of temporary classrooms so that the damaged school could reopen in September.

London Borough of Harrow and Kier used an FAC-1 prototype in conjunction with *Project Contracts* based on the PPC2000 standard form project alliance contract.

Case Study 30. Haringey housing alliance, building safety and net zero.
Haringey Council has launched an £800 million housing procurement using the FAC-1 *Framework Alliance Contract* to deliver and integrate the work of four contractors over a 10.5 year programme running from November 2023 to March 2034.

The council is using FAC-1 to deliver its *Objectives*, *Success Measures* and *Targets* for a range of ambitious investment plans that include

- ensuring that all its housing meets the UK 'Decent Homes Standard' by 2025;
- energy improvements to deliver its zero-carbon targets and ensure that all council-owned homes have a minimum rating of EPC B by 2035;
- regeneration works at the Broadwater Farm estate;
- new homes including infill, conversions and rooftop developments; and
- meeting and maintaining statutory safety standards in all blocks.

The works are split into four geographic lots, and key FAC-1 *Objectives* include

- providing employment and training opportunities,
- supporting and enabling the SME *Supply Chain* in the borough to benefit from the investments, and
- involving residents at all stages of the procurement and delivery process.

Haringey is using FAC-1 in conjunction with multiple TAC-1 term alliance contracts.

See also Case Study 12.

CHAPTER 35

What are the duties of care between *Alliance Members*?

[FAC-1 clauses 10, 13.1 and 13.6]

F AC-1 provides for a duty of reasonable skill and care that is linked to each *Alliance Member*'s agreed role, expertise and responsibilities. FAC-1 clause 10.1 states that, subject to any amendments stated in the *Framework Alliance Agreement*, in all matters governed by the *Framework Alliance Contract* the *Alliance Members* shall use reasonable skill and care appropriate to their respective roles, expertise and responsibilities as stated in the *Framework Documents*. The FAC-1 provisions governing duties of care are summarised in Checklist 14.

Any amendments to the FAC-1 duty of reasonable skill and care are stated in the *Framework Alliance Agreement* by reference to clause 10.1 and/ or clause 10.2 (page iv). Amendments to the duty of reasonable skill and care could reflect, for example,

- a statutory duty of care required by the laws of the jurisdiction where an FAC-1 *Alliance* is established,
- an exclusion of liability or other limit on liability agreed under particular *Project Contract Conditions*, or
- a fitness-for-purpose obligation agreed under particular *Project Contract Conditions*.

FAC-1 specifies certain matters where a duty of care is owed only between specific *Alliance Members,* e.g. as to the confidential FAC-1 *Framework Prices* and *Framework Proposals* submitted by prospective industry *Alliance Members* when seeking a place on the *Alliance*. The clauses limiting the duty of care to specific *Alliance Members* are as follows:

| 1.3.3 | *Framework Prices* and *Framework Proposals* bind only the *Client*, any *Additional Clients*, the *Alliance Manager* and the industry *Alliance Member* who provides them |

| 1.4 | An *Alliance Member* is responsible only for the *Framework Documents* it prepares or contributes to, except to the extent of its stated reliance on other *Alliance Members* |

| 1.11.3 | Only the implementing *Client* or *Additional Client* is liable for its *Direct Award Procedure*, *Competitive Award Procedure*, *Project Contracts*, *Orders* and agreed payments |

| 10.1 | *Alliance Members* use reasonable skill and care appropriate to their roles, expertise and responsibilities as stated in the *Framework Documents* except as agreed otherwise |

| 10.2 | A duty of care is owed between all *Alliance Members* except as stated in 1.11.3, 10.3, 10.4, 10.5, 11.2 and except as amended in the *Framework Alliance Agreement* |

| 10.3 | A duty of care in respect of *Framework Proposals*, *Framework Prices*, *Project Proposals*, *Agreed Prices* is only owed to the *Client*, any *Additional Clients* and the *Alliance Manager* |

| 10.4 | Only the *Client* and any *Additional Clients* owe a duty of care to the *Alliance Manager* in respect of *Alliance Manager Payment Terms* |

| 10.5 | In an *Order* for *Pre-Contract Activities* only the issuing *Client* or *Additional Client*, the signing *Alliance Member* and the *Alliance Manager* owe each other a duty of care |

| 10.6 | An *Alliance Member's* duty of care may be extended to other parties as stated in the *Framework Alliance Agreement* or otherwise agreed |

| 11.2 | Those *Alliance Members* implementing a *Direct Award Procedure* or *Competitive Award Procedure* or *Pre-Contract Activities* warrant/indemnify *Intellectual Property Rights* only to each other |

Checklist 14. FAC-1 duties of care.

- FAC-1 clause 10.2 states that, subject to clauses 1.11.3, 10.3–10.5 and 11.2 and any amendments stated in the *Framework Alliance Agreement*, the *Alliance Members* shall owe each other a duty of care under the *Framework Alliance Contract*.
- FAC-1 clause 10.3 states that an *Alliance Member* shall owe a duty of care in respect of its *Framework Proposals*, *Framework Prices*, *Project Proposals* and *Agreed Prices* only to the *Client*, any *Additional Clients* and the *Alliance Manager* and not to the remaining *Alliance Members*.
- FAC-1 clause 10.4 states that only the *Client* and any *Additional Clients* owe a duty of care to the *Alliance Manager* in respect of the *Alliance Manager Payment Terms*.
- FAC-1 clause 10.5 states that under an *Order* for *Pre-Contract Activities* only the *Client* or *Additional Client* who issues it, the other *Alliance Member* who signs it and the *Alliance Manager* shall owe each other a duty of care.

Any amendments to the *Alliance Members* between whom a duty of care is owed under FAC-1 are stated in the *Framework Alliance Agreement* by reference to clause 10.2 (page iv).

A duty of care can be extended to parties other than *Alliance Members* as agreed, e.g. by third-party collateral warranties or through other permitted third-party rights. FAC-1 clause 10.6 states that the duty of care of an *Alliance Member* may be extended to other parties by the means stated in the *Framework Alliance Agreement* or as otherwise agreed. When extending a duty of care to any parties other than *Alliance Members*, the following details should be stated in the *Framework Alliance Agreement* by reference to clauses 10.6 (page iv):

- the *Alliance Members* who extend the FAC-1 duty of care to other parties,
- the other parties to whom the FAC-1 duty of care is extended, and
- the means by which the FAC-1 duty of care is extended.

The duty of care under each *Project Contract* is stated in the relevant *Project Contract Conditions* as set out or referred to in the *Template Project Documents*. Where third-party rights are to be created in respect of *Project Contracts*, these are stated in the *Project Contract Conditions* or other *Template Project Documents*.

CHAPTER 36

How are *Intellectual Property Rights* and confidentiality protected?

[FAC-1 clauses 11 and 13.3]

The multiparty structure of FAC-1 facilitates exchange of information so as to ensure that all *Alliance Members* participate in the investigation and submission of proposals for *Improved Value* consistent with the agreed *Objectives* of the *Alliance* and of the *Framework Programme* (clause 2.2). Exchanges of information under FAC-1 include lessons learned on specific *Projects* so that all *Alliance Members* can apply those lessons on subsequent *Projects*.

However, in order to attract innovations and other *Alliance Member* proposals for *Improved Value* and effective *Risk Management* solutions, it is important to make clear the ways in which the *Client,* any *Additional Clients,* the *Alliance Manager* and the contractor/consultant/supplier *Alliance Members* may agree to share those innovations, proposals and solutions for the benefit of the *Framework Programme* as a whole.

> **Practice Note 43. *Intellectual Property Rights.***
> Gold Standard participants expressed concern that many framework contracts
>
> - 'do not recognise the importance of intellectual property rights to supplier business models and do not take a balanced approach to the licensing and protection of those rights'; and
> - 'do not include joint decision-making machinery among clients, managers and suppliers which would enable the agreement of a fair and equitable approach to cross-framework adoption of improved solutions'.

The FAC-1 provisions governing *Intellectual Property Rights* are summarised in Checklist 15, and, when combined with the protection of confidentiality, they provide balanced rights and obligations for *Alliance Members* by means of

- protection and licensing of *Intellectual Property Rights* under clause 11;
- confidentiality provisions under clause 13.3;
- any amended confidentiality provisions stated in the *Framework Alliance Agreement,* by reference to clause 13.3 (page iv), e.g. by reason of the identity of the *Client* or the nature of the *Projects* comprising the *Framework Programme*; and
- particular confidentiality of *Framework Prices* and other *Framework Proposals* between the relevant *Alliance Member,* the *Client/Additional Clients* and the *Alliance Manager* under clause 13.3.2.

11.1	Each *Alliance Member* warrants and indemnifies the other *Alliance Members* that its contributions to *Alliance Activities* do not infringe *Intellectual Property Rights*
11.2	Warranty and indemnity only between the *Client* or *Additional Client* and other *Alliance Members* implementing a *Direct Award Procedure*, a *Competitive Award Procedure* or *Pre-Contract Activities*
11.3	Each *Alliance Member* retains *Intellectual Property Rights* in all documents that it prepares forming part of or pursuant to the *Framework Alliance Contract*
11.3	*Alliance Members* grant to each other an irrevocable, non-exclusive, royalty-free licence to copy and use documents that each prepares for agreed *Alliance Activities*
11.3	Mutual licences include a right to transfer and sub-license for the same purposes, and have the benefit of rights from third parties to allow the grant of the licence
11.4	No *Alliance Member* is liable for any document other than in relation to the use of that document for the purpose for which it was agreed to be prepared
Sched. 5	*Intellectual Property Rights* in relation to individual *Projects* are not covered in FAC-1 and should be protected and licensed in the relevant *Project Contracts*

Checklist 15. FAC-1 *Intellectual Property Rights.*

FAC-1 clause 11.1 states that, subject to clause 11.2, each *Alliance Member* warrants to the other *Alliance Members* that nothing it contributes to *Alliance Activities* shall infringe any *Intellectual Property Rights*, and undertakes to indemnify the other *Alliance Members* in respect of any legal liability and related costs arising out of or in connection with any infringement.

FAC-1 clause 11.2 states that the *Client* or any *Additional Client* and each other *Alliance Member* implementing a *Direct Award Procedure* or *Competitive Award Procedure* or undertaking *Pre-Contract Activities* warrant to each other (but not to the other *Alliance Members*) that nothing that each of them contributes to the *Direct Award Procedure, Competitive Award Procedure* or *Pre-Contract Activities* shall infringe any *Intellectual Property Rights*, and undertake to indemnify each other (but not the other *Alliance Members*) in respect of any legal liability and related costs arising out of or in connection with any infringement.

FAC-1 clause 11.3 states that each *Alliance Member* shall retain *Intellectual Property Rights* in all documents that it prepares forming part of or pursuant to the *Framework Alliance Contract* and each *Alliance Member* grants to the other *Alliance Members* an irrevocable, non-exclusive, royalty-free licence to copy and use all those documents for any agreed *Alliance Activities*, in all cases with the right to transfer and sub-license those rights for the same purposes, and shall ensure that licence shall have the benefit of the same rights from third parties as necessary to allow the grant of that licence.

FAC-1 clause 11.4 states that no *Alliance Member* shall be liable in respect of any document that it prepares forming part of or pursuant to the *Framework Alliance Contract* to the extent of any use for any purpose other than the purpose for which it was agreed to be prepared as stated in, or which can reasonably be inferred from, the *Framework Documents*.

FAC-1 clause 13.3 states that, subject to any amendments stated in the *Framework Alliance Agreement*, the *Alliance Members* shall not reveal to any third party (except as expressly agreed or as obliged by law) any information exchanged between them, if and to the extent that it is stated or known by them to be confidential, and shall use that information only for the purposes of the *Framework Programme*. Without limitation to this general rule,

- the *Alliance Manager Payment Terms* are confidential as between the *Alliance Manager*, the *Client* and any *Additional Clients* (clause 13.3.1); and
- the *Framework Prices* and *Framework Proposals* of an *Alliance Member* are confidential as between that *Alliance Member*, the *Client*, any *Additional Clients* and the *Alliance Manager* (clause 13.3.2).

CHAPTER 37

What are the FAC-1 insurances?

[FAC-1 clause 12]

FAC-1 clause 12.1 states that each *Alliance Member* shall take out insurances of the types and for the amounts stated against its name in the *Framework Alliance Agreement* or any *Joining Agreement* for matters governed by the *Framework Alliance Contract*.

The types and levels of insurance cover in respect of the activities and obligations governed by FAC-1 can include third-party liability insurance and professional indemnity insurance in respect of *Alliance Manager Services*, *Alliance Activities* and *Pre-Contract Activities*.

These FAC-1 insurances are separate from the insurances required in respect of each *Project*, which are governed by the *Project Contracts* and which should be stated in the *Template Project Documents*.

The types and amounts of insurance cover to be taken out by each *Alliance Member* under FAC-1 are inserted in the *Framework Alliance Agreement* by reference to clause 12 (page iv).

The agreed requirements as to insured risks, exclusions, deductibles and other terms should be stated in the *Framework Brief*. FAC-1 clause 12.2 requires that all insurances stated in the *Framework Alliance Agreement* or any *Joining Agreement* shall be placed with insurers for those risks, with those exclusions and deductibles, and on those other terms as shall be stated in the *Framework Brief* or otherwise agreed by the *Client*, and all those insurances shall be maintained from the date of the *Framework Alliance Agreement* or the relevant *Joining Agreement* until the expiry or earlier termination of the *Framework Alliance Contract* and no *Alliance Member* shall do anything to invalidate those insurances.

FAC-1 clause 12.3 states that each *Alliance Member* shall provide to another *Alliance Member* upon request copy policies or detailed certification as evidence of its agreed insurances.

CHAPTER 38

How does FAC-1 state applicable laws, *Legal Requirements* and *Special Terms*?

[FAC-1 clauses 13.4, 13.5 and 15.5 and the Schedule 6 *Legal Requirements* and *Special Terms]*

FAC-1 is designed for use in any jurisdiction, and the applicable law is inserted in the *Framework Alliance Agreement* by reference to clauses 13.4 and 15.5 (page v). The stated applicable law governs all aspects of the *Framework Alliance Contract*, and the FAC-1 provisions governing laws and regulations are summarised in Checklist 16.

FAC-1 provides for the *Contract Terms* to be supplemented or amended to state particular *Legal Requirements* in order to comply with the laws of the jurisdiction stated in the *Framework Alliance Agreement* (clause 13.4 and Schedule 6, Part 1).

FAC-1 also provides for the *Contract Terms* to be supplemented or amended by *Special Terms* that are not *Legal Requirements* but that reflect the particular needs of the *Client* or other *Alliance Members* or are required by reason of the nature of the *Framework Programme* (clause 13.5 and Schedule 6, Part 2).

FAC-1 does not include any *Contract Terms* that state or refer to specific provisions of English law. Although clause 8 ('Payment') and clause 15.3 ('Adjudication') are drafted to conform to the requirements of the UK Housing Grants, Construction and Regeneration Act 1996 as amended, they do not specifically refer to that legislation.

The *Client/Additional Clients* and other *Alliance Members* need to decide

- which specific legislative provisions, if any, of any jurisdiction need to be restated in the *Legal Requirements*; and
- whether the selected applicable laws (stated in the *Framework Alliance Agreement* by reference to clauses 13.4 and 15.5) give rise to the need for additional provisions to be set out in the *Legal Requirements*.

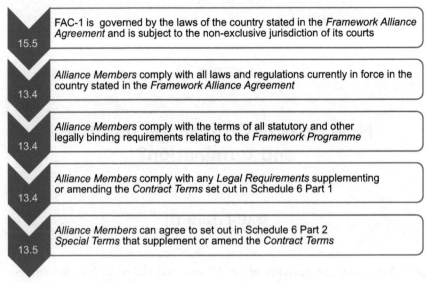

Checklist 16. FAC-1 laws and regulations.

Collaborative work on translations in Germany, Italy, Spain, Bulgaria, Brazil, Chile and Peru has shown that few amendments are required to reflect the legal requirements of these countries. Such amendments as are needed are illustrated in Annex E of this handbook (in relation to Italian law) and they can include

- an amendment to the duty of care by reference to clause 10.1 (page iv) in the *Framework Alliance Agreement* where this is necessary to reflect the statutory duty of care of a particular jurisdiction;
- an amendment to *Intellectual Property Rights* by reference to clause 11 in the Schedule 6, Part 2 *Legal Requirements* where this is necessary to reflect the statutory definitions of a particular jurisdiction; and
- amendments to the dispute resolution procedures by reference to clause 15 (page v) and Appendix 4 in the *Framework Alliance Agreement* where these are necessary to reflect the statutory requirements of a particular jurisdiction.

CHAPTER 39

How does FAC-1 manage duration and termination?

[FAC-1 clause 14]

Clarifying the duration of an *Alliance* and the provisions for an open and orderly exit process are essential for the *Alliance Members* to invest in and commit to their long-term relationships. The *Alliance Members* will recognise that any *Alliance*, however successful, will be time-limited, and they need to know

- the date of commencement of the *Framework Alliance Contract*, its duration and any extension procedures; and
- the circumstances under which the appointment of an *Alliance Member* may be terminated before expiry of the *Framework Alliance Contract* and the procedures governing termination.

FAC-1 provides for details to be set out in the *Framework Alliance Agreement* by reference to clause 14.1 (page v), stating

- the agreed commencement date and duration of the *Framework Alliance Contract* and
- any provisions for extension or earlier termination by agreement of the *Alliance Members* or as otherwise stated.

The FAC-1 duration and termination provisions are summarised in Checklist 17, and clause 14.1 states that the duration of the *Framework Alliance Contract* is stated in the *Framework Alliance Agreement*, subject to the remainder of this clause 14 and subject to extension or earlier termination by agreement of all *Alliance Members* or in accordance with the procedures set out in the *Framework Alliance Agreement*.

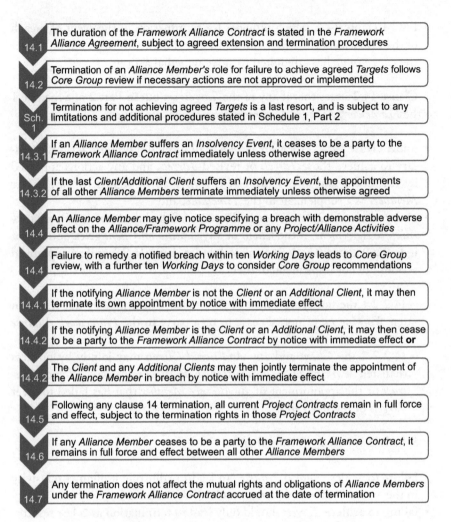

14.1 The duration of the *Framework Alliance Contract* is stated in the *Framework Alliance Agreement*, subject to agreed extension and termination procedures

14.2 Termination of an *Alliance Member's* role for failure to achieve agreed *Targets* follows *Core Group* review if necessary actions are not approved or implemented

Sch. 1 Termination for not achieving agreed *Targets* is a last resort, and is subject to any limtitations and additional procedures stated in Schedule 1, Part 2

14.3.1 If an *Alliance Member* suffers an *Insolvency Event*, it ceases to be a party to the *Framework Alliance Contract* immediately unless otherwise agreed

14.3.2 If the last *Client/Additional Client* suffers an *Insolvency Event*, the appointments of all other *Alliance Members* terminate immediately unless otherwise agreed

14.4 An *Alliance Member* may give notice specifying a breach with demonstrable adverse effect on the *Alliance/Framework Programme* or any *Project/Alliance Activities*

14.4 Failure to remedy a notified breach within ten *Working Days* leads to *Core Group* review, with a further ten *Working Days* to consider *Core Group* recommendations

14.4.1 If the notifying *Alliance Member* is not the *Client* or an *Additional Client*, it may then terminate its own appointment by notice with immediate effect

14.4.2 If the notifying *Alliance Member* is the *Client* or an *Additional Client*, it may then cease to be a party to the *Framework Alliance Contract* by notice with immediate effect **or**

14.4.2 The *Client* and any *Additional Clients* may then jointly terminate the appointment of the *Alliance Member* in breach by notice with immediate effect

14.5 Following any clause 14 termination, all current *Project Contracts* remain in full force and effect, subject to the termination rights in those *Project Contracts*

14.6 If any *Alliance Member* ceases to be a party to the *Framework Alliance Contract*, it remains in full force and effect between all other *Alliance Members*

14.7 Any termination does not affect the mutual rights and obligations of *Alliance Members* under the *Framework Alliance Contract* accrued at the date of termination

Checklist 17. FAC-1 duration and termination.

Rights of earlier termination arise under

- FAC-1 clause 14.2, which provides for termination of an *Alliance Member*'s appointment if it fails to meet specific, agreed performance *Targets*, but subject to any limitations and additional procedures stated in Schedule 1, Part 2 and only after the *Core Group* has attempted to agree remedial actions;
- FAC-1 clause 14.3, which provides for automatic termination if an *Alliance Member* suffers an *Insolvency Event* unless the other *Alliance Members* agree otherwise; and

- FAC-1 clause 14.4, which provides for termination in the event of breach of the *Framework Alliance Contract* by any *Alliance Member*, but only after the *Core Group* has attempted to agree remedial actions.

Clause 14.2 states that if any of the *Targets* set out in Part 2 of Schedule 1 to the *Framework Alliance Agreement* are not achieved, then

- under clause 14.2.1, the *Core Group* shall meet and propose actions necessary to achieve those *Targets* or revised *Targets*, and any actions approved by the *Client* and any *Additional Clients* shall be signed by all *Alliance Members* as a supplement to the *Timetable*; and
- under clause 14.2.2, subject to Part 2 of Schedule 1 to the *Framework Alliance Agreement*, if the *Client* or any *Additional Client* gives notice that it does not approve actions proposed under clause 14.2.1 or if any approved actions are not implemented, then:

  o 14.2.2.1 the notifying *Client* or *Additional Client* may by not less than ten *Working Days'* notice cease to be a party to the *Framework Alliance Contract*; or
  o 14.2.2.2 the *Client* and any *Additional Clients* may jointly by not less than ten *Working Days'* notice terminate the *Framework Alliance Contract* or the appointment of an *Alliance Member* that has failed to meet *Targets* or revised *Targets*.

Schedule 1, Part 2 provides that

- failure to achieve agreed *Targets* can lead to adjustment of any exclusivity in the award of *Project Contracts* under FAC-1 clause 5.7;
- failure to achieve *Targets* should only lead to termination as 'a last resort';
- rights of termination may apply only to stated *Success Measures* and *Targets*; and
- rights of termination may be subject to stated additional procedures.

FAC-1 clause 14.3 states that if any *Alliance Member* suffers an *Insolvency Event*, then, unless otherwise agreed by all other *Alliance Members*,

- the relevant *Alliance Member* shall, under clause 14.3.1, cease to be a party to the *Framework Alliance Contract* with immediate effect; or
- if the relevant *Alliance Member* is the only or last remaining *Client* or *Additional Client*, then, under clause 14.3.2, the appointment of all other *Alliance Members* shall automatically terminate with immediate effect.

FAC-1 clause 14.4 states that if any *Alliance Member* breaches the *Framework Alliance Contract* in a way that has a demonstrable, adverse effect on the *Alliance* or on the *Framework Programme* or any *Project* or *Alliance Activities*, and if that *Alliance Member* does not remedy that breach within ten *Working Days* from the date of notice from another *Alliance Member* specifying the breach, then, after notifying the *Core Group* and allowing a period of ten *Working Days* from the date of that notification to receive and consider its recommendations,

- if the notifying *Alliance Member* is not the *Client* or an *Additional Client*, the notifying *Alliance Member* may terminate its own appointment under the *Framework Alliance Contract* by notice with immediate effect (clause 14.4.1); and
- if the notifying *Alliance Member* is the *Client* or an *Additional Client*, then either it may cease to be a party to the *Framework Alliance Contract* or the *Client* and any *Additional Clients* may jointly terminate the appointment of the *Alliance Member* in breach, in either case by notice with immediate effect (clause 14.4.2).

FAC-1 provisions describe the impact of termination:

- on existing *Project Contracts* (under clause 14.5),
- on other *Alliance Members* (under clause 14.6), and
- on accrued rights and obligations (under clause 14.7).

FAC-1 clause 14.5 states that, notwithstanding any termination under this clause 14, all *Project Contracts* in existence at the time of termination shall remain in full force and effect, subject to the termination rights in those *Project Contracts*.

FAC-1 clause 14.6 states that, notwithstanding an *Alliance Member* for any reason ceasing to be a party to the *Framework Alliance Contract*, as between all other *Alliance Members* the *Framework Alliance Contract* shall remain in full force and effect, and, in the event of termination of the appointment of the *Alliance Manager*, the *Client* and any *Additional Clients* shall jointly identify a replacement and all *Alliance Members* shall enter into a *Joining Agreement* with the replacement *Alliance Manager*.

FAC-1 clause 14.7 states that any termination under this clause 14 shall not affect the mutual rights and obligations of the *Alliance Members* under the *Framework Alliance Contract* accrued at the date of termination.

CHAPTER 40

What are the FAC-1 processes for problem-solving and dispute resolution?

**[FAC-1 clause 15 and the Appendix 4 'Conciliation',
'Adjudication' and 'Arbitration' procedures]**

Any problem or dispute risks the failure of an *Alliance* and demands urgent attention in accordance with procedures that enable *Alliance Members* to resolve the problem or dispute by agreement or by relying on the decision of a third party. FAC-1 includes systems that are designed to enable the *Alliance Members* to avoid or resolve disputes effectively.

FAC-1 clause 15.1 requires that, as soon as it is aware of any dispute, an *Alliance Member* shall give notice to the other *Alliance Members* involved in the dispute and to the *Alliance Manager* who shall convene a *Core Group* meeting, notifying all available information and inviting all involved *Alliance Members* who shall all attend (with any *Independent Adviser*) and who shall make constructive proposals in seeking to achieve an agreed solution.

The agreement of solutions by *Core Group Consensus* has averted the need for many disputes to be referred for third-party resolution (see Chapters 21 and 34).

Practice Note 44. Collaborative problem-solving.
Reporting on their FAC-1 prototype highways alliance, Surrey County Council stated: 'With the size of the task (delivering over 500 major schemes in the first 3 years) this commitment was always tested in regard to disputes. Through the cultural workshops face to face discussions showed the team shared the same goals and desires to succeed and issues were discussed and agreed through open challenge and honest conversations.'
See also Case Study 5.

Practice Note 45. *Core Group* **dispute resolution.**
The SCMG FAC-1 prototype housing alliance used the *Core Group* to resolve 'potential disputes with the benefit of full cost and time information plus the motive to retain long-term relationships.'
See also Case Study 12.

The FAC-1 provisions governing problem-solving and dispute resolution are summarised in Checklist 18.

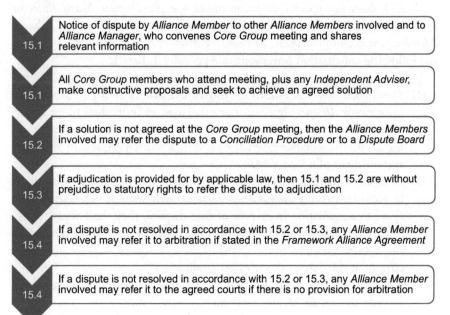

15.1 Notice of dispute by *Alliance Member* to other *Alliance Members* involved and to *Alliance Manager,* who convenes *Core Group* meeting and shares relevant information

15.1 All *Core Group* members who attend meeting, plus any *Independent Adviser,* make constructive proposals and seek to achieve an agreed solution

15.2 If a solution is not agreed at the *Core Group* meeting, then the *Alliance Members* involved may refer the dispute to a *Conciliation Procedure* or to a *Dispute Board*

15.3 If adjudication is provided for by applicable law, then 15.1 and 15.2 are without prejudice to statutory rights to refer the dispute to adjudication

15.4 If a dispute is not resolved in accordance with 15.2 or 15.3, any *Alliance Member* involved may refer it to arbitration if stated in the *Framework Alliance Agreement*

15.4 If a dispute is not resolved in accordance with 15.2 or 15.3, any *Alliance Member* involved may refer it to the agreed courts if there is no provision for arbitration

Checklist 18. FAC-1 problem-solving and dispute resolution.

If a dispute is not resolved by the *Core Group* in accordance with clause 15.1, then FAC-1 clause 15 and Appendix 4 describe the following systems of dispute resolution.

- The option to refer a dispute to a *Conciliation Procedure* or a *Dispute Board* (clause 15.2 and Appendix 4, Part 1).
- The right to refer a dispute to adjudication if provided for under the laws of the country stated in the *Framework Alliance Agreement* (clause 15.3 and Appendix 4, Part 2).
- The option to refer a dispute to arbitration if it is not resolved in accordance with the clause 15.2 *Conciliation Procedure* or a *Dispute Board* or in accordance with clause 15.3 adjudication (clause 15.4 and Appendix 4, Part 3).

Clause 15.2 states that if any dispute is not resolved in accordance with clause 15.1 and provided that no *Alliance Member* has by reason of that dispute exercised a right of termination under clause 14, then, if stated in the *Framework Alliance Agreement*, the *Alliance Members* involved in a dispute may refer it to conciliation in accordance with Part 1 of Appendix 4 and the *Conciliation Procedure* stated in the *Framework Alliance Agreement* or to a *Dispute Board* in accordance with the *Dispute Board Rules* stated in the *Framework Alliance Agreement*.

FAC-1 does not specify or recommend specific *Dispute Board Rules* or a *Conciliation Procedure*, leaving these matters to be agreed by the *Alliance Members* when completing the *Framework Alliance Agreement*. FAC-1 sets out the following conciliation provisions in Appendix 4, Part 1.

(1) The '*Conciliator*' shall mean the individual named in or pursuant to the *Framework Alliance Agreement* or otherwise an individual to be agreed between the *Alliance Members* seeking conciliation within ten *Working Days* after one has given the other(s) a written request to agree the appointment of a *Conciliator*.

(2) If, at any time before reference of a dispute to litigation or arbitration in accordance with the *Contract Terms*, the *Alliance Members* in dispute agree to conciliation in respect of that dispute, they shall apply jointly to the *Conciliator* who shall conduct the conciliation in accordance with the '*Conciliation Procedure*' stated in the *Framework Alliance Agreement* current at the date of the relevant application

(3) Any written agreement signed by the *Alliance Members* in dispute, which records the terms of any settlement reached during the conciliation, shall be final and binding and they shall comply with that settlement in accordance with its terms. If any of them fails to do so, then the other(s) shall be entitled to take legal proceedings to secure compliance.

In jurisdictions such as the UK, adjudication is a statutory right that can be exercised at short notice, and it may be difficult to ensure that *Alliance Members* first undertake other more collaborative processes. Questions may arise as to the enforceability of an agreement to refer a dispute to the *Core Group* and any *Independent Adviser* in accordance with clause 15.1 or to a *Conciliation Procedure* or a *Dispute Board* in accordance with clause 15.2 before referring the dispute to adjudication. Therefore, FAC-1 clause 15.3 states that, if adjudication is provided for under the laws of the country stated in the *Framework Alliance Agreement*, then the procedures under clauses 15.1 and 15.2 are without prejudice to the rights of any *Alliance Member* involved in a dispute to refer it to adjudication in accordance with Part 2 of Appendix 4 and the procedure stated in the *Framework Alliance Agreement.*

FAC-1 does not specify or recommend an adjudication procedure, leaving this to be agreed by the *Alliance Members* when completing the *Framework Alliance Agreement.* FAC-1 sets out the following adjudication provisions in Appendix 4, Part 2.

(1) The *'Adjudicator'* shall mean the individual named in or pursuant to the *Framework Alliance Agreement* or otherwise an individual to be appointed in accordance with the model adjudication procedure stated in the *Framework Alliance Agreement* and current at the date of the relevant notice of adjudication (the *'Model Adjudication Procedure'*) and the following provisions shall override the *Model Adjudication Procedure* in the event of any conflict.

(2) Any *Alliance Member* has the right to refer a dispute for adjudication by giving notice at any time of its intention to do so. The notice shall be given and the adjudication shall be conducted under the *Model Adjudication Procedure.*

(3) The *Adjudicator* shall be appointed and the dispute referred to him or her within seven days following notice by any *Alliance Member* under paragraph 2 above.

(4) The *Adjudicator* shall reach his or her decision within twenty-eight days following the date of referral, or any longer period agreed by the *Alliance Members* in dispute after the dispute has been referred. The *Adjudicator* may extend the period of twenty-eight days by up to fourteen days with the consent of the *Alliance Member* who referred the dispute.

(5) The *Adjudicator* shall act impartially and may take the initiative in ascertaining the facts and the law.

(6) The *Adjudicator* may correct his or her decision so as to remove a clerical or typographical error arising by accident or omission within five days following the date of communicating his or her decision to the *Alliance Members* in dispute.

(7) The *Adjudicator*'s decision shall be binding until the dispute is finally determined by legal proceedings, by arbitration (if provided for in the *Framework Alliance Agreement*) or by agreement.

(8) The *Adjudicator* shall be required to give reasons for his or her decision.

(9) Without prejudice to their rights under the *Framework Alliance Contract,* the *Alliance Members* in dispute shall comply with any decision of the *Adjudicator.* If any of them fails to do so, then the other(s) shall be entitled to take legal proceedings to secure compliance pending final determination of the dispute.

If any dispute cannot be resolved in accordance with clauses 15.2 and 15.3, then clause 15.4 states that it may be referred by any *Alliance Member* involved in that dispute either to the courts stated in the *Framework Alliance Agreement* or, if stated in the *Framework Alliance Agreement*, to one or three arbitrators as stated in the *Framework Alliance Agreement* who shall be appointed as stated in the *Framework Alliance Agreement* and who shall conduct that arbitration in the location and in accordance with Part 3 of Appendix 4 and the rules stated in the *Framework Alliance Agreement*.

FAC-1 does not specify or recommend one or three arbitrators, an appointment procedure, a location or a choice of arbitration rules, leaving these matters to be agreed by the *Alliance Members* when completing the *Framework Alliance Agreement*. FAC-1 sets out the following arbitration provisions in Appendix 4, Part 3.

(1) If arbitration is provided for in the *Framework Alliance Agreement*, any *Alliance Member* may give notice to the one or more other *Alliance Members* in dispute, requiring that the matter be referred to arbitration by one or more arbitrators, in accordance with the rules and at the location as are stated in the *Framework Alliance Agreement*.

(2) If, in the opinion of any *Alliance Member* in dispute, any dispute to be referred to arbitration under the *Framework Alliance Contract* raises matters which are connected with matters raised in another dispute between the same and/or other *Alliance Members* that has already been referred to arbitration under the *Framework Alliance Contract*, then the *Alliance Members* in dispute shall arrange for their dispute to be referred to the arbitrator(s) first appointed who shall have the power to deal with all those connected disputes as he or she or they think most just and convenient.

(3) The arbitrator(s) appointed under the *Framework Alliance Contract* shall have full power to open up, review and revise any notice, decision, consent, approval, valuation, opinion or instruction of any *Alliance Member*, and his or her or their award shall be final and binding on the *Alliance Members* in dispute.

Practice Note 46. FAC-1 and dispute avoidance.
The Arcadis Global Disputes Report 2020 recorded survey responses that suggest 'contract obligations are drafted in a manner which makes it difficult for all parties to follow' and concluded that 'greater use of more collaborative standard forms of contract [such as] FAC-1 might provide more confidence in project delivery'.

ANNEXES

FAC-1 definitions

Additional Alliance Member – an additional *Alliance Member* with which the *Alliance Members* enter into a *Joining Agreement* under clause 1.11

Additional Client – an additional *Client* with which the *Alliance Members* enter into a *Joining Agreement* under clause 1.11

Adjudicator – an individual identified as an adjudicator under the *Framework Alliance Agreement*, the *Model Adjudication Procedure* and Part 2 of Appendix 4

Agreed Prices – prices in respect of a *Project* as proposed by an *Alliance Member* and as may be agreed pursuant to a *Direct Award Procedure* or a *Competitive Award Procedure*

Alliance – the framework alliance created between the *Alliance Members* and governed by the *Framework Alliance Contract*

Alliance Activities – any activities agreed to be performed by *Alliance Members* under clause 6 in order to achieve *Improved Value* consistent with the *Objectives*, including agreed *Supply Chain Collaboration*, agreed innovation and education, agreed exchanges of information, and agreed integration, adaptation and standardisation of roles, expertise and responsibilities

Alliance Manager – the party named in the *Framework Alliance Agreement* to fulfil the role of *Alliance Manager* as described in clauses 3.1 and 3.2, subject to replacement in accordance with clause 14.6

Alliance Manager Payment Terms – a document forming part of the *Framework Alliance Contract* describing the amounts payable to the *Alliance Manager* and the terms of payment including any agreed fluctuations

Alliance Manager Services – the services described in the *Alliance Manager Services Schedule*

Alliance Manager Services Schedule – a document forming part of the *Framework Alliance Contract* describing the role, expertise and responsibilities of the *Alliance Manager*

Alliance Members – the *Client*, the *Alliance Manager*, all other parties who execute the *Framework Alliance Agreement* and any *Additional Clients* and other *Additional Alliance Members* who execute *Joining Agreements*

BIM – building information modelling

Budget – the *Client's* or any *Additional Client's* monetary allowance for a *Project* referred to in clause 4.1.4 as may be stated in a *Direct Award Procedure* or *Competitive Award Procedure*

Client – the party named in the *Framework Alliance Agreement* to fulfil the role of *Client* as described in the *Framework Documents*

Competitive Award Procedure – the competitive procedure leading to the award of a *Project Contract* as set out in Part 2 of Schedule 4 to the *Framework Alliance Agreement*

Conciliation Procedure – the procedure governing the work of a *Conciliator* as may be stated in the *Framework Alliance Agreement* and Part 1 of Appendix 4

Conciliator – an individual who may be identified as a conciliator under the *Framework Alliance Agreement*, the *Conciliation Procedure* and Part 1 of Appendix 4

Consensus – unanimous agreement following reasoned discussion

Contract Terms – the contract terms, including appendices, as annexed to the *Framework Alliance Agreement*

Core Group – the individuals identified in the *Framework Alliance Agreement* or in a *Joining Agreement* as *Core Group* members, subject only in each case to agreement of changes and alternates in accordance with clause 1.6.1

Definitions – the definitions set out in this Appendix 1

Direct Award Procedure – the procedure leading to the award of a *Project Contract* without further competition among *Alliance Members* as set out in Part 1 of Schedule 4 to the *Framework Alliance Agreement*

Dispute Board – a group of individuals who may be identified in the *Framework Alliance Agreement* to advise the *Alliance Members* on the avoidance or resolution of any dispute

Dispute Board Rules – the rules governing the work of a *Dispute Board* as may be stated in the *Framework Alliance Agreement*

Due Date – the date of receipt by the *Client* of an application for payment submitted in accordance with clause 8.3

Early Warning – early warning in accordance with clause 1.8

Environment – all and any land, water and air including air within any natural or man-made structure above or below ground

Final Date for Payment – the final date for payment pursuant to clauses 8.6.1 and 8.6.2

Framework Alliance Agreement – the agreement executed by the *Alliance Members*

Framework Alliance Contract – the framework alliance contract created by and between the *Alliance Members* by executing the *Framework Alliance Agreement* and any *Joining Agreements*

Framework Brief – one or more documents forming part of the *Framework Alliance Contract* describing the scope and nature of the *Alliance* and of the *Projects* comprising the *Framework Programme* and setting out the *Client*'s and any *Additional Clients*' technical, management and commercial requirements including the required approach to design, supply chain engagement, costing, *Risk Management* and programming and all other relevant procedures and expected outcomes and where appropriate the required approach to *BIM*

Framework Documents – the documents comprising the *Framework Alliance Contract* as set out in the *Framework Alliance Agreement* subject to addition and amendment in accordance with any *Joining Agreements* and the *Contract Terms*

Framework Prices – each of the documents forming part of the *Framework Alliance Contract* describing the prices of an *Alliance Member* in response to the *Framework Brief*, agreed confidentially between that *Alliance Member*, the *Client*, any *Additional Clients* and the *Alliance Manager*

Framework Programme – the works and/or services and/or supplies governed by the *Framework Alliance Contract*, as described in the *Framework Documents*

Framework Proposals – each of the documents forming part of the *Framework Alliance Contract* describing the proposals of an *Alliance Member* in response to the *Framework Brief*, agreed confidentially between that *Alliance Member*, the *Client*, any *Additional Clients* and the *Alliance Manager*

Improved Value – improved value consistent with the *Objectives*, which may include (if and as stated in the *Objectives*) improved cost and/or time certainty, cost and/or time savings, improved quality, improved *Operation*, improved staff and other resources, improved health and safety and other working procedures, improved *Sustainability*, improved efficiency, improved profitability and other benefits to *Alliance Members*, *Users* and *Stakeholders*

Incentives – the incentives set out in Part 3 of Schedule 1 to the *Framework Alliance Agreement*

Independent Adviser – an independent adviser who may be identified in the *Framework Alliance Agreement* and appointed on terms agreed by the *Alliance Members* to provide fair and constructive advice to the *Alliance Members* on the implementation of the *Framework Alliance Contract* and the avoidance or resolution of any dispute

Insolvency Event – an event of insolvency as referred to in clause 14.3, arising under the laws of the country in which an *Alliance Member* is incorporated or established and including:

- any event where any *Alliance Member* being a corporate body has an order made for its winding up or a petition is presented or a meeting is convened for purpose of considering a resolution for its winding up or that resolution is passed (except for any members' voluntary winding up for the purposes of amalgamation or reconstruction on terms previously approved in writing by all the other *Alliance Members*); or has a receiver (including an administrative receiver) or manager appointed in respect of the whole or any part of its property, assets or undertaking; or has an administrator appointed (whether by the court or otherwise) or any step taken (whether in or out of court) for the appointment of an administrator or any notice given of an intention to appoint an administrator; or has any distress, execution or other process levied or applied for in respect of the whole or any part of its property, assets or undertaking; or has any composition in satisfaction of its debts or any scheme of arrangement of its affairs or any compromise or arrangement between it and its creditors and/ or members or any class of its creditors and/or members proposed, sanctioned or approved; or

- any event where any *Alliance Member* being an individual is the subject of a bankruptcy order, or has a bankruptcy petition filed against him or her; or enters into an individual voluntary arrangement, a deed of arrangement or any other composition or arrangement with his or her creditors in satisfaction of his or her debts; or has any distress, execution or other process levied or applied for in respect of the whole or any part of any of his or her property or assets; or
- any event equivalent to any of the above in any jurisdiction outside England and Wales

Intellectual Property Rights – all intellectual property rights (including, without limitation, patents, trade marks, designs, design rights, copyright, inventions, trade secrets, know-how and confidential information) and all applications for protection of any of those rights

Joining Agreement – an agreement executed by the *Alliance Members* with an *Additional Client* or other *Additional Alliance Member* based on the form set out in Appendix 2

Legal Requirements – any legal requirements supplementing or amending the *Contract Terms* pursuant to clause 13.4, as set out in Part 1 of Schedule 6 to the *Framework Alliance Agreement*

Model Adjudication Procedure – the procedure governing the work of an *Adjudicator* as may be stated in the *Framework Alliance Agreement* and Part 2 of Appendix 4

Objectives – the agreed objectives of the *Alliance* and the *Framework Programme* and of the *Alliance Members* in respect of the *Alliance* and the *Framework Programme* as set out in Part 1 of Schedule 1 to the *Framework Alliance Agreement*

Operation – use, occupation, operation, maintenance, repair, alteration and demolition of a *Project*

Order – an order governing *Alliance Activities* or *Pre-Contract Activities* issued under clause 7 and based on the form set out in Appendix 3

Overheads – overhead levels set in accordance with the *Framework Prices* and/or in accordance with a *Direct Award Procedure* or *Competitive Award Procedure*

Partnership – a business entity creating joint and several liability between its members

Pay Less Notice – a notice issued in accordance with clause 8.8

Payment Notice – a notice specifying the amount that the *Alliance Manager* considers to be due in accordance with clause 8.4 or that the *Client* or an *Additional Client* as applicable considers to be due in accordance with clause 8.5

Pre-Contract Activities – any activities agreed to be performed by an *Alliance Member* in relation to a *Project* before the award of a *Project Contract*

Profit – profit levels set in accordance with the *Framework Prices* and/or in accordance with a *Direct Award Procedure* or *Competitive Award Procedure*

Project – a project forming part of the *Framework Programme* as described in the *Framework Brief* and in a *Project Brief* issued pursuant to a *Direct Award Procedure* or *Competitive Award Procedure*

Project Brief – one or more documents forming part of the *Template Project Documents* and each *Direct Award Procedure* or *Competitive Award Procedure*, describing the scope and nature of a *Project*, setting out the *Client's* technical, management and commercial requirements and expected outcomes in respect of the *Project*, including all required quality standards and warranties, including all requirements in respect of insurances and securities, including all processes and procedures for management of communication, performance, quality, design, *Supply Chain* engagement, cost, payment, time, change, risk, health and safety and all other project management processes and procedures, including the required approach to *BIM* as appropriate, and including all requirements in respect of *Sustainability*, *Operation*, and engagement with *Stakeholders* and *Users*

Project Contract – a contract awarded by the *Client* or an *Additional Client* to any *Alliance Member* in respect of a *Project* in accordance with clause 5 and based on the *Template Project Documents*

Project Contract Conditions – the terms and conditions governing a *Project Contract*

Project Proposals – proposed *Agreed Prices* and other proposals in respect of a *Project* submitted by an *Alliance Member* under a *Direct Award Procedure* or a *Competitive Award Procedure*

Risk Management – a structured approach to ensure that risks are identified at the earliest opportunity, that their potential impacts are allowed for and that by agreed actions those risks and/or their impacts are eliminated, reduced, insured, shared or apportioned

Risk Register – the risk register set out in Schedule 3 to the *Framework Alliance Agreement* and updated in accordance with clause 9.4, describing recognised risks and agreed *Risk Management* actions in relation to the *Framework Programme* and agreed *Alliance Activities*

Special Terms – any terms supplementing or amending the *Contract Terms* pursuant to clause 13.5, as set out in Part 2 of Schedule 6 to the *Framework Alliance Agreement*

Stakeholders – any one or more organisations or groups of individuals, as stated in the *Framework Alliance Agreement* by reference to clause 1.10, who are not *Alliance Members* and who have an interest relating to the *Framework Programme*

Success Measures – the success measures in respect of achievement of the *Objectives* and the performance of the *Alliance Members* as set out in Part 2 of Schedule 1 to the *Framework Alliance Agreement*

Supply Chain – any party or parties providing to one or more *Alliance Members* works or services or supplies of goods, materials or equipment

Supply Chain Collaboration – any activities agreed to be performed by *Alliance Members* under clause 6.3 in order to achieve *Improved Value* through more consistent, longer term, larger scale *Supply Chain Contracts* and through other improved *Supply Chain* commitments and working practices

Supply Chain Contract – a contract entered into between an *Alliance Member* and any of its *Supply Chain*

Sustainability – measures intended to reduce carbon emissions, to reduce use of energy and or natural and manmade resources, to improve waste management, to improve employment and training opportunities, and otherwise to protect or improve the condition of the *Environment* or the well-being of people

Targets – the targets in respect of the *Success Measures* as set out in Part 2 of Schedule 1 to the *Framework Alliance Agreement*

Template Project Documents – the template documents used in each *Direct Award Procedure* and *Competitive Award Procedure* and in creating each *Project Contract* as described in Schedule 5 to the *Framework Alliance Agreement* including the *Project Contract Conditions*

Timetable – the timetable set out in Schedule 2 to the *Framework Alliance Agreement* and updated in accordance with clause 2.6 stating agreed deadlines, gateways and milestones in respect of the *Framework Programme*, achievement of the *Objectives* and the timescales for *Alliance Activities*

User – any person or party using a *Project*

Working Day – any day other than a weekend or public holiday recognised in the country where the *Framework Programme* is located

FAC-1 as a Gold Standard
Framework Contract

This Annex B comprises two sections, namely 'The twenty-four Gold Standard recommendations' and 'Creating a Gold Standard *Framework Contract*'.

The first part of this annex states the twenty-four Gold Standard recommendations and the rationale for each of them using extracts that are quoted from 'Constructing the Gold Standard' along with cross-references to the relevant chapters of this handbook. The second part states the requirements for 'Creating a Gold Standard *Framework Contract*' using extracts that are quoted from Annex 4 of 'Constructing the Gold Standard' along with cross-references to the relevant clauses of FAC-1 and to relevant *Framework Documents*.

THE TWENTY-FOUR GOLD STANDARD RECOMMENDATIONS

1. Use the Gold Standard features of frameworks, framework contracts and action plans to measure Construction Playbook implementation on a 'comply or explain' basis. [Chapter 2]
To provide an objective and measurable basis for implementation of Construction Playbook policies on a 'comply or explain' basis, this review recommends that Cabinet Office assesses the ways in which public sector clients and suppliers adopt and apply the features of a Gold Standard framework, a Gold Standard framework contract and a Gold Standard action plan.

2. Ensure that all Gold Standard features are adopted by clients and suppliers when comparing the different construction frameworks on offer. [Chapter 2]
For clients and suppliers to make informed decisions when comparing the many construction frameworks on offer, this review recommends that they adopt the features of a Gold Standard framework, a Gold Standard framework contract and a Gold Standard action plan to identify the questions they need to ask and the answers they should expect.

3. Require that all public sector construction frameworks prioritise safety, net zero carbon and the Compact with Industry. [Chapter 8]
In order to deliver government priorities and the Compact with Industry, this review recommends that framework providers, clients and suppliers make clear how their framework strategy, procurement, contract and management will achieve improved building safety, net zero carbon targets, long-term relationships, fair returns, equitable treatment of risk, rewards for faster, better and greener delivery and collaboration at all levels of the supply chain.

4. Reduce procurement costs, improve value and reduce risks by wider adoption of a standard form Gold Standard framework alliance contract. [Chapter 3]
To achieve efficiency savings by reducing waste, confusion and duplication, and to replicate the substantial value improvements shown in collaborative framework case studies, this review recommends the wider adoption of a standard form framework alliance contract that:

- Aligns the objectives, success measures, targets and incentives of clients and suppliers
- Provides transparent performance measurement and work allocation procedures
- Requires joint work by clients and suppliers to improve value and reduce risks
- Translates framework objectives into actions with clear timescales and outcomes.

5. Create contractually binding Gold Standard action plans to convert framework objectives into actions and timetables that deliver improved economic, social and environmental outcomes. [Chapter 13]
In response to the need for urgent implementation of Construction Playbook policies in ways that achieve the ambitions of government and industry, this review recommends that framework providers, clients and suppliers create contractually binding action plans that convert improved value objectives under their existing framework contracts into shared strategic commitments and that state agreed actions and timetables.

6. Invest in framework management that demonstrates value for money for clients and suppliers. [Chapter 25]
In response to industry concerns regarding varying levels of framework leadership and management, this review recommends that framework providers invest in framework management responsibilities which demonstrate value for money for clients and suppliers and which include integration of strategic

interests, support for collaborative joint working and assurance that framework commitments and opportunities are understood and implemented, including where consultants are appointed from outside the framework.

7. Capture improved value by identifying SME strengths and use Supply Chain Collaboration systems to maximise social value. [Chapter 9]
To capture improved value from the contributions of SMEs, this review recommends that framework providers, clients and managers make framework appointments using evaluation criteria that identify SME strengths, and also use 'Supply Chain Collaboration' to create supplier-led alliances with supply chains that include local and regional businesses. To maximise social value, including improved employment, skills and environmental sustainability and the combatting of Modern Slavery, framework contracts should convert social value objectives into shared action plans with timescales and expected outcomes.

8. Avoid wasted procurement costs and improve supplier commitments by ensuring that frameworks offer sustainable pipelines of work. [Chapter 11]
In response to industry concerns regarding the significant cost and time wasted by clients and suppliers in procuring speculative frameworks, and in order to optimise competitive bids and strategic commitments from prospective suppliers, this review recommends that framework providers and clients make clear in all their framework procurements the pipelines of work to which they commit and the preconditions to implementing those commitments.

9. Use pre-procurement framework consultation to explore emerging technologies and innovations and to identify opportunities in the market. [Chapter 5]
To incentivise improved outcomes, to optimise competition and to improve market health and capability, this review recommends that framework providers and clients use pre-procurement framework consultation to explore emerging technologies and innovations and to identify relevant opportunities and limitations in the market, and that their framework strategies, procurements and contracts embody this pre-procurement learning.

10. Reduce procurement costs and improve value through the award of longer-term call-off contracts and the incentive of additional work. [Chapter 23]
In response to industry concerns regarding inefficient and costly mini-competitions, this review recommends that framework providers and clients establish as part of their framework strategy the optimum duration, scope and continuity of framework call-offs, including the potential benefits of awarding

long-term project contracts or additional project contracts without additional mini-competitions, and that framework providers and clients obtain supplier proposals as to how these awards will lead to innovations and investments that deliver improved productivity and efficiency savings.

11. Improve supplier investments in MMC and other offsite technologies by awarding framework call-off contracts for portfolios of work. [Chapter 15] To obtain improved value from suppliers planning, investing in and delivering MMC and other offsite manufacturing technologies, this review recommends that framework providers, clients and managers use their framework strategies, procurements and contracts to explore and agree the benefits of MMC and other offsite manufacturing technologies and the additional benefits of one or more clients calling off aggregated portfolios of work.

12. Create a whole life golden thread of asset information using BIM and other digital technologies integrated under a framework alliance contract. [Chapter 14] To improve performance, safety, sustainability and value for money over the whole life of built assets, this review recommends that framework providers, clients, managers and suppliers use BIM and other digital technologies to standardise data generation, classification, security and exchange and to retain and manage a golden thread of building information, and that framework alliance contracts support these actions by integrating the information management systems of clients, suppliers and supply chain members.

13. Improve economic, social and environmental outcomes through framework early supply chain involvement (ESI), using Supply Chain Collaboration systems in all framework contracts. [Chapter 30] To maximise the improved value demonstrated by ESI in collaborative framework case studies, including efficiency savings, improved quality and safety, improved social value and reduced GHG emissions, this review recommends that framework providers, clients and managers use framework ESI to obtain and evaluate supplier and supply chain insights, innovations and proposals, including a contractual 'Supply Chain Collaboration' system through which to create strategic supply chain relationships that improve project outcomes.

14. Incentivise innovative solutions by creating specifications for frameworks and call-offs that focus on required client outcomes. [Chapter 18] To identify and incentivise improved project outcomes through a mutually beneficial approach to sharing ideas and innovative solutions, this review recommends that framework providers, clients and managers use specifications that focus on required client outcomes, that they include a whole life carbon assessment which minimises GHG emissions, that they use a 'Project Outcome Profile' linking performance criteria to supplier incentives, and that they clarify which intellectual property rights are relevant to the needs of clients and suppliers.

15. Use delivery model assessments to inform and support framework strategies, procurement, contracting, management and call-off. [Chapter 10]
To identify the best delivery model for each prospective framework project or programme of work, this review recommends that framework providers and clients include in their framework strategies an evidence-based delivery model assessment, that they reflect the chosen delivery model or models in their framework procurement, call-off and management systems, and that framework managers provide guidance to clients on how to choose the most appropriate delivery model when calling off each project.

16. Assess and control the costs of framework deliverables through the use of evidence-based benchmarks and whole life Should Cost Models. [Chapter 27]
To assess framework deliverables in respect of cost, schedule, GHG emissions and other expected outcomes, and in order to maintain cost controls that support call-off, ESI, performance measurement, value improvement and other framework processes, this review recommends that framework providers, clients and managers use benchmarks based on information from past projects and programmes and that they create 'Should Cost Models' forecasting what each framework project or programme should cost over its whole life.

17. Integrate the mutual commitments of framework providers, clients, managers and suppliers through the terms of a Gold Standard framework alliance contract. [Chapter 2]
To integrate the mutual commitments of framework providers, clients, managers and suppliers, this review recommends that effective framework contracts incorporate:

- An outcome-based strategic brief that drives economic, social and environmental value with strategic supplier proposals for delivering that brief
- Multi-party relationships that align objectives, success measures, targets and incentives with commitments to joint work on improving value and reducing risk
- Enterprise contract systems and a timetable of strategic actions that improve information, integration, value and outcomes, for example using MMC, digital technologies, ESI and Supply Chain Collaboration

- Transparent costing, call-off, performance measurement and incentives that provide a fair return for suppliers and drive value rather than a race to the bottom
- Framework management systems that support collaboration and dispute avoidance.

18. Allocate risks based on framework market engagement and use joint framework systems for early risk mitigation and efficient responses to risk events. [Chapter 34]
To address industry concerns regarding costly and unsustainable risk transfer, this review recommends that framework providers, clients and managers implement risk allocation informed by market engagement, that they create and update a shared contractual risk register with suppliers to jointly manage risks at framework level and help eliminate, reduce and mitigate potential risks on framework projects, and that they respond efficiently to framework risk events through a framework early warning system and joint decision-making group.

19. Create transparent pricing mechanisms for frameworks and call-offs that maximise cost certainty and ensure prompt payment. [Chapter 26]
In order to drive improved value and fair treatment, this review recommends that framework providers, clients and managers create payment and pricing mechanisms for framework projects and programmes of work that maximise cost certainty, that identify agreed fees, profit and overheads separately from other costs, that incentivise desired outcomes and that require clients and suppliers always to pay their supply chain promptly.

20. Reduce procurement costs by consistent and proportionate assessment of economic and financial standing using 'PAS91' or the 'Common Assessment Standard'. [Chapter 5]
In response to industry proposals that more consistent and proportionate procedures for assessing the economic and financial standing of framework suppliers will reduce waste and duplication, creating efficiency savings for clients and industry, this review recommends that all framework providers and clients use 'PAS91' or the 'Common Assessment Standard', with levels of stringency established by a 'Contract Tiering' tool that applies higher thresholds to more critical projects.

21. Evaluate proposals for frameworks and call-offs proportionately and consistently using balanced criteria that include quality, social value and net zero GHG emissions. [Chapter 5]

In response to industry proposals that more proportionate and consistent evaluation systems for framework procurement and call-off will reduce waste and duplication and will create efficiency savings for clients and industry, this review recommends that framework providers, clients and managers establish and apply balanced evaluation criteria that examine all relevant aspects of value, that enable differentiation between qualitative bids, that reflect expected client outcomes and that incentivise improved value objectives aligned to government priorities including social value and net zero GHG emissions by 2050.

22. Establish shared and transparent framework systems through which to manage and mitigate the risks of a supplier's financial distress. [Chapter 34]
So that framework providers, clients, managers and suppliers use the stability of their long-term framework relationships to manage a supplier's financial distress and to mitigate its impact, this review recommends that framework providers and clients establish flexible and transparent systems for resolution planning in their framework contracts, including rapid response to early warnings.

23. Improve framework outcomes by creating collaborative systems for the management of framework relationships and strategic supply chain relationships. [Chapter 6]
To drive improved framework outcomes through clear mutual understanding, effective problem-solving and dispute avoidance, this review recommends that framework providers, clients and managers create collaborative systems for managing framework relationships and that these are mirrored by suppliers in strategic supply chain relationships. These systems should include a 'Core Group' or equivalent joint decision-making group through which to manage strategic planning, value improvement, risk reduction and dispute avoidance.

24. Support the adoption of Gold Standard frameworks, framework contracts and action plans through government-led training and guidance. [Chapter 3]
In order to help framework providers, clients, managers and suppliers implement Construction Playbook policies through the widespread adoption of Gold Standard frameworks, Gold Standard framework contracts and Gold Standard action plans, this review recommends that Cabinet Office leads the development of accessible, cross-disciplinary training and guidance, and that clients and industry contribute their experience, feedback and case studies to create a compelling body of shared knowledge.

Creating a Gold Standard *Framework Contract.*

'Construction Playbook' Principles for Successful Framework Contracts	Components of a Gold Standard for *Framework Contracts*
An outcome-based strategic brief that drives economic, social and environmental value with strategic supplier proposals for delivering that brief.	Provide an outcome-based framework brief that explains the framework strategy and the required and desired outcomes, including the framework provider's and clients' technical, management and other commercial requirements in relation to the framework programme, their approaches to design, costing, risk management, programming, MMC, digital technologies and ESI and their commitments to the delivery of net zero carbon, social value and all other expected outcomes. **[FAC-1 *Framework Brief*]**
	State the committed and planned pipelines of work and any minimum value or type of project contracts that will be awarded to suppliers so that they have a clear picture as to the level of certainty in the flow of work. **[FAC-1 *Framework Brief* and clause 5.6]**
	State any exclusivity granted to suppliers and any adjustment of exclusivity according to achievement of agreed targets. **[FAC-1 clause 5.7 and Schedule 1 Part 2]**
	Provide commercial protections for suppliers in respect of exchanges of information by means of mutual intellectual property rights, confidentiality and data security in respect of shared information and the use of digital technologies. **[FAC-1 clauses 11 and 13.3]**
	State which proposals and other information provided by a supplier are the exclusive property of that supplier and which can be used for the benefit of the framework. **[FAC-1 clauses 6.1, 11.1 and 11.3]**
	State the rights and obligations of the framework provider, clients, manager and suppliers to use: • The outputs from *Supply Chain Collaboration* and other framework activities • Lessons learned on other projects. **[FAC-1 clauses 6.1, 6.3, 11.1 and 11.3]**
	Provide flexibility for clients to reflect their specific requirements. **[FAC-1 clauses 13.4 and 13.5 and Schedule 6]**

Multiparty relationships that align objectives, success measures, targets and incentives with commitments to joint work on improving value and reducing risks. The Playbook recommends that a successful framework 'should be based around principles that align objectives, success measures, targets and incentives so as to enable joint work on improving value and reducing risk'.	State the commitments of the framework provider, clients, manager and suppliers to aligned objectives, success measures, targets and incentives, and consider how a multiparty framework alliance contract can support this alignment. **[FAC-1 clauses 2.1, 2.3 and 2.4 and Schedule 1]** State the commitments of the framework provider, clients, manager and suppliers to implement joint work on improving value and reducing risk, to a timetable of agreed actions, to a shared risk register and to a joint decision-making forum, and consider how a multiparty framework alliance contract can support these systems. **[FAC-1 clauses 1.6, 1.7, 2.2, 6 and 9, Schedule 2 and Schedule 3]** Integrate the relationships and commitments of the framework provider, clients, manager and suppliers, with the facility to add additional clients and suppliers by agreement at any time. **[FAC-1 clauses 1.1 and 1.11]** State the scope and duration of the framework, the clients who will use it, the commercial pipelines of work it will govern, the range and types of work within its scope and how that work will be awarded. **[FAC-1 clauses 1.1 and 14.1 and *Framework Brief*]** State: • The objectives for which the framework is created and a system of early warning, consultation and action plans if the objectives are not fulfilled **[FAC-1 clauses 1.8, 2.1, 2.3 and 14.2 and Schedule 1, Parts 1 and 2]** • The outcome-based success measures/KPIs which determine the success of the framework and are used to measure the performance **[FAC-1 clause 2.3 and Schedule 1, Part 2]** • The agreed targets for each success measure/KPI, the method of recording relevant data, the party responsible for measuring against that data and the system for reporting to other clients and suppliers **[FAC-1 clause 2.3 and Schedule 1, Part 2]** Include a shared risk register recording the commitment of the framework provider, clients, manager and suppliers to risk management actions and setting out: **[FAC-1 clause 9 and Schedule 3]** • The nature of each risk, its likelihood and impact on the framework programme, on achievement of the agreed objectives and success measures and on the progress of agreed value improvement activities, including any anticipated financial impact • The framework provider, clients, manager and suppliers responsible for each risk management action • The agreed risk management actions, including actions to reduce the likelihood of each risk and to reduce its financial and other impact • The agreed periods or deadlines for completing those actions.

'Construction Playbook' Principles for Successful Framework Contracts	Components of a Gold Standard for Framework Contracts
A timetable of strategic systems to improve integration and outcomes, for example using MMC, digital technologies, ESI and *Supply Chain Collaboration*.	Include a shared timetable setting out how and when the framework provider, clients, manager and suppliers will seek improved value and stating **[FAC-1 clauses 2.5 and 2.6 and Schedule 2]** • Agreed deadlines, gateways and milestones for achieving framework objectives and success measures • Agreed deadlines, gateways and milestones for value improvement activities, including *Supply Chain Collaboration* • Timescales for the contributions of the framework provider, clients, manager and suppliers to value improvement activities, including the nature, sequence and duration of the agreed actions of each party and any consents or approvals that are pre-conditions to subsequent actions.
Framework pricing systems and incentives that provide a fair return for suppliers and that drive value rather than a race to the bottom.	Provide for framework prices and proposals to be submitted confidentially by each supplier in response to the framework brief, on the basis that these are binding only between the framework provider, clients, manager and the supplier who submits them. **[FAC-1 clauses 1.3.3 and 13.3.2]** State the system for agreeing project prices, for the use of Should Cost Models and for agreeing costs established through framework activities. **[FAC-1 clause 4 and the *Framework Prices*]** Include options for framework prices to state the fees, profit and overheads of suppliers and to state separately the net costs comprising the framework prices and the agreed prices for each project. **[FAC-1 clause 4.3]** State prompt payment commitments and requirements at all levels of the supply chain. **[FAC-1 clause 8]**

| Transparent performance measurement and work allocation procedures. | State the links between work allocation procedures and performance incentives. [FAC-1 clauses 2.3 and 2.4 and Schedule 1, Parts 2 and 3]

Consider how a multiparty framework alliance contract can improve the transparency of performance measurement and work allocation procedures. [FAC-1 multiparty structure]

State a shared system of open performance measurement and rewards. [FAC-1 clauses 2.3 and 2.4 and Schedule 1, Parts 2 and 3]

Set out the procedures for awarding contracts for projects and programmes of work. [FAC-1 clauses 5.1 and 5.2 and Appendix 4]

State the template project documents to be used in each award procedure and make clear: [FAC-1 clause 5.3 and Schedule 5 Template Project Documents]
• The standard form JCT2016, NEC3, NEC4 or PPC2000/TAC-1 contract conditions to be used for call-off
• The structure and standard components of each project brief
• Proportionate requirements in respect of insurances and securities
• Processes and procedures for managing communication, performance, quality, design, supply chain engagement, costs, payment, time, change, risk, health and safety, in each case including the required approaches to MMC, digital information and ESI
• Requirements in respect of net zero carbon, social value, operation of the completed project and engagement with stakeholders and users
• The required structure and content of agreed prices and other project proposals forming part of each project contract |

'Construction Playbook' Principles for Successful Framework Contracts	Components of a Gold Standard for *Framework Contracts*
Management systems that support collaboration and avoid disputes.	Describe the role of an in-house or external framework manager who integrates the work of the framework provider, clients and suppliers and who: **[FAC-1 clause 3]** •Implements the project award procedures •Monitors and supports achievement of agreed objectives, success measures and targets •Monitors and supports achievement of deadlines in a shared timetable and prepares updates of the timetable for approval by the framework provider, clients and suppliers •Organises meetings of the core group or the equivalent joint decision-making forum •Organises, supports and monitors Supply Chain Collaboration and other value improvement activities. Provide for consensus-based governance by a core group or equivalent joint decision-making forum made up of named individuals representing the framework provider, clients, manager and suppliers. **[FAC-1 clause 1.6]** State the terms of reference for the core group in terms of how it meets and makes decisions. **[FAC-1 clause 1.7]** Provide for the core group to be used by the framework provider, clients, manager and suppliers to consider and agree proposals for improved value, to raise early warning of issues, to resolve problems before they become disputes and to consider options for resolution planning in the event of supplier distress. **[FAC-1 clauses 1.8, 2.2, 2.6, 9.4, 14.2, 14.4 and 15.1]**

Completing an FAC-1
Framework Alliance Agreement

The details inserted in the FAC-1 *Framework Alliance Agreement* and its schedules set out the specific requirements and expectations of the *Alliance Members* and the processes that they will implement in order to bring their *Alliance* to life. Words and expressions in italics are defined in Appendix 1 of FAC-1.

Question	Framework Alliance Agreement page number and Contract Terms clause number	Details to be inserted
What is the scope of works, services or supplies comprising the *Framework Programme* and the name of the *Client*?	Page (i)	**State** the title of the *Framework Programme*. Details are set out in the *Framework Brief* and in the Schedule 1 *Objectives* and the Schedule 5 *Template Project Documents*. **State** the name of the *Client*. Details are stated at signature page (vi).
What are the names of the other *Alliance Members*?	Page (i) Clause 1.1	**State** the *Alliance Members*. In addition to the *Client*, any *Additional Clients* and the *Alliance Manager*, the *Alliance Members* may include one or more consultants, contractors, *Supply Chain* subcontractors, suppliers, manufacturers, operators or other providers of works, services and supplies in any combination. **State** the roles of each *Alliance Member* such as an architect, an engineer, a contractor, a *Supply Chain* member, an organisation responsible for *Operation*, a *BIM* information manager or an *Alliance Manager*. Details are stated at signature pages (vi) and (vii).
What are the *Framework Documents*?	Page (i) Clauses 1.3, 1.4 and 1.5	**Complete** the *Framework Documents* listed in the *Framework Alliance Agreement* and arrange for them to be signed for identification where necessary. In addition to the details completed in the *Framework Alliance Agreement*, relevant details are completed in the following Schedules and *Framework Documents*: • **Insert** in Schedule 1 the *Objectives, Success Measures, Targets and Incentives* The *Objectives, Success Measures, Targets and Incentives* stated at FAC-1 Schedule 1 clarify why the *Alliance* is created, how its success will be measured and what motivates the *Alliance Members* to deliver *Improved Value* and reduced risks. Examples of *Objectives and Success Measures* are listed in Chapter 22.

What are the Framework Documents? [Continued]	Page (i) Clauses 1.3, 1.4 and 1.5	• **Complete** the Schedule 2 Timetable

The shared *Timetable* in FAC-1 Schedule 2 sets out the ways in which the *Alliance Members* agree to seek *Improved Value* through

  • agreed deadlines, gateways and milestones in respect of *Alliance Activities* and achievement of the *Objectives*; and
  • timescales for the agreed *Alliance Activities*, including the nature, sequence and duration of the agreed actions of each *Alliance Member* and any consents or approvals (whether required from *Alliance Members* or third parties) that are preconditions to subsequent actions.

The FAC-1 *Timetable* integrates the commitments of *Alliance Members* to agreed deadlines and interfaces for all agreed contributions, reviews and approvals in accordance with the *Framework Documents*. The *Timetable* integrates the deadlines that are separately agreed with each *Alliance Member* under their individual *Project Contracts*. The *Timetable* is regularly updated by the *Alliance Manager* for *Core Group* approval in accordance with FAC-1 clause 2.6.

• **Complete** the Schedule 3 Risk Register

The shared *Risk Register* in FAC-1 Schedule 3 integrates and identifies the risks perceived by the *Client* and the other *Alliance Members*, and it states the actions they agree to mitigate those risks. The *Risk Register* is regularly updated by the *Alliance Manager* for *Core Group* approval in accordance with FAC-1 clause 9.4.

• **Complete** the Schedule 4 Direct Award Procedure and/or Competitive Award Procedure

FAC-1 Schedule 4 states the agreed system for awarding *Project Contracts*. If some or all *Project Contracts* are awarded by procedures that are not governed by FAC-1, this should be stated in Schedule 4.

• **List** the Schedule 5 Template Project Documents

For all *Project Contracts* that are awarded in accordance with the Schedule 4 *Direct Award Procedure* and/or *Competitive Award Procedure*, Schedule 5 describes the *Project Contract Conditions* and other *Template Project Documents* that will govern the award of each *Project Contract*. For any *Project Contracts* that are awarded by procedures not governed by FAC-1, Schedule 5 enables the *Alliance Members* to share relevant details from those *Project Contracts* as *Template Project Documents*.

FAC-1 does not increase the roles and responsibilities of any *Alliance Member* under its *Project Contract*, and the details shared in Schedule 5 do not add to or alter the scope or nature of the services, works and supplies governed by each *Project Contract*. |

Question	Page and clause no.	Details to be inserted
What are the Framework Documents? [Continued]	Page (i) Clauses 1.3, 1.4 and 1.5	• **Insert** any Schedule 6 *Legal Requirements* and *Special Terms* that give rise to additions and amendments to the *Contract Terms*
		The FAC-1 Schedule 6, Part 1 *Legal Requirements* state any additional or amended *Contract Terms* required for the *Framework Alliance Contract* to comply with specific laws of England and Wales or of any other jurisdiction stated in the *Framework Alliance Agreement.*
		The FAC-1 Schedule 6 Part 2 *Special Terms* state any additional or amended *Contract Terms* required by reason of the particular needs of the *Client* or other *Alliance Members* or by reason of the nature of the *Framework Programme.* Additions and amendments can be kept to a minimum by not including matters that are clarified in other provisions of the *Framework Alliance Agreement* and in Schedules 1, 2, 3, 4 and 5.
		• **Identify and sign** the *Framework Brief*
		The *Framework Brief* enables the *Alliance Members* to work collaboratively by integrating relevant parts of the separate *Project Briefs* that form the basis for the appointment of each *Alliance Member* under its *Project Contract.* The *Framework Brief* is defined in FAC-1 Appendix 1 as including the *Client's* 'technical, management and commercial requirements, including the required approach to design, *Supply Chain* engagement, costing, *Risk Management* and programming and all other relevant procedures and expected outcomes and where appropriate the required approach to *BIM'.*
		• **Identify and sign** the *Framework Prices* and *Framework Proposals*, each agreed confidentially between the *Client,* any *Additional Clients,* the *Alliance Manager* and another *Alliance Member*
		The *Framework Prices* describe any agreed amounts agreed to be payable to each *Alliance Member* for *Alliance Activities* and *Pre-Contract Activities* under FAC-1. These amounts are separate from *Agreed Prices,* which are payable under the terms of each *Project Contract.*
		The *Framework Proposals* describe the proposals submitted by each *Alliance Member* in response to the *Framework Brief.*

What are the Framework Documents? [Continued]	Page (i) Clauses 1.3, 1.4 and 1.5	• **Identify and sign** any Alliance Manager Services Schedule The Alliance Manager is identified in FAC-1 clause 3 and may be an employee of the Client or a separate Alliance Member. An Alliance Manager Services Schedule is only required if the Alliance Manager is a separate Alliance Member. • **Identify and sign** any Alliance Manager Payment Terms. These are agreed confidentially between the Client, any Additional Clients and the Alliance Manager. Alliance Manager Payment Terms are only required if the Alliance Manager is a separate Alliance Member.
What are the names of the Core Group members, including any alternates?	Page (ii) Clause 1.6	**Insert** the names of the Core Group members including any alternates. The FAC-1 Core Group is a collaborative governance system that supports Alliance relationships, assesses proposals for Improved Value, resolves problems and avoids disputes. The FAC-1 Core Group provides a collaborative decision-making forum through which the agreed representatives of the Client and the other Alliance Members meet to reach agreement on • proposals in respect of the design, supply, construction or Operation of the Framework Programme or Projects; • proposals in respect of quality, safety, Sustainability, cost, time and risk relating to the Framework Programme or Projects; and • resolution of clashes, conflicts or potential disputes between the proposals of Alliance Members. The Core Group comprises named individuals or agreed alternates appointed by each of Alliance Members, who reach decisions unanimously by Consensus among those members who attend the meeting (FAC-1 clause 1.6.1). The work of the Core Group does not restrict the agreed authority of the Client and the Alliance Manager.
What are the agreed communications systems?	Page (ii) Clause 1.9.3	**Insert** details of the agreed communication systems. These may comprise, for example, electronic information exchange systems for all communications, for management of the Alliance, for the Project Contract award procedures and in connection with BIM.
What are the names of any Stakeholders and what is the nature of their intended involvement?	Page (ii) Clause 1.10	**Insert** the names of any Stakeholders and cross-refer to the Framework Brief for their interest in the Framework Programme and the ways in which Alliance Members agree to engage with them. Alliance Members do not owe a direct duty of care to Stakeholders other than pursuant to clause 10.6 of the Contract Terms.

Question	Page and clause no.	Details to be inserted
Are there any named Additional Clients and/or other Additional Alliance Members that it is agreed may join the Alliance?	Page (ii) Clause 1.11	**Insert** the names or descriptions of any *Additional Clients* and/or other *Additional Alliance Members* that it is agreed may join the *Alliance*. The form of *Joining Agreement* is set out in Appendix 2 to the *Contract Terms*.
What is the name of the Alliance Manager and are there any restrictions on his/her/its authority?	Page (ii) Clause 3.1	**Insert** the name of the *Alliance Manager*, who may be a *Client* employee or an independent consultant. **Insert** any limits on the authority of the *Alliance Manager* by reference to clause 3.1 of the *Contract Terms*.
In what matters can the Alliance Manager act on behalf of the Client?	Page (ii) Clause 3.2	In addition to the matters described in clause 3.1, **insert** any authority delegated by the *Client* to the *Alliance Manager* to act on its behalf.
Is there an Independent Adviser?	Page (iii) Clause 3.3	The role of the *Independent Adviser* is an optional source of fair and constructive advice to *Alliance Members* on implementation of the *Framework Alliance Contract*, including avoidance or resolution of disputes. **Insert** details or **delete** as required.
Will Framework Prices state separately an Alliance Member's agreed levels of Profit and Overheads?	Page (iii) Clauses 4.3 and 4.4	The separate agreement of *Profit* and *Overheads* enables the analysis and agreement of cost reductions through *Alliance Activities* such as *Supply Chain Collaboration* without eroding *Alliance Member* margins. **Delete** if not applicable.

Question	Reference	Content
Will any minimum value or type of *Projects* be awarded to *Alliance Members*?	Page (iii) Clause 5.6	By reference to the procedures in Schedule 4, **insert** any minimum value or type of *Projects* that will be awarded to any one or more *Alliance Members*.
Will all or any part of the *Framework Programme* be awarded exclusively to any one or more *Alliance Members*?	Page (iii) Clause 5.7	**Insert** details of any agreed exclusivity. **Insert** details of any contract in relation to a *Project* that may be awarded to a party who is not an *Alliance Member* **Insert** also in Part 2 of Schedule 1 to the *Framework Alliance Agreement* any provision for adjustment of exclusivity according to achievement of agreed *Targets*.
What *Supply Chain Collaboration* and other *Alliance Activities* will be undertaken by *Alliance Members* in accordance with the *Timetable* or as otherwise agreed?	Page (iii) Clause 6	*Alliance Activities* describe the agreed work of *Alliance Members* in seeking to achieve *Improved Value*. *Alliance Activities* include *Supply Chain Collaboration* under FAC-1 clause 6.3 by which *Alliance Members* • revisit any *Supply Chain* proposals obtained when *Alliance Members* are selected; • develop new *Supply Chain* proposals; • seek improvements through joint engagement with *Supply Chain* members under shared systems monitored by the *Client* and the *Alliance Manager*; and • agree improved and more consistent commitments with *Supply Chain* members, including *Improved Value* and reduced risks. If the FAC-1 *Supply Chain Collaboration* systems are led by a contractor *Alliance Member*, they enable a *Client* to influence *Supply Chain* appointments on public sector *Projects* without the need for additional public procurement procedures. Selected *Supply Chain* members can become *Alliance Members* if the current *Alliance Members* agree to this in accordance with FAC-1 clause 1.11 and Appendix 2. **Insert** details of the agreed *Supply Chain Collaboration* and other *Alliance Activities* including joint processes and shared working practices intended to achieve improved efficiency, cost savings and other *Improved Value*. *Supply Chain Collaboration* and other *Alliance Activities* are linked to dates and periods of time set out in the *Timetable*.

Question	Page and clause no.	Details to be inserted
Are there amended payment periods in respect of amounts agreed to be paid for Alliance Manager Services, Alliance Activities and Pre-Contract Services?	Page (iii) Clause 8.6	**Insert** any amended payment periods in respect of amounts agreed to be paid for *Alliance Manager Services, Alliance Activities* and *Pre-Contract Activities*. These clauses relate only to any amounts that are agreed to be paid under FAC-1. All amounts that are payable for works, services and supplies under each *Project Contract* are paid in accordance with the terms of each *Project Contract*.
Is there an agreed rate of interest on any late payment?	Page (iii) Clause 8.11	**Insert** the agreed rate of interest that is due in the event of a delay in a payment due to an *Alliance Member* under FAC-1 clause 8.
Are there any amendments to the duty of reasonable skill and care or to the parties between whom a duty of care is owed?	Page (iv) Clauses 10.1 and 10.2	**Insert** any agreed amendments to the duty of reasonable skill and care owed between *Alliance Members*. FAC-1 creates a duty of care only in respect of the rights and obligations of *Alliance Members* under FAC-1 and does not affect the duty of care of any *Alliance Member* under any *Project Contract*. The FAC-1 duty of care can be adjusted • to be consistent with the duty of care under the *Project Contracts* and • to increase or decrease the extent to which the agreed mutual commitments are binding between *Alliance Members*. The duty of reasonable skill and care is described in clauses 10.1 and 10.2. A duty of care is owed between limited *Alliance Members* in respect of certain documents and activities under clauses 1.11.3, 10.3, 10.4, 10.5 and 11.2. **Insert** any amendments in respect of the parties between whom a duty of care is owed.
Is a duty of care extended to any other parties?	Page (iv) Clause 10.6	**Insert** any agreed commitments of *Alliance Members* to provide a duty of care under FAC-1 to a party who is not an *Alliance Member*.

What types and levels of insurance cover are to be taken out by each *Alliance Member*?	Page (iv) Clause 12	**Insert** the agreed types and levels of insurance cover in respect of obligations under FAC-1, which can include, for example, third-party liability insurance and professional indemnity insurance in respect of *Alliance Manager Services, Alliance Activities* and *Pre-Contract Activities*.
		Details of insured risks, exclusions, deductibles and other relevant insurance terms are stated in the *Framework Brief*.
		These insurances are separate from insurances under *Project Contracts*, which should be stated in the *Template Project Documents*.
		FAC-1 does not affect the insurances agreed in each *Project Contract* in relation to the services, works and supplies provided by each *Alliance Member*, and this section relates only to the insurance of agreed activities under FAC-1 that are not governed by each *Project Contract*. The insurances required under FAC-1 should be consistent with the insurances required under the *Project Contracts*.
Is any *Alliance Member* entitled to assign or subcontract its rights or obligations under the *Framework Alliance Contract* to another party?	Page (iv) Clause 13.2	**Insert** any agreed entitlement of an *Alliance Member* to assign or subcontract rights under FAC-1.
Are there amended confidentiality provisions?	Page (iv) Clause 13.3	**Insert** the agreed mutual commitments of *Alliance Members* in relation to confidentiality and other aspects of data security, based on the *Client's* requirements. These commitments can extend or relax the confidentiality provisions set out in clause 13.3, e.g. by reason of the identity of the *Client* or the nature of the *Projects* comprising the *Framework Programme*.
What are the commencement date and duration of the *Framework Alliance Contract*, and are there any extension procedures?	Page (v) Clause 14.1	**Insert** the date of commencement of the *Framework Alliance Contract*, its duration and any agreed extension procedures.

Question	Page and clause no.	Details to be inserted
Is there an agreed *Conciliator* and *Conciliation Procedure* or a *Dispute Board*?	Page (v) Clause 15.2	These are optional non-adversarial dispute resolution approaches and are additional to the role of the *Core Group* and any *Independent Adviser*. **Insert** details and **edit** or **delete** as required and see also Part 1 of Appendix 4 to the *Contract Terms* regarding conciliation. FAC-1 clause 15 does not amend the dispute resolution procedures that apply under each *Project Contract*. The dispute resolution procedures under FAC-1 clause 15 can be amended for consistency with the dispute resolution procedures in the *Project Contracts*.
Is there an agreed *Adjudicator* and *Model Adjudication Procedure*?	Page (v) Clause 15.3	Adjudication is a statutory right in respect of the resolution of construction contract disputes in the UK and in certain other jurisdictions. **Insert** details and **edit** or **delete** as required and see also Part 2 of Appendix 4 to the *Contract Terms*.
Are there agreed arrangements for the appointment of arbitrators, and as to applicable arbitration rules, and the location and language of arbitration?	Page (v) Clause 15.4	Arbitration is an optional dispute resolution approach. **Insert** details or **delete** as required and see also Part 3 of Appendix 4 to the *Contract Terms*.
What is the country whose laws govern the *Framework Alliance Contract* and whose courts have jurisdiction?	Page (v) Clauses 13.4 and 15.5	**Insert** the country whose laws govern the *Framework Alliance Contract*. The *Alliance Members* shall comply with the laws, regulations and other legally binding requirements currently in force in the stated country, and the courts of that country have non-exclusive jurisdiction in respect of any dispute. Particular *Legal Requirements* may amend or supplement the FAC-1 *Contract Terms*, and these are set out in Part 1 of Schedule 6 of the *Framework Alliance Agreement*.

The FAC-1 *Timetable* and time limits

F AC-1 *Alliance Members* commit to act 'without delay' in all matters governed by the *Framework Alliance Contract* (clause 1.1). The timing of the *Alliance Members*' FAC-1 commitments should be stated in the Schedule 2 *Timetable*, and where appropriate in the Schedule 3 *Risk Register*, and certain FAC-1 timescales are stated in the *Contract Terms*.

The timing of the following FAC-1 commitments depends on stating periods and deadlines for agreed actions, consents and approvals in the third column of the Schedule 2 *Timetable* (subject to updates of the *Timetable* prepared by the *Alliance Manager* for *Core Group* approval):

- the deadlines, gateways and milestones in respect of the *Framework Programme* and achievement of the *Objectives*;
- the timescales for *Supply Chain Collaboration* and other *Alliance Activities*, including the nature, sequence and duration of the agreed actions of each *Alliance Member* and any consents or approvals (whether required from *Alliance Members* or third parties) that are preconditions to subsequent actions; and
- the frequency of *Core Group* meetings.

The timing of the following FAC-1 commitments depends on stating the timescales for actions in the sixth column of the Schedule 3 *Risk Register* (subject to updates of the *Risk Register* prepared by the *Alliance Manager* for *Core Group* approval):

- the periods and deadlines for completing agreed *Risk Management* actions, including actions intended to reduce the likelihood of each risk and to reduce its financial and other impact.

The timing of the following FAC-1 commitments depends on stating timescales in the Schedule 4 *Direct Award Procedure* and *Competitive Award Procedure*:

- the issuing of each *Project Brief*;
- the submission of proposed *Agreed Prices* and other *Project Proposals*;
- all other steps leading to award of *Project Contracts*; and
- the 'procurement model for each *Project* including the sources and timing of all contributions to design, *Supply Chain* engagement, costing, programming and *Risk Management*, and incorporating the required approach to *BIM* as appropriate'.

The timing of the following FAC-1 commitments is subject to timescales stated in specific *Contract Terms*:

- notice of a *Core Group* meeting is not less than five *Working Days*, unless all *Core Group* members agree a shorter period (clause 1.7.1);
- the convening of a *Core Group* meeting is within five *Working Days* following an *Early Warning*, unless all *Core Group* members agree a shorter period or agree a course of action without a meeting (clause 1.8.2);
- the execution and return by an *Alliance Member* of a *Project Contract* prepared in accordance with the *Framework Documents* is within ten *Working Days* following its receipt from the *Alliance Manager* (clause 5.5);
- the option of the *Client* or *Additional Client* to terminate an *Order* is by not less than ten *Working Days'* notice at any time (clause 7.5);
- payment applications are submitted at the end of each calendar month (being the *Due Date*) unless different periods are agreed in the *Alliance Manager Payment Terms* or in the *Framework Brief* (clause 8.3);
- a *Payment Notice* is issued within five days from each *Due Date* (clauses 8.4 and 8.5);
- payment is made within twenty *Working Days* from receipt of each application (being the *Final Date for Payment*) subject to any revised periods stated in the *Framework Alliance Agreement* (clause 8.6);
- a *Pay Less Notice* is issued not less than five *Working Days* before the relevant *Final Date for Payment* (clause 8.8);
- a right to suspend performance arises if failure to pay an amount due continues for seven days after an *Alliance Member* has given notice of intention to suspend performance (clause 8.10);
- termination for an *Alliance Member*'s failure to achieve agreed *Targets* is by not less than ten *Working Days'* notice following a *Core Group* meeting

to propose remedial actions and is subject to other agreed procedures and limitations (clause 14.2 and Part 2 of Schedule 1); and

- termination for a breach having a demonstrable adverse effect on the *Alliance* or the *Framework Programme* arises after notice to an *Alliance Member* specifying the breach and allowing ten *Working Days* for the breach to be remedied, and after that period notifying the *Core Group* of the breach and allowing a further period of ten *Working Days* from the date of that notification to receive and consider the *Core Group*'s recommendations (clause 14.4).

Amendments to FAC-1 for use in Italy

The table on the pages that follow was prepared by Professor Sara Valaguzza for Chapter 24 of *Collaborative Construction Procurement and Improved Value* (Wiley, 2019).

Table of differences between the English and Italian versions of FAC-1.

Reference	English Version	Italian Version (translated into English)	Explanations
Title	*Framework Alliance Contract*	Framework dell'Accordo Collaborativo.	The acronym of both definitions is 'FAC-1'.
Inside cover	*Description of the nature and origin of FAC-1 and details about intellectual property rights on the document and publication*	A preface was added, explaining the contents and the structure of FAC-1.	The explanatory preface is intended to bring the operators closer to the model contract, which is far from the way that contracts are structured in Italy.
FAA, reference to clause 1.6	*The Core Group members are:*	Added footnote: 'Every *Alliance Member* should appoint a delegate to be part of the *Core Group*.'	The footnote was added – answering the request of the sector to clarify that individual *Alliance Members* should not fear the decisions of the *Core Group*, since they are all represented in the same body.
FAA, clauses 10.1 and 10.2	*The following amendments apply to the duties of care under clauses 10.1 and/or 10.2*	Added in italics: '(only to provide a higher, additional or more specific duty than the one established by the *Contract Terms*)'.	Italian law does not permit us to derogate from the duty of care.

FAA, reference to clause 15.3	Adjudication	Deleted.	Adjudication does not exist in Italian law and is arguably not compatible with the approaches to alternative dispute resolution permitted in the Italian system.
FAA, signatures	Or executed as a deed by …	Signed and authenticated by …	In Italian law execution as a deed does not exist. The typical approaches are signature, authenticated signature and a public act drafted by a notary public.
Clause 10	Duty of care	10.1 makes reference to a suitable duty of care, according to the roles, expertise and responsibilities of the *Alliance Members*. 10.2 makes reference to a duty of 'fairness and bona fide'. 10.3 and 10.4 make reference to the duty owed in respect of contractual obligations.	The clause has been adapted to the Italian contractual duty, which cannot be derogated from by the parties.

Reference	English Version	Italian Version (translated into English)	Explanations
Clause 14	Termination	14.2.2.1 In case an *Alliance Member* does not meet an *Objective* or a revised *Objective*, the *Client* or the *Additional Client* will have the power to terminate the contract or (only if the performance of said *Alliance Member* is not considered essential) the appointment of that *Alliance Member*, only after the notification of an invitation to remedy within 20 *Working Days*. If the objective is not reached after that period, the contract or that appointment will be automatically terminated. 14.3.1 The other *Alliance Members* shall have the right to cease to be a party, to require immediate execution of the *Client's* performance and to suspend their own performance unless adequate warranty is provided. 14.3.2 The norms contained in the Italian bankruptcy law shall apply. 14.4 In case of breach, every *Alliance Member* shall notify it to the *Core Group*, which shall provide guidance and recommendations; in parallel, the *Alliance Member* shall invite the breaching *Alliance Member* to remedy within 20 *Working Days*. If the breach is not resolved within that period, the FAC-1 contract or (only if the performance of said *Alliance Member* is not considered essential) the appointment of the breaching *Alliance Member* will be automatically terminated.	The clause has been adapted to the Italian rules on termination which cannot be derogated from by the parties. The Italian bankruptcy law forbids termination in case of insolvency events.
Clause 15	• Adjudication • Conciliation or Dispute Board • Arbitration	• No adjudication. • Conciliation or amicable agreement (i.e. a contract by which the parties, through mutual agreement, define an imminent or actual difference). • Arbitration, as it is described in the English version.	Adjudication does not exist in Italian law. Amicable agreement is a common tool to solve disputes in Italy. Arbitration may not be applicable to public administrations but it is only facilitative.

Definition: Independent Adviser	An *Independent Adviser* who may be identified in the *Framework Alliance Agreement* and appointed on terms agreed by the *Alliance Members* to provide fair and constructive advice to the *Alliance Members* on the implementation of the *Framework Alliance Contract* and the avoidance or resolution of any dispute.	There can be more than one *Independent Adviser*, of different expertise. This reflects the fact that differences and disputes could arise both on technical issues and on legal issues.
Definition: insolvency event	• Any case in which (where the *Alliance Member* is a legal person) events or other exterior facts demonstrate that it is not able to regularly satisfy its obligations; or • any case in which (where the *Alliance Member* is a natural person) he/she has filed a restructuring plan in court; • any other event equivalent to those indicated above, in any other jurisdiction outside Italy.	The definition has been adapted to the Italian insolvency rules which cannot be derogated from by the parties.
Appendix 4	Does not refer to adjudication.	
Final page	Signatures	A double signature is required for clauses 1.3, 1.4, 5.6, 7.5, 8.10, 13.1, 13.2, 14 and 15.	According to the Italian Civil Code, such clauses – where inserted in a document such as the *Contract Terms* – should be expressly double-signed for acceptance.

Sources of case studies and relevant guidance

Alliance Contracts website, 'News and Users' (https://allianceforms.co.uk). (This provides more information on Case Studies 7, 10, 11, 13, 18, 19, 20, 26 and 30.)

Arcadis, 'Global Construction Disputes Report 2020' (https://majorprojects. org/resources/global-construction-disputes-report/).

Association of Consultant Architects, 'PPC2000 Standard Form of Contract for Project Partnering' (2000; amended 2013).

Association of Consulting Architects, '10 Years of Partnering Contracts: PPC2000/TPC2005' (2010) (https://bit.ly/3ZW2Mtv). (This provides more information on Case Studies 6, 15, 27, 28 and 29.)

Association of Consultant Architects, 'FAC-1 Framework Alliance Contract' (2016).

Association of Consultant Architects, 'TAC-1 Term Alliance Contract' (2016).

Cabinet Office, 'Procurement Trial Case Study Report – Highways Maintenance' (2014) (https://bit.ly/3R9huZV). (This provides more information on Case Study 5.)

Cabinet Office, 'Procurement Trial Case Study: New Prison North Wales' (2014) (https://bit.ly/3wrmIGY). (This provides more information on Case Study 23.)

Cabinet Office, 'Procurement Trial Case Study: Social Housing Refurbishment' (2014) (https://bit.ly/3XBk0L1). (This provides more information on Case Study 12.)

Cabinet Office, 'Constructing the Gold Standard: An Independent Review of Public Sector Construction Frameworks' (2021). (This provides more information on Case Studies 1, 2, 4, 5, 7, 12, 14, 21, 23 and 28.)

Cabinet Office, 'Construction Playbook: Government Guidance on Sourcing and Contracting Public Works Projects and Programmes' (2022) (https:// bit.ly/3XBgQXL).

Cabinet Office, 'Promoting Net Zero Carbon and Sustainability in Construction', Guidance Note (2022) (https://bit.ly/3Hadns7).

Constructing Excellence, 'Connect Plus Sustainable Business Culture Model', PPP Trial Project case study (https://bit.ly/3J8z9Pl).

Construction Innovation Hub, 'Value Toolkit' (2022) (https://constructioninnovationhub.org.uk/our-projects-and-impact/value-toolkit/).

De'Ath, M., and Farmer, M., 'Build Homes, Build Jobs, Build Innovation: A Blueprint for a Housing Led Industrial Strategy' (September 2020) (https://bit.ly/3j3134H).

Department for Levelling Up, Housing and Communities, 'Collaborative Procurement Guidance for Design and Construction to Support Building Safety' (2022) (https://bit.ly/3j1h0IP).

Fuchs, S., and Jackson, S., 'Good Faith: An Anglo-German Comparison', *International Construction Law Review* Volume 32, Part 4 (2015).

Government Commercial Function, 'Longer Term Contracting Programmes, Projects and Portfolios in Construction', Guidance Note (2022) (https://bit.ly/3iZYG2S). (This provides more information on Case Study 16.)

Government Commercial Function, 'Market, Supplier & Supply Chain Engagement in Construction', Guidance Note (2022) (https://bit.ly/3kKABNJ). (This provides more information on Case Study 16.)

International Organization for Standardization, 'ISO 44001: Collaborative Business Relationship Management Systems – Requirements and Framework' (2017) (https://www.iso.org/standard/72798.html).

International Organization for Standardization, 'ISO 19650-1:2018: Organization and Digitization of Information about Buildings and Civil Engineering Works, including Building Information Modelling (*BIM*) — Information Management Using Building Information Modelling' (2018) (https://www.iso.org/standard/68078.html).

Mosey, D., *Early Contractor Involvement in Building Procurement* (Wiley, 2009).

Mosey, D., *Collaborative Construction Procurement and Improved Value* (Wiley, 2019). (This provides more information on Case Studies 2, 3, 4, 5, 6, 8, 12, 15, 17, 21, 22, 23, 24, 25, 27, 28 and 29.)

Mosey, D., Vornicu, R., Bahram, D., and Giana, P., 'White Paper on Procurement Strategies for Incentivizing Collaborative Delivery to Optimize Whole-Life Outcomes', Centre for Digital Built Britain (2022) (https://bit.ly/3j4nIOc). (This provides more information on Case Studies 1, 4, 5, 9, 12, 23, 24 and 28.)

Mosey, D., Vornicu, R., Bahram, D., and Giana, P., 'Procuring Net Zero Construction', Society of Construction Law (2022) (https://bit.ly/3kI-2HcE). (This provides more information on Case Studies 9 and 10.)

Procurement/Lean Client Task Group, 'Government Construction Strategy' (2012) (https://bit.ly/3XD9NxG). (This provides more information on Case Study 4.)
Project 13, 'About Project 13' (https://www.project13.info/about-project13/).